THE BEDSIDE BOOK OF BEER

Barrie Pepper

ALMA
BOOKS

Author: **Barrie Pepper**

Design: **Opus Design Group**

Cover illustration: **Andrzej Krauze**

Typeset and printed by: **Cambridge University Press**

ISBN **1-85249-106-X**

Published by **Alma Books Ltd.**, a wholly-owned
subsidiary of the Campaign for Real Ale Ltd., 34 Alma Road,
St Albans, Herts.

Thanks

I am most grateful to my many colleagues in the Campaign for Real Ale, the British Guild of Beer Writers, the Brewery History Society and the National Union of Journalists for their ready help and cooperation in the preparation of this book. Many of them have allowed me to use their published material without charge and it is fair to say that without their generous assistance this book would never have happened. All of them are suitably acknowledged in the book. In particular I would like to thank Jill Adam and Roger Protz for their continued support throughout the production process and their help and advice and Roger's personal contribution.

CONTENTS

CHAPTER I

A PERSONAL JOURNEY

If with water you fill up your glasses,
You'll never write anything wise,
For Ale is the horse of Parnassus
Which hurries a bard to the skies.

Thomas Moore

This is a personal journey through time and space. It takes in much of a life and a good spread of distance.

Three things stand out. At the age of 12 or 13 I drank a couple of mouthfuls of Melbourne Bitter on a form outside the Cross Keys in Darfield near Barnsley whilst my uncle was preoccupied. It was a pleasant and memorable experience.

Then I was walking above Windermere enjoying the air. A pub was just part of that day but its sign remains in the memory many years on when the rest including the welcome pint of bitter has opaqued:

Oh, Mortal Man, that lives by bread,
What is it makes thy nose so red?
Thou silly fool that art so pale,
'tis drinking Sally Birkett's ale.

Later my father moved into a pub at Sowerby Bridge in the West Riding called The Wharf. Or was it The Wharfe? It doesn't really matter but what it did do was to kindle my interest in the value of beer as a recuperative, fulfilling drink and in the public house as an institution and start me off on a voyage of exploration that has been fascinating, educative and wholly pleasing.

The desire to seek out whatever is chronicled and documented on the topic has brought me a room full of guides, magazines and other printed matter, a collection of mats, labels and other breweriana, thousands of photographs and slides and a library of close on 400 books on the subject.

My experience as a journalist had taught me several things, not least that while you can seldom judge a book by its cover it is often unnecessary to take in the whole lot to enjoy it. I have been reading *The Wind in the Willows* for years and have never read through the book at one go yet I must have read the whole several times over and some parts many times. The curate's egg theory applies.

So I would never suggest, for example, that you should read the whole of *Tom Jones* simply to find out what Fielding had to say about The Bell at Gloucester although you may well enjoy it for the doing. An anthology such as this attempts to do such difficult tasks for you:

'. . . an excellent house indeed, and which I do most sincerely recommend to every reader who shall visit this ancient city.'

Books like *Tom Jones* point up the fact that of the many million words that have been written on the subject not all are to be found in books about beer and pubs. So in seeking out the selection for this book I have scoured many other anthologies, much fiction and some less likely sources such as newspapers, diaries, the odd play script and even the spoken word.

Arranging the selections proved less of a problem than I first imagined. The all too obvious ways of using a chronological or alphabetical order were soon rejected. The first would have been too patchy and the second would have started with many pages of Anons with often little relevance to one another. So I opted for a subject division with some overriding groups. Pubs, beer and drinking are the main and obvious sectors to which I have added the modern phenomenon of campaigning. From these I have separated out most of the poetry and songs and all the lengthier fiction. A final section is a series of original essays by colleagues in the British Guild of Beer Writers. The illustrations come from colleagues and historical sources.

My personal journey in search of good ale, good pubs and good writing has taken me a good number of years and to many parts of the world although I was often there for other reasons. In the vastness of the United States it is almost impossible to be 'just passing' but it happened when I came upon the Catamount brewery at White River Junction in Vermont and similar conditions applied when I visited the Solan brewery, eight thousand feet into the Himalayas. But my journey has been mainly confined to England and Ireland with occasional forays elsewhere – the Chalice in Prague is remembered by the book *The Good Soldier Švejk* and the Hofbräuhaus in Munich by Patrick Leigh Fermor's *A Time of Gifts,* and to Harry's Bar in Paris where Scott Fitzgerald, Hemingway, Faulkner and Thornton Wilder drank and Gershwin composed. There have been other places too – Edinburgh, Vienna, Brussels, even the Isle of Man. But the island of Ireland and England, specifically Yorkshire, have been my happier hunting grounds.

In the heady days ten years before everybody voted Green in the 1989 Euro-elections, Richard Boston brought out Vole and Miles Kington invented the Dublin Underground – Toob Lingus he called it. It had a special section for writers and artists that was licensed for the sale of stout and whiskey. The first owner was G Rafferty from whom 'graffiti' is said to be derived and which the law says shall be written in both English and Irish. It reflected, in the best satirical way of the Irish, the relationship that exists between Irish writers and the mighty art of drinking.

I once wrote an essay on drinking in Dublin; I was certainly not the first to do so and will not be the last. It was really a paean to water, homage to the Liffey and the effect that that moving road can have upon a dilatory drinker. I used the phrase: 'Last night's Guinness was still a potent force but its appeal was waning fast.' It reflected a real state of mind and body and later that day I read Joyce on morality and Yeats on spirituality and failed to find anything to

assuage my conscience or my throbbing temples. Better I should have tried
Flann O'Brien who determined that:

> When things go wrong and will not come right,
> Though you do the best you can,
> When life looks black as the hour of night –
> A PINT OF PLAIN IS YOUR ONLY MAN.

Flann O'Brien, Brian O'Nolan, Miles nagCopaleen, call him what you will,
wrote well of the pub and of drinking. He did it in the Irish tradition and in a
slightly more refined way than Brendan Behan. Pubs and drinking were
wound up in Behan's life, and his death. He drank in what he called 'the
literary pubs of Grafton Street'. This, no doubt would include Davy Byrnes
which James Joyce called: 'moral pub' though I could never understand why.
Not moral to Behan.

His respect for the customers of these literary pubs was often directly
related to their ability to buy him a drink. On the whole though he had great
love for his fellow man most of which he met in pubs be they literary or
otherwise. Brendan Behan once wrote briefly of Kruger Kavanagh's pub at
Dunquin on the Dingle peninsula in County Kerry. It was here that
CAMRA – the Campaign for Real Ale – was formed in 1971.

I dragged my teenage son there to pay homage. We were told the story of
how Kruger had his photograph taken with President Kennedy and President
de Valera and it was captioned: 'Who are those two men with Kruger
Kavanagh?' While we were there the peninsula was invaded by an Italian
Caravan Club and a visiting American declared: 'Holy Cow, its World War
three!' It was hot and the Guinness was very potable – a time to enjoy.

Drinking in Ireland is an entirely different experience to anywhere else.
The country is compact, almost like a village, with the result that dropping in
for a quiet pint somewhere can often lead to a meeting with someone of note
and always with someone who knows someone of note. Irish pubs – so unlike
their British counterparts – are for conversation and are much more
democratic.

I can name drop and say that I have drunk and chatted with a former
Taoiseach (Prime Minister) and a Euro-politician in as informal a way as it is
possible to imagine. And it happened in the same pub – Comber's in Lahinch
on the west coast of Clare. In the same place I have met other politicians,
diplomats, the literati of Ireland, actors, golfers, musicians [inevitably] and
even what Flann O'Brien chose to call 'the Plain People of Ireland'.

Comber's is a way of life. When it left the family three or four years ago it
made the pages of the dailies and there was some concern as to its future. But
they needn't have worried; John Galvin, the new owner, opened it up a bit
and started to sell sandwiches on a regular basis; the Victorian telephone box
has gone, it has a new sign but little else has changed. Mary Comber lives
next door and retains her corner seat, the curtains are drawn at closing
time, the priests sing bawdy songs and everything is welcome except pretension.

Round the bay in Liscannor is Joe McHugh's pub. This is an experience, total and sufficient. The uniqueness requires your presence but some have attempted descriptions – the actor Donal Farmer calls it '. . . the smallest emporium in the world.' Its very shape encourages conviviality –three feet wide by twenty feet long. And Joe, with his flat cap at an angle, reigns supreme.

Dublin and Belfast apart, and Cork is well beyone my pale, the only pubs of character in Ireland are those you discover yourself, as with my gems in West Clare. But I was pointed to one by a mentor of mine who takes pleasure in quoting great chunks of O'Casey at me as the stout flows – '. . . oh he's a darlin' man, a daarlin' man'. Chris Clarken took me to Abbeyleix to Morrisseys. On the fourth visit I met the man who owned it, grocer's shop, cockroach trap, biscuit tins and all. Paddy Mulhall is also a funeral director, auctioneer and valuer, estate agent and newsagent and, as is the way of these things, probably a poet.

Pepys enjoyed drinking and to read him you can enjoy the company and experience the atmosphere of the metropolitan tavern in the days of Charles II. James Joyce once said that if Dublin was ever wiped off the world it would be possible to rebuild it from the pages of his *Ulysses* and so I suspect you could do the same for seventeenth-century London from Pepys's diaries. Shakespeare preceded Pepys in writing of the London public house such as the Boars Head Tavern where Mistress Quickly kept house in the two parts of *Henry IV*. But while they were amongst the first they were followed by many more.

A literary tour of London's pubs is a worthwhile experience; many authors used actual pubs in their works either with their original names or disguised ones whilst others used actual pubs to do their works. Dickens could be found all over the capital. He wrote of several pubs and he drank in many more including the Lamb and Flag in Covent Garden. Dryden had been a regular there many years before and has a room named after him. And Dickens was just one of the literati that frequented the Olde Cheshire Cheese off Fleet Street, presumably in his journalist days. Others included Congreve, Voltaire and William Butler Yeats.

Plays have been performed for centuries in the courtyard of the George at Southwark – Shakespeare's strolling players will have been there for the Globe Theatre is nearby, and so is the Anchor where Boswell and Johnson are commemorated. They also drank at the Holly Bush in Hampstead and so did Charles Lamb – it was once the home of George Romney the artist.

Karl Marx knew several pubs and the Museum Tavern opposite the British Museum was just one of them but he shared it with the Bloomsbury set including Virginia Woolf. The Sherlock Holmes in Northumberland Avenue is described by Roger Protz in *The Best Pubs in London* as: '. . . a shrine to the greatest detective and to his creator: Sir Arthur Conan Doyle . . .'

Modern writers are remembered too, Graham Greene, whose family own a brewery, and Ernest Hemingway drank at the Dove in Hammersmith which had William Morris for a next door neighbour. Dylan Thomas used the George in Great Portland Street and George Orwell's membership card of the National Union of Journalists is displayed at the Fitzroy Tavern in Charlotte Street where he was a regular.

Charles Dickens didn't restrict himself to the pubs of London and travelled widely including four times to Yorkshire The visit most remembered was that in 1838 to Greta Bridge and the Bowes area in search of information for his forthcoming book *Nicholas Nickleby*.

Greta Bridge was the second night stop for coaches on the London to Carlisle route. Dickens and his friend Hablot K Browne, 'Phiz' the cartoonist, arrived there on a freezing, snowblind night in January 1838. He was later to refer to what was then called the New Inn as: '. . . the best inn I have ever put up at', but it was not his first impression, as he wrote to his wife:

'. . . we have driven through snow from Grantham . . . arrived 11 pm, we reached a bare place with a house standing alone in the midst of a dreary moor . . . it was fearfully cold, and there was no outward signs of anyone being up in the house. But to our great joy we discovered a comfortable room with drawn curtains and a most blazing fire . . . in half an hour, they gave us a smoking supper and a bottle of mulled port . . . then we retired to a couple of capital bedrooms, in each of which there was a roaring fire halfway up the chimney.'

He went on to describe their most fulsome breakfast:

'. . . toast, cakes, a Yorkshire pie, a piece of beef about the size and much the shape of my portmanteau, tea, coffee, ham and eggs.'

When the journey was repeated in the novel, things were a little different. Nickleby stayed outside the 'George and New Inn' and noted that Wackford Squeers, his new master, had gone inside to 'stretch his legs'. He continued:

'After some minutes he returned with his legs thoroughly stretched, if the hue of his nose and a short hiccup afforded any criterion.'

Dickens journeyed from Greta Bridge to the Unicorn at Bowes, where he found the model for Dotheboys Hall and where he wrote part of *Nicholas Nickleby*.

The Wordsworths, too, were intrepid travellers and their journeys are interspersed with visits to country inns in Lakeland and in Yorkshire. Dorothy's journal is full of references to inns and her descriptions are superb. She wrote more than once of the Black Swan at Helmsley:

'My heart danced at the sight of its cleanly outside bright yellow walls, casements overshadowed with jasmine, and its low, double gavel-ended front.'

J B Priestley was a great man for the pub and shared his company between his birth-town of Bradford, often called Bruddersford, and the Yorkshire Dales. I happily confess to having chosen a phrase he used to describe one for the title of one of my books. He referred to the Spotted Cow in the Manningham district of Bradford as 'a haunt of rare souls'. But he was writing of Edward VII's days. When he returned in the fifties all the character had gone to be replaced by what he called 'bogus plastic luxury'. He would be even more disappointed today where part of the place is a night club called 'Spotties'!

Priestley continued to buy his wine in Bradford long after he left the city. When the city council belatedly conferred on him the freedom he took advantage of the visit to call on his wine merchant. 'How are you Mr Priestley?' he was asked. 'Oh, a little older and a little fatter', he replied. 'That's what you said the last time you were here', said the victualler. 'Well then', said the author, 'a little older, a little fatter and more repetitive'.

James Herriot, if the television series of *All Creatures Great and Small* tells all, enjoys a pint of beer. The pubs in his books are identifiable even if they do not represent the actual places he drank in his early days of practice. He is one of many authors who have happily fitted the comfort and pleasures of the public house into his writings. Even Charlotte Brontë managed it in *Jane Eyre* and Walter Scott with the *Heart of Midlothian*. Wilkie Collins toured Yorkshire and wrote to Dickens about the standard of inns in Whitby and Daniel Defoe wrote much of *Robinson Crusoe* in a Halifax pub and had the hero of the story born in York.

My journey has been enhanced by discovering the writings of Alfred J Brown, who is little known outside his own county. He recognised the fullness of Yorkshire in a book called *Broad Acres* and a half a dozen others beside. He glorifies the joys of walking – he sometimes calls it tramping – but for him the great delight is the pub at the end of the journey: '. . . the inn is the essential culmination to the day's achievement: and I cannot but think that those who have not fallen under the spell of inns on such occasions, much as I respect them, miss a great deal.' These are magic words and their enchantment brings my journey to a close. The rest is for you.

'... grocer's shop, cockroach trap, biscuit tins and all!'

CHAPTER 2

POETRY AND SONGS

From: The Ingoldsby Legends

For both now came loaded with Meux's entire;
Combe's, Delafield's, Hanbury's, Truman's – no stopping –
Goding's, Charrington's, Whitbread's continued to drop in
With Hodson's pale ale, from the Sun Brewhouse, Wapping.
(The firms differed then, but I can't put a tax on
My memory to say what their names were in Saxon).
    To be sure the best beer
    Of all did not appear,
For I've said 'twas June, and so late in the year
The 'Trinity Audit Ale' is not come-at-able,
As I've found to my great grief when dining at that table.

Richard Harris Barham

Bar Room Conversation

A lorry made the windows shake
And noon light on the sour spilt beer
Quivered. 'A widow's an easy make,'

He said, 'you pedal and let her steer;
Or the next best is a girl inclined
To play, but her man's away for a year.

'And she's too shy or he's too blind.
None of your nattering flirts – they're hard –
But one of the Sunday school teacher kind

Ripe and ready behind her guard.'
Gently the other sipped his drink;
The barman wrote on a doubles card.

He said, 'I saw her first at the rink,
Danced and yarned and took it slow.
She's come to trust me now, I think.

'Ten weeks of bringing her home by moonglow
With a kiss and cuddle at the gate –
No more. Tonight we'll go to a show

'At Dan's – I bet you a dollar, mate,
With a drink or two she'll turn it up.'
In the yard a lorry unloaded a crate;
The barman polished a football cup.

James K. Baxter

Good English Hospitality

This city & this country has brought forth many mayors,
To sit in state & give forth laws out of their old oak chairs,
With face as brown as any nut with drinking of strong ale;
Good English hospitality, O then it did not fail!

With scarlet gowns & broad gold lace would make a yeoman sweat,
With stockings roll'd above their knees & shoes as black as jet,
With eating beef & drinking beer, O they were stout & hale!
Good English hospitality, O then it did not fail!

Thus sitting at the table wide, the Mayor & Aldermen
Were fit to give law to the city; each eat as much as ten.
The hungry poor enter'd the hall, to eat good beef & ale.
Good English hospitality, O then it did not fail!

William Blake

The Fleur-de-Lys

In Cranborne Town two Inns there are,
And one the Fleur-de-Lys is hight,
And one, the inn Victoria,
Where, for it was alone in sight,
We turned in tired and tearful plight,
Seeking for warmth, and company,
And food, and beds so soft and white –
These things are at the Fleur-de-Lys.

Where is the ointment for the scar?
Slippers?: and table deftly dight?
Sofas? tobacco? soap? and ah!
Hot water for the weary wight?
Where is the food, in toils despite?
The golden eggs? the toast? the tea?
The maid so pretty and polite?
These things are at the Fleur-de-Lys.

Oh, we have wandered far and far,
We are fordone and wearied quite.
No lamp is lit: there are no star.
Only we know that in the night
We somehow missed the faces bright,
The lips and eyes we longed to see;
And Love, and Laughter, and Delight.
These things are at the Fleur-de-Lys.

Prince, it is dark to left and right.
Waits there an inn for you and me?
Fine hoppy ale and red firelight?
These things are at the Fleur-de-Lys.

Rupert Brooke

John Barleycorn

There was three Kings into the east,
   Three Kings both great and high,
And they hae sworn a solemn oath
   John Barleycorn should die.

They took a plough and plough'd him down,
   Put clods upon his dead,
And they hae sworn a solemn oath
   John Barleycorn was dead.

But the cheerfu' Spring came kindly on,
   And show'rs began to fall;
John Barleycorn got up again,
   And sore surpris'd them all.

The sultry suns of Summer came,
   And he grew thick and strong,
His head weel arm'd wi' pointed spears,
   That no one should him wrong.

The sober Autumn enter'd mild,
   When he grew wan and pale;
His bending joints and drooping head
   Show'd he began to fail.

His colour sicken'd more and more,
   He faded into age;
And then his enemies began
   To shew their deadly rage.

They've ta'en a weapon, long and sharp,
    And cut him by the knee;
Then tied him fast upon a cart,
    Like a rogue for forgerie.

They laid him down upon his back,
    And cudgell'd him full sore;
    They hung him up before the storm,
    And turn'd him o'er and o'er.

They fillèd up a darksome pit
    With water to the brim,
They heavèd in John Barleycorn,
    There let him sink or swim.

They laid him out upon the floor,
    To work him farther woe,
And still, as signs of life appear'd,
    They toss'd him to and fro.

They wasted, o'er a scorching flame,
    The marrow of his bones;
But a miller us'd him worst of all,
    For he crush'd him between two stones.

And they hae ta'en his very heart's blood,
    And drank it round and round;
And still the more and more they drank,
    Their joy did more abound.

John Barleycorn was a hero bold,
    Of noble enterprise,
For if you do but taste his blood,
    'Twill make your courage rise;

'Twill make a man forget his woe;
    'Twill heighten all his joy:
'Twill make the widow's heart to sing,
    Tho' the tear were in her eye.

Then let us toast John Barleycorn,
    Each man a glass in hand;
And may his great posterity
    Ne'er fail in old Scotland!

Robert Burns

John Barleycorn – an alternative version

There was three men came out of the west,
Their fortunes for to try,
And these three men made a solemn vow,
John Barleycorn should die.
They ploughed, they sowed, they harrowed him in,
Throwed clods upon his head,
And these three men made a solemn vow,
John Barleycorn was dead.

Then they let him lie for a very long time
Till the rain from heaven did fall,
Then little Sir John sprung up his head,
And soon amazed them all.
They let him stand till midsummer
Till he looked both pale and wan,
And little Sir John he growed a long beard
And so became a man.

They hired men with the scythes so sharp
To cut him off at the knee,
They rolled him and tied him by the waist,
And served him most barbarously.
They hired men with the sharp pitchforks
Who pricked him to the heart,
And the loader he served him worse than that,
For he bound him to the cart.

They wheeled him round and round the field
Till they came unto a barn,
And there they made a solemn mow
Of poor John Barleycorn.
They hired men with the crab-tree sticks
To cut him skin from bone,
And the miller he served him worse than that,
For he ground him between two stones.

Here's little Sir John in a nut-brown bowl,
And brandy in a glass;
And little Sir John in the nut-brown bowl
Proved the stronger man at last.
And the huntsman he can't hunt the fox,
Nor so loudly blow his horn,
And the tinker he can't mend kettles or pots
Without a little of Barleycorn.

Anon

Beer

In those old days which poets say were golden –
    (Perhaps they laid the gilding on themselves:
And, if they did, I'm all the more beholden
    To those brown dwellers in my dusty shelves,
Who talk to me 'in language quaint and olden'
    Of gods and demigods and fauns and elves,
Pan with his pipes, and Bacchus with his leopards,
And staid young goddesses who flirt with shepherds:)

In those old days, the Nymph called Etiquette
    (Appalling thought to dwell on) was not born.
They had their May, but no Mayfair as yet,
    No fashions varying as the hues of morn.
Just as they pleased they dressed and drank and ate,
    Sang hymns to Ceres (their John Barleycorn)
And danced unchaperoned, and laughed unchecked,
And were no doubt extremely incorrect.

Yet do I think their theory was pleasant:
    And oft, I own, my 'wayward fancy roams'
Back to those times, so different from the present;
    When no one smoked cigars, nor gave At-homes,
Nor smote a billiard-ball, nor winged a pheasant,
    Nor 'did' her hair by means of long-tailed combs,
Nor migrated to Brighton once a year,
Nor – most astonishing of all – drank Beer.

No, they did not drink Beer, 'which brings me to'
    (As Gilpin said) 'the middle of my song.'
Not that 'the middle' is precisely true,
    Or else I should not tax your patience long:
If I had said 'beginning' it might do;
    But I have a dislike to quoting wrong:
I was unlucky – sinned against, not sinning –
When Cowper wrote down 'middle' for 'beginning'.

So to proceed. That abstinence from Malt
    Has always struck me as extremely curious.
The Greek mind must have had some vital fault,
    That they should stick to liquors so injurious –
(Wine, water, tempered p'raps with Attic salt) –
    And not at once invent that mild, luxurious,
And artful beverage, Beer. How the digestion
Got on without it, is a startling question.

Had they digestions? and an actual body
    Such as dyspepsia might make attacks on?
Were they abstract ideas – (like Tom Noddy
    And Mr Briggs) – or men, like Jones and Jackson?
Then nectar – was that beer, or whisky-toddy?
    Some say the Gaelic mixture, I the Saxon:
I think a strict adherence to the latter
Might make some Scots less pigheaded, and fatter.

Besides, Bon Gaultier definitely shows
    That the real beverage for feasting gods on
Is a soft compound, grateful to the nose
    And also to the palate, known as 'Hodgson'.
I know a man – a tailor's son – who rose
    To be a peer: and this I would lay odds on,
(Though in his memoirs it may not appear,)
That that man owed his rise to copious Beer.

O Beer! O Hodgson, Guinness, Allsopp, Bass!
    Names that should be on every infant's tongue!
Shall days and months and years and centuries pass,
    And still your merits be unrecked, unsung?
Oh! I have gazed into my foaming glass,
    And wished that lyre could yet again be strung.
Which once range prophet-like through Greece, and taught her
Misguided sons that the best drink was water.

How would he now recant that wild opinion,
    And sing – as would that I could sing – of you!
I was not born (alas!) the 'Muses' minion',
    I'm not poetical, not even blue:
And he, we know, but strives with waxen pinion,
    Who'er he is that entertains the view
Of emulating Pindar, and will be
Sponsor at last to some now nameless sea.

Oh! when the green slopes of Arcadia burned
    With all the lustre of the dying day,
And on Cithaeron's brow the reaper turned,
    (Humming, of course, in his delightful way,
How Lycidas was dead, and how concerned
    The Nymphs were when they saw his lifeless clay;
And how rock told to rock the dreadful story
That poor young Lycidas was gone to glory:)

What would that lone and labouring soul have given,
    At that soft moment for a pewter pot!
How had the mists that dimmed his eye been riven,
    And Lycidas and sorrow all forgot!
If his own grandmother had died unshriven,
    In two short seconds he'd have recked it not;
Such power hath Beer. The heart which Grief hath canker'd
Hath one unfailing remedy – the Tankard.

Coffee is good, and so no doubt is cocoa;
    Tea did for Johnson and the Chinamen:
When 'Dulce est desipere in loco'
    Was written, real Falernian winged the pen.
When a rapt audience has encored 'Fra Poco'
    Or 'Casta Diva', I have heard that then
The Prima Donna, smiling herself out,
Recruits her flagging powers with bottled stout.

But what is coffee, but a noxious berry,
    Born to keep used-up Londoners awake?
What is Falernian, what is Port or Sherry,
    But vile concoctions to make dull heads ache?
Nay stout itself – (though good with oysters, very) –
    Is not a thing your reading man should take.
He that would shine, and petrify his tutor,
Should drink draught Allsopp in its 'native pewter'.

But hark! a sound is stealing on my ear –
    A soft and silvery sound – I know it well.
Its tinkling tells me that a time is near
    Precious to me – it is the Dinner Bell.
O blessed Bell! Thou bringest beef and beer,
    Thou bringest good things more than tongue may tell:
Seared is, of course, my heart – but unsubdued
Is, and shall be, my appetite for food.

I go. Untaught and feeble is my pen:
    But on one statement I may safely venture:
That few of our most highly gifted men
    Have more appreciation of the trencher.
I go. One pound of British beef, and then
    What Mr Swiveller called a 'modest quencher';
That home-returning, I may 'soothly say',
'Fate cannot touch me: I have dined to-day.'

C S Calverley

Wine and Water

Old Noah he had an ostrich farm and fowls on the largest scale,
He ate his egg with a ladle in an egg-cup big as a pail,
And the soup he took was Elephant Soup and the fish he took was
   Whale.
But they all were small to the cellar he took when he set out to sail,
And Noah he often said to his wife when he sat down to dine,
'I don't care where the water goes if it doesn't get into the wine.'

The cataract of the cliff of heaven fell blinding off the brink
As if it would wash the stars away as suds go down a sink,
The seven heavens came roaring down for the throats of hell to
   drink,
And Noah he cocked his eye and said, 'It looks like rain, I think.
The water has drowned the Matterhorn as deep as a Mendip mine,
But I don't care where the water goes if it doesn't get into the wine.'

But Noah he sinned, and we have sinned; on tipsy feet we trod,
Till a great big black teetotaller was sent for us for a rod,
And you can't get wine at a P.S.A., or chapel, or Eisteddfod,
For the Curse of Water has come again because of the wrath of God,
And water is on the Bishop's board and the Higher Thinker's shrine,
But I don't care where the water goes if it doesn't get into the wine.

G K Chesterton

I Went to the Alehouse

I went to the Alehouse as an honest Woman should
And a Knave followed after, as you know Knaves would
Knaves will be Knaves in every degree
I'll tell you by-and-by how this Knave served me.

I called for my Pot as an honest Woman should
And the Knave drank it up as you know Knaves would
Knaves will be Knaves etc.

I went into my Bed as an honest Woman should
And the Knave crept into it, as you know Knaves would
Knaves will be Knaves etc.

I proved with child as an honest Woman should
And the Knave ran away as you know Knaves would
Knaves will be Knaves in every Degree:
And thus I have told you how this Knave served me.

Thomas D'Urfey

Birth of a Plastic Pub

First they tore out the original oak beams
And slapped in olde plastic facsimiles.
Then they rooted out the jovial red-faced shire-horse of a landlord.
And replaced him with a surly glove-puppet, with a carved-in snarl.
Then they flushed out the good strong draught ale down into the
  sewers
And piped in what had previously been in the sewers.
Then they booted out the old concertina man
And installed a head-throbbing juke-box
(To stop people talking about what was happening).
This forced out all the customers with any character
And in their place, came ...
Well; suffice it to say that one night
A member of the new clientele stood too near a lamp
And melted.

Dave Dutton

Yes, this used to be a modern pub until they modernised it.

Downtown Boozers – Pre-War

Above the reeking taproom's door
The pregnant clock stood close on ten.
I heard the jangle of the glass;
The cackle of a tipsy ass;
The raucous, uncouth shouts again;
The inane shrill of female soaks;
The maudlin songs of sodden men.
How foul the atmosphere within
That den! The smell of beer, the din,
Filled me with nausea, and then
The clock struck, and the publican,
That bloodshot-eyed and bloated man,
To sweeter air the door flung wide.
Ye Gods! those wretches staggered out,
All slack of tongue and bleary-eyed,
Discordantly to sing and shout
And babble by the gutterside.
Homecoming for that drunken crew:
Sated *nostalgie de la boue*.

John Fraser

Public Bar

Now beginneth Sir Glutton to go to his shrift;
His course is to kirkward, as culprit to pray.
But Betty the brewster just bade him 'Good-morrow',
And asked him therewith as to whither he went.

'To holy church haste I, to hear me a mass,
And straight to be shriven, and sin nevermore.'
'Good ale have I, gossip; Sir Glutton, assay it!'
'But has thou hot spices at hand, in thy bag?'
'I have petter and paeony-seed, and a pound of garlick,
And a farthingworth of fennel-seed, for fasting days.'

Then Glutton goes in, and with him great oaths.
Cicely the shoe-seller sat on the bench,
The warrener Wat, and his wife also,
Timothy the tinker, with two of his lads,
The hackney-man Hick, the needle-man Hugh,
Clarice of Cock Lane, the clerk of the church,
Davy the Ditcher, and a dozen others;
Sir Piers the priest, and Parnel of Flanders,

A fiddler, a ratcatcher, a Cheapside raker,
A rider, a rope-seller, dish-selling Rose,
Godfrey of Garlickhithe, Griffin of Wales;
And a heap of upholsterers, early assembled,
Gave Glutton, with glad cheer, a treat of good ale.

William Langland

From: Tales of a Wayside Inn

One Autumn night, in Sudbury town,
Across the meadows bare and brown,
The windows of the wayside inn
Gleamed red with firelight through the leaves
Of woodbine, hanging from the eaves
Their crimson curtains rent and thin.

As ancient is this hostelry
As any in the land may be,
Built in the old Colonial day,
When men lived in a grander way.
With ampler hospitality;
A kind of old Hobgoblin Hall,
Now somewhat fallen to decay,
With weather-stains upon the wall,
And stairways worn, and crazy doors,
And creaking and uneven floors,
And chimneys huge, and tiled and tall.
A region of repose it seems,
A place of slumber and of dreams,
Remote among the wooded hills!
For there no noisy railway speeds,
Its torch-race scattering smoke and gleeds;
But noon and night, the panting teams
Stop under the great oaks, that throw
Tangles of light and shade below,
On roofs and doors and windowsills.
Across the road the barns display
Their lines of stalls, their mows of hay;
Through the wide doors the breezes blow,
The wattled cocks strut to and fro,
And, half effaced by rain and shine,
The Red Horse prances on the sign.

Henry Wadsworth Longfellow

The man who waters the workers beer

Oh I'm the man, the very fat man, that waters the workers beer,
I'm the man, the very fat man, that waters the workers beer,
And what do I care if it makes 'em ill
If it makes 'em terribly queer,
I've a car, a yacht and an aeroplane
And I water the workers beer.

Now when I makes the workers beer I puts in strychnine,
Some methylated spirits and a gallon of paraffin.
But since the brews so terribly strong
Might make 'em horribly queer,
I reach me hand for the watering can
And I waters the workers beer.

But I'm the man, the very fat man, etc.,

Now a drop of good beer is good for a man who is thirsty, tired and
    hot,
I sometimes has a drop meself of a very special lot.
But a fat and healthy working class
Is a thing that I must fear,
So I reach me hand for the watering can
And I water the workers beer.

But I'm the man, the very fat man, etc.

Now ladies fair beyond compare and be ye maid or wife,
Sometimes give a thought for one who leads a wandering life.
The water rates are shockingly high
And the meths is terrible dear
There isn't the profit there used to be
In watering workers beer.

But I'm the man, the very fat man, etc.,

                                                    Paddy Ryan

At an Inn in Henley

To thee, fair Freedom! I retire,
    From flattery, feasting, dice and din;
Nor art thou found in domes much higher
    Than the lone cot or humble Inn.

'Tis here with boundless power I reign,
    And every health which I begin,
Converts dull port to bright champagne;
    For Freedom crowns it, at an Inn.

I fly from pomp, I fly from plate,
    I fly from falsehood's specious grin;
Freedom I love, and form I hate,
    And choose my lodgings at an Inn.

Here, waiter! take my sordid ore,
    Which lacqueys else might hope to win;
It buys what Courts have not in store,
    It buys me Freedom, at an Inn.

And now once more I shape my way
    Through rain or shine, through thick or thin,
Secure to meet, at close of day,
    With kind reception at an Inn.

Whoe'er has travelled life's dull round,
    Where'er his stages may have been,
May sigh to think how oft he found
    The warmest welcome – at an Inn.

William Shenstone

At Elinor Rumming's Ale-House

Then Margery Milkduck
Her kirtle she did uptuck
An inch above her knee
Her legs that ye might see;
But they were sturdy and stubbéd,
Mighty pestles and clubbéd,
As fair and as white
As the foot of a kite:
She was somewhat foul,
Crooked-necked like an owl;
And yet she brought her fees,
A cantel of Essex cheese,
Was well a foot thick
Full of maggots quick:
It was huge and great,
And mighty strong meat
For the devil to eat
It was tart and pungete!

Another set of sluts:
Some brought walnuts,
Some apples, some pears,
Some brought their clipping shears,
Some brought this and that,

Elinovr Rvmmin,

The famous Ale-wife of *England*.

Written by Mr. *Skelton*, Poet Laureat to King

Henry the egiht.

When Skelton *wore the* Lawrell Crowne,
My Ale put all the *Ale-wiues' downe.*

LONDON

Printed for *Samuel Rand* 1624.

Some brought I wot n'ere what;
Some brought their husband's hat,
Some puddings and links,
Some tripes that stinks.
But of all this throng
One came them among,
She seemed half a leech,
And began to preach
Of the Tuesday in the week
When the mare doth kick,

Of the virtue of an unset leek,
Of her husband's breek;
With the feathers of a quail
She could to Bordeaux sail;
And with good ale barme
She could make a charme
To help withal a stitch:
She seemed to be a witch.

Another brought two goslings
That were naughty froslings;
She brought them in a wallet,
She was a comely callet:
The goslings were untied,
Elinor began to chide,
'They be wretchocks thou hast brought,
They are sheer shaking nought!'

John Skelton

Drinking Song

There are people, I know, to be found,
    Who say, and apparently think,
That sorrow and care may be drowned
    By a timely consumption of drink.

Does not man, these enthusiasts ask,
    Most nearly approach the divine,
When engaged in the soul-stirring task
    Of filling his body with wine?

Have not beggars been frequently known,
    When satisfied, soaked and replete,
To imagine their bench was a throne
    And the civilised world at their feet?

Lord Byron has finely described
    The remarkably soothing effect
Of liquor, profusely imbibed,
    On a soul that is shattered and wrecked.

In short, if your body or mind
    Or your soul or your purse come to grief,
You need only get drunk, and you'll find
    Complete and immediate relief.

For myself, I have managed to do
    Without having recourse to this plan,
So I can't write a poem for you,
    And you'd better get someone who can.

J K Stephen

A Glass of Beer (Righteous Anger)

The lanky shank of a she in the inn over there
Nearly killed me for asking the loan of a glass of beer;
May the devil grip the whey-faced slut by the hair,
And beat bad manners out of her skin for a year.

That parboiled ape, with the toughest jaw you will see
On virtue's path, and a voice that would rasp the dead,
Came roaring and raging the minute she looked at me,
And threw me out of the house on the back of my head!

If I asked her master he'd give me a cask a day;
But she, with the beer at hand, not a gill would arrange!
May she marry a ghost and bear him a kitten, and may
The High King of Glòry permit her to get the mange.

James Stephens

Some Anonymous Contributions

Ale, Glorious Ale

When I was a young man me father did say,
The summer is coming it's time to make hay,
And when hay's been carted don't you ever fail,
For to drink gaffer's health in a pint of good ale.

Ale, ale, glorious ale,
Served up in pewter, it tells its own tale,
Some folk like radishes, some curly kale,
But give I boiled parsnips
and a gert dish of taties
and a lump of fatty bacon,
And a pint of good ale.

Our MPs in parliament our faith for to keep,
I hopes now we've put him there he won't sit and sleep.
But he'll always get my vote if he never fail
For to keep down the price of our good English ale.

Ale, ale, glorious ale, etc.,

Now take all teetotallers they drink water neat,
Well it must rot their guts's and give them damp feet.
But I always say that a chap can't grow stale,
On broad beans and bacon and a pint 'a good ale.

Ale, ale, glorious ale, etc.

I Likes a Drop of Good Beer

Come one and all, both great and small,
With voices loud and clear,
And let us sing 'Bless Billy the King',
Who baited the tax upon beer.

For I likes a drop of good beer,
I likes a drop of good beer,
And damn his eyes whoever tries
To rob a poor man of his beer.

Let Ministers shape the duty on Cape
And cause port wine to be dear,
So that they keep the bread and meat cheap
And give us a drop of good beer.

For I likes a drop etc.,

Me wife and I feel always dry,
In market on Saturday night.
But a noggin of beer I never did fear,
For me wife always says that its right.

For I likes a drop etc.,

In harvest field there's nothing can yield,
The labouring man so much cheer.
To plough and sow and make them all grow,
Than to give him a skinful of beer.

For I likes a drop etc.,

Then long may Queen Victoria reign,
And be to her subjects most dear.
Where ever she goes we'll wallop her toes
Only give us a skinful of beer.

For I likes a drop etc.,

Doll thy Ale

"Doll thy ale, doll, doll thy ale, doll
Ale make many a man to have a doty poll.

Ale make many a man to stik at a brere;
Ale make many a man to lie in the miere;
And ale make many a man to slepe by the fiere
    With doll!

Ale make many a man to stomble at a stone;
Ale make many a man to go dronken home;
And ale make man to breke his tone
    With doll!

Ale make many a man to draw his knife;
Ale make many a man to make grete strife;
And ale make many a man to bete his wife
    With doll!

Ale make many a man to wet his chekes;
Ale make many a man to lie in the stretes,
And ale make many a man to wet his sheetes,
    With doll!

Ale make many a man to stombell at the blokkes;
Ale make many a man to make his head have knokkes,
And ale make many a man to sit in the stokkes
   With doll!

Ale make many a man to rine over the falows;
Ale make many a man to swere by God and Allhalows;
And ale make many a man to hang upon the galows
   With doll!"

Bryng us in Good Ale

Bryng us in no browne bred, fore that is made of brane,
Nor bryng us in no whyt bred, for therein is no game;
   But bryng us in good ale.

Bryng us in no befe, for ther is many bonys (bones),
But bryng us in good ale, for that goth downe at onys (once)
   And bryng us in good ale.

Bryng us in no bacon, for that is passing fate,
But bryng us in good ale, and gyfe us i-nough of that;
   And bryng us in good ale.

Bryng us in no mutton, for that is often lene,
Nor bryng us in no trypes, for thei be syldom clene;
   But bryng us in good ale.

Bryng us in no eggs, for ther ar many schelles,
But bryng us in good ale, and gyfe us no(th)yng ellys;
   And bryng us in good ale.

Bryng us in no butter, for therin ar many herys (hairs),
Nor bryng us in no pygges flesch, for that wyl mak us borys;
   But bryng us in good ale.

Bryng us in no podynges, for therein is al Godes good,
Nor bryng us in no venesen, for that is not for owr blod;
   But bryng us in good ale.

Bryng us in no capons flesch, for that is ofte der,
Nor bryng us in no dokes (duck's) flesch, for thei slober in the mer
(mire);
   But bryng us in good ale.

Drinking Song (c 1757)

Ye true honest Britons who love your own land
  Whose sires were so brave, so victorious, so free,
Who always beat France when they took her in hand –
  Come join honest Britons in chorus with me.
    Let us sing our own treasures, Old England's good cheer,
    The profits and pleasures of stout British beer;
    Your wine-tippling, dram-sipping fellows retreat,
    But your beer-drinking Britons can never be beat.

The French with their vineyards are meagre and pale,
  They drink of the squeezings of half-ripened fruit;
But we, who have hop-yards to mellow our ale,
  Are rosy and plump, and have freedom to boot.
    Chorus.

Should the French dare invade us, thus armed with our poles,
  We'll bang their bare ribs, make their lantern jaws ring;
For your beef-eating, beer-drinking Britons are souls
  Who will shed their last blood for their country and King.
    Chorus.

The Leather Bottel

God bless the cow and the old cow's hide,
And ev'ry thing in the world beside,
For when we've said and done all we can,
'Tis all for the good and use of man;
So I hope his soul in heaven may dwell
That first devised the leather bottel.

What say ye, to these glasses fine?
Faith! they shall have no praise of mine;
For if you touch your glass on the brim,
The liquor falls out and leaves none therein,
And though your table-cloth be ever so fine,
There lies your beer, your ale, your wine;
Whereas had it been the leather bottel,
And the stopper been in, it had been well.
So I hope in heaven his soul may dwell
That first devised the leather bottel.

What say ye, to these tankards fine?
Faith! they shall have no praise of mine,
For when the master doth send his man
To fill it with liquor as fast as he can,
The bearer thereof then runneth away
And is ne'er heard again of for many a day.
Whereas had it been the leather bottel,
And the stopper been in, why all had been well.
So I hope his soul in heaven will dwell
That first devised the leather bottel.

What say ye, to these black-jacks three?
Faith they shall have no praise from me;
For when a man and wife are at strife,
Which much too often is the case in life,
Why, then they seize on the black-jack both,
And in the scuffle they spoil the broth;
Not thinking that at a future day
They must account for throwing good liquor away;
Whereas had it been the leather bottel,
And the stopper been in, they could have banged away well.
So I hope his soul in heaven may dwell
That first devised the leather bottel.

And when this bottel is quite grown old,
And no more good liquor it will hold,
All off its sides you may cut a clout,
That will serve to mend your old shoes about;
T'other end, hang it on to a pin,
'Twill serve to put your odd trifles in;
Here's a save-all for your candles' ends,
For young beginners have need of such things;
So I hope his soul in heaven may dwell
That first devised the leather bottel.

In Praise of Ale

Come all you brave wights
That are dubbed ale-knights,
   Now set yourself in fight;
And let them that crack
In the praises of Sack
   Know Malt is of mickle might.

Though Sack they define
To be holy, divine,
    Yet is it but natural liquor;
Ale hath for its part
An addition of art
    To make it drink thinner or quicker.

Sack's fiery fume
Doth waste and consume
    Men's *humidum radicale*;
It scaldeth their livers,
It breeds burning fevers,
    Proves *vinum venenum reale*.

But history gathers
From aged forefathers
    That Ale's the true liquor of life;
Men lived long in health,
And preserved their wealth,
    Whilst barley-broth only was rife.

Sack quickly ascends
And suddenly ends
    What company came for at first;
And that which yet worse is
It empties men's purses
    Before it half quenches their thirst.

Sack makes men from words
Fall to drawing of swords,
    And quarrelling endeth their quaffing;
Whilst dagger-ale barrels
Bear off many quarrels,
    And oft turn chiding to laughing.

Sack's drink for our masters;
All may be ale-tasters.
    Good things the more common the better;
Sack's but single broth,
Ale's meat, drink, and cloth,
    Say they that know never a letter.

But not to entangle
Old friends till they wrangle,
    And quarrell for other men's pleasure,
Let Ale keep his place,
And let Sack have his grace,
    So that neither exceed the true measure.

The Ploughman

A ploughman dresses fine, he drinks strong beer, ale, and wine,
And the best of tobacco he do smoke.
'Pretty maids don't think amiss a ploughman for to kiss,
For his breath smells as sweet as a rose, a rose, a rose,
His breath smells as sweet as a rose.'

A ploughman in his shirt he completely does his work,
And so loudly to the little boy do call,
Saying: 'Be nimble and be quick by the swishing of your whip.'
And so merrily he'll rattle them along, along, along,
And so merrily he'll rattle them along.

When our shears are shod, to the blacksmith off we wad,
And so loudly to the blacksmith we do call,
Saying: 'Be nimble and be quick, and throw your blows in thick.'
And so merrily he will swing his hammer round, around, around,
And so merrily he'll swing his hammer round.

When our shears are done, to the ale-house we will run,
And so loudly to the landlord we do call;
Saying: 'Bring to us some beer, for while I am here,
A ploughman is always a-dry, a-dry, a-dry,
A ploughman is always a-dry.'

Ratcliffe Highway

As I was a-walking down London,
From Wapping to Ratcliffe Highway,
I chanced to pop into a gin-shop,
To spend a long night and a day.

A young doxy came rolling up to me,
And asked if I'd money to sport.
For a bottle of wine changed a guinea,
And she quickly replied: 'That's the sort.'

When the bottle was put on the table,
There was glasses for everyone.
When I asked for the change of my guinea,
She tipped me a verse of her song.

This lady flew into a passion,
And placed both her hands on her hip,
Saying: 'Sailor, don't you know our fashion?
Do you think you're on board of your ship?'

'If this is your fashion to rob me,
Such a fashion I'll never abide.
So launch out the change of my guinea,
Or else I'll give you a broadside.'

A gold watch hung over the mantel,
So the change of my guinea I take,
And down the stairs I run nimbly,
Saying: 'Darn my old boots, I'm well paid.'

The night being dark in my favour,
To the river I quickly did creep,
And I jumped in a boat bound for Deptford,
And got safe aboard of my ship.

So come all you bold young sailors,
That ramble down Ratcliffe Highway,
If you chance to pop into a gin-shop,
Beware, lads, how long you do stay.

For the songs and the liquors invite you,
And your heart will be all in a rage;
If you give them a guinea for a bottle,
You can go to the devil for change.

The Widow that Keeps the Cock Inn

A traveller for many long years I have been,
    But I never went over to France –
Most cities and all market towns I've been in,
    From Berwick on Tweed to Penzance,
Many hotels and taverns I've been in my time,
    And many fair landladys seen –
But of all the fair charmers who other outshine
        Give me the sweet widow –
        The dear little widow,
I mean the sweet widow that keeps the Cock Inn.

Her lips are as roses as e'en is her wine,
    And like all her liquors, she's neat,
She's full of good spirits, that's really devine
    And while serving her bitters, looks sweet,
Excuse these outpourings, they spring from the heart,
    You may laugh – so shall I, if I win,
One smile of consent, how 'twould lessen the smart,
        From the active young widow,
        The spruce little widow.
The little widow that keeps the Cock Inn.

There's Bet at the 'Blossom' and Poll of the 'Crown',
   Fat Dolly who owns the 'Red Heart'.
There's Kate of the 'Garter and Star', of renown
   And Peggy who keeps the 'Skylark'.
Spruce Fan of the 'Eagle' and Nan of the 'Bell'
   Pretty Jane of the 'Man drest in Green'
But of all the fair creatures that others excel.
     Give me the sweet widow,
     The nice little widow.
My neat pretty widow who keeps the Cock Inn.

There's Nance at 'the Old Woman clothed in Gray'
   I look black upon her I vow,
Even Letty who graces 'the Old Load of Hay',
   I don't care a straw for her now,
There's another decanter'd just now in my heart
   I for none of the rest care a pin.
Oh, that Cupid the rogue, would but let fly his dart,
     At the plump little widow,
     The gay little widow,
The spirited widow that keeps the Cock Inn.

When last in her little bar parlour I sat
   I joked her about her lone state,
A brood of young chicken's dear widow mind that,
   Would be better around you prate,
Says she, pray don't reckon 'fore they are hatch'd,
   says I, where's the harm or the sin?
You can manage a second, we're very well match'd
     You dear little widow,
     You charming young widow,
You're a nice little widow to keep the Cock Inn.

Then here's to the dear little charmer I prize,
   In a bumper now filled to the brim,
For who could resist such a pair of black eyes,
   As in rich liquid moisture they swim,
Away, then away, with my bachelor's vow
   My hand then is hers, with the ring,
For if she be willing to take me in tow,
     I'll marry the widow,
     The dear little widow,
I'll marry the widow, and keep the Cock Inn.

Wassails

Wassail! wassail! all over the town,
Our toast it is white and our ale it is brown;
Our bowl it is of the good maplin tree,
So here's, good fellow, I'll drink to thee.

Gloucestershire

Here we come a-wassailing,
 Among the leaves so green;
Here we come a-wandering,
 So fair to be seen.

Chorus.

Love and joy come to you
 And to your wassail, too,
And God send you a happy New Year,
 A New Year,
And God send you a happy New Year,
Our wassail cup is made of rosemary-tree,
So is your beer of the best barley.

Staffordshire

Have you noticed how the whole country seems to grind to a halt this time of year?

Limericks and the Like

There was an old man of Dundee,
Who came home as drunk as can be;
    He wound up the clock
    With the end of his cock,
And buggered his wife with the key.

One the chest of a barmaid in Sale
Were tattooed the prices of ale,
    And on her behind,
    For the sake of the blind,
Was the same information in Braille.

There was a young girl of St Cyr,
Whose reflex reactions were queer;
    Her escort said: 'Mabel,
    Get up off the table!
That money is there for the beer.'

The exquisite bartender at Sweeney's
Is famed for his ale and free wienies,
    But I thought him uncouth
    To gulp gin and vermouth,
Chill the glasses and piddle Martinis.

'COME TO NOAH'S for wine and strong waters,
And for diddling in clean classy quarters.
    I assure every guest
    I've made personal test
Of my booze and my beds and my daughters.'

A Plumber's Plea to all Peers

Have you heard of our plumbers dilemma,
It's driving them right round the bend.
The Urinals run slow
Elbows deep our lads go
Then they find it's just a fag end.

Inscribed on a Pint-Pot

There are several reasons for drinking,
And one has just entered my head;
If a man cannot drink when he's living
How the Hell can he drink when he's dead?

A Toast

Here's to a temperance supper,
    With water in glasses tall,
And coffee and tea to end with –
    And me not there at all!

David Copperfield, by 'Phiz'

CHAPTER 3

FICTION

Charles Dickens

From: David Copperfield

"There's half a pint of ale for you. Will you have it now?"

I thanked him and said, "Yes." Upon which he poured it out of a jug into a large tumbler, and held it up against the light, and made it look beautiful.

"My eye!" he said. "It seems a good deal, don't it?"

"It does seem a good deal," I answered with a smile. For it was quite delightful to me to find him so pleasant. He was a twinkling-eyed, pimple-faced man, with his hair standing upright all over his head; and as he stood with one arm a-kimbo, holding up the glass to the light with the other hand, he looked quite friendly.

"There was a gentleman here yesterday," he said – "a stout gentleman, by the name of Topsawyer – perhaps you know him?"

"No," I said, "I don't think – "

"In breeches and gaiters, broad brimmed hat, grey coat, speckled choker," said the waiter.

"No," I said bashfully, "I haven't the pleasure – "

"He came in here," said the waiter, looking at the light through the tumbler, "ordered a glass of this ale – WOULD order it – I told him not – drank it, and fell dead. It was too old for him. It oughtn't to be drawn; That's the fact."

I was very much shocked to hear of this melancholy accident, and said that I thought I had better have some water.

"Why, you see," said the waiter, still looking at the light through the tumbler, with one of his eyes shut up, "our people don't like things being ordered and left. It offends 'em. But I'll drink it if you like. I'm used to it, and use is everything. I don't think it'll hurt me, if I throw my head back, and take if off quick. Shall I?"

I replied that he would much oblige me by drinking it, if he thought he could do it safely, but by no means otherwise. When he did throw his head back, and take it off quick, I had a horrible fear, I confess, of seeing him meet the fate of the lamented Mr Topsawyer, and fall lifeless on the carpet. But it didn't hurt him. On the contrary, I thought he seemed the fresher for it.

"What have we got here?" he said, putting a fork into my dish. "Not chops?"

"Chops," I said.

"Lord bless my soul!" he exclaimed, "I didn't know they were chops. Why a chop's the very think to take the head off the bad effects of that beer! Ain't it lucky?"

And he proceeded to demolish the chops and the pudding too.

"What is your best – your VERY BEST – ale a glass?"

"Twopence-halfpenny," says the landlord, "is the price of the Genuine Stunning ale."

"Then," says I, producing the money, "just draw me a glass of the Genuine Stunning, if you please, with a good head to it."

The landlord looked at me in return over the bar, from head to foot, with a strange smile on his face; and instead of drawing the beer, looked round the screen and said something to his wife. She came out from behind it, with her work in her hand, and joined him in surveying me. Here we stand, all three, before me now. The landlord in his shirtsleeves, leaning against the bar window-frame; his wife looking over the little half-door; and I, in some confusion, looking up at them from outside the partition. They asked me a good many questions; as, what my name was, how old I was, where I lived, how I was employed, and how I came there. To all of which, that I might commit nobody, I invented, I am afraid, appropriate answers. They served me with ale, though I suspect it was not the Genuine Stunning: and the landlord's wife, opening the little half-door of the bar, and bending down, gave me my money back, and gave me a kiss that was half admiring, and half compassionate, but all womanly and good, I am sure.

Pickwickian Inns: The Blue Lion

'We are about to partake of a plain dinner at the Blue Lion, sir; we hope you and your friends will join us.'

'Of course,' said Mr Wardle, 'among our friends, we include Mr –'; and he looked towards the stranger.

'Jingle,' said that versatile gentleman, taking the hint at once. 'Jingle – Alfred Jingle, Esq., of No Hall, Nowhere.'

'I shall be very happy, I am sure,' said Mr Pickwick.

'So shall I,' said Mr Alfred Jingle, drawing one arm through Mr Pickwick's, and another through Mr Wardle's, as he whispered confidentially in the ear of the former gentleman:

'Devilish good dinner – cold, but capital – peeped into the room this morning – fowls and pies, and all that sort of thing – pleasant fellows these – well behaved, too – very.'

There being no further preliminaries to arrange, the company straggled into the town in little knots of twos and threes; and within a quarter of an hour were all seated in the great room of the Blue Lion Inn, Muggleton – Mr Dumkins acting as chairman, and Mr Luffey officiating as vice.

There was a vast deal of talking and rattling of knives and forks, and plates: a great running about of three ponderous headed waiters, and a rapid disappearance of the substantial viands on the table; to each and every of which item of confusion, the facetious Mr Jingle lent the aid of half-a-dozen ordinary men at least. When everybody had eaten as much as possible, the cloth was removed, bottles, glasses, and dessert were placed on the table; and the waiters withdrew to 'clear away', or in other words, to appropriate to their own private use and emolument whatever remnants of the eatables and drinkables they could contrive to lay their hands on.

Amidst the general hum of mirth and conversation that ensued, there was a little man with a puffy Say-nothing-to-me, – or-I'll-contradict-you sort of countenance, who remained very quiet; occasionally looking round him when the conversation slackened, as if he contemplated putting in something very weighty; and now and then bursting into a short cough of inexpressible grandeur. At length, during a moment of comparative silence, the little man called out in a very loud, solemn voice, –

'Mr Luffey!'

'Everybody was hushed into a profound stillness; as the individual addressed, replied –

'Sir!'

'I wish to address a few words to you, sir, if you will entreat the gentlemen to fill their glasses.'

Mr Jingle uttered a patronizing 'hear, hear', which was responded to by the remainder of the company; and the glasses having been filled the Vice-President assumed an air of wisdom in a state of profound attention, and said –

'Mr Staple.'

'Sir,' said the little man, rising, 'I wish to address what I have to say to *you* and not to our worthy chairman, because our worthy chairman is in some measure – I may say in a great degree – the subject of what I have to say, or I may say – to – '

'State,' suggested Mr Jingle.

– 'Yes, to state,' said the little man. 'I thank my honourable friend, if he will allow me to call him so (four "hears" and one certainly from Mr Jingle) – for the suggestion. Sir, I am a Deller – a Dingley Deller (cheers). I cannot lay claim to the honour of forming an item in the population of Muggleton; nor, sir, I will frankly admit, do I covet that honour; and I will tell you why, sir – (hear); to Muggleton I will readily concede all those honours and distinctions to which it can fairly lay claim – they are too numerous and too well known to require aid or recapitulation from me. But, sir, while we remember that Muggleton has given birth to a Dumkins and a Podder, let us never forget that Dingley Dell can boast a Luffey and a Struggles. (Vociferous cheering.) Let me not be considered as wishing to detract from the merits of the former gentlemen. Sir, I envy them the luxury of their own feelings on this occasion. (Cheers.) Every gentleman who hears me, is probably acquainted with the reply made by an individual, who – to use an ordinary figure of speech – "hung out" in a tub, to the emperor Alexander: "If I were not Diogenes," said he, "I would be Alexander." I can well imagine these gentlemen to say, ordinary men at least. When everybody had eaten as much as possible, the cloth was removed, bottles, glasses, and dessert were placed on the table; and that your fellowtownsmen stand pre-eminent? Have you never heard of

Dumkins and determination? Have you never been taught to associate Podder with property? (Great applause.) Have you never, when struggling for your rights, your liberties, and your privileges, been reduced, if only for an instant, to misgiving and despair? And when you have been thus depressed, has not the name of Dumkins laid afresh within your breast the figure which had just gone out; and has not a word from that man lighted it again as brightly as if it had never expired? (Great cheering.) Gentlemen, I beg to surround with a rich halo of enthusiastic cheering, the united names of "Dumkins and Podder".'

Here the little man ceased, and here the company commenced a raising of voices, and thumping of tables, which lasted with little intermission during the remainder of the evening. Other toasts were drunk. Mr Luffey and Mr Struggles, Mr Pickwick and Mr Jingle, were, each in his turn, the subject of unqualified eulogium; and each in due course returned thanks for the honour.

Enthusiastic as we are in the noble cause to which we have devoted ourselves, we should have felt a sensation of pride which we cannot express and a consciousness of having done something to merit immortality of which we are now deprived, could we have laid the faintest outline of these addresses before our ardent readers. Mr Snodgrass, as usual, took a great mass of notes, which would no doubt have afforded most useful and valuable information, had not the burning eloquence of the words or the feverish influence of the wine made that gentleman's hand so extremely unsteady, as to render his writing nearly unintelligible, and his style wholly so. By dint of patient investigation, we have been enabled to trace some characters bearing a faint resemblance to the names of the speakers; and we can also discern an entry of a song (supposed to have been sung by Mr Jingle), in which the words 'bowl', 'sparkling', 'ruby', 'bright', and 'wine' are frequently repeated at short intervals. We fancy too, that we can discern at the very end of the notes, some indistinct reference to 'broiled bones'; and then the words 'cold' 'without' occur; but as any hypothesis we could found upon them must necessarily rest upon mere conjecture, we are not disposed to indulge in any of the speculations to which they may give rise.

We will therefore return to Mr Tupman: merely adding that within some few minutes before twelve o'clock that night, the convocation of worthies of Dingley Dell and Muggleton were heard to sing, with great feeling and emphasis, the beautiful and pathetic national air of

> We won't go home 'till morning,
> We won't go home 'till morning,
> We won't go home 'till morning,
>   'Till daylight doth appear.

Pickwickian Inns: The Magpie and Stump

This favoured tavern, sacred to the evening orgies of Mr Lowten and his companions, was what ordinary people would designate a public-house. That the landlord was a man of a money-making turn, was sufficiently testified by the fact of a small bulk-head beneath the tap-room window, in size and shape not unlike a sedan-chair, being underlet to a mender of shoes: and that he was a being of a philanthropic mind, was evident from the protection he afforded to a pieman, who vended his delicacies without fear of interruption on the very door-step. In the lower windows, which were decorated with curtains of a saffron hue, dangled two or three printed cards, bearing reference to Devonshire cyder and Dantzic spruce, while a large black board, announcing in white letters to an enlightened public that there were 500,000 barrels of double stout in the cellars of the establishment, left the mind in a state of not unpleasing doubt and uncertainty as to the precise direction in the bowels of the earth, in which this mighty cavern might be supposed to extend. When we add, that the weather-beaten sign-board bore the half-obliterated semblance of a magpie intently eyeing a crooked streak of brown paint, which the neighbours had been taught from infancy to consider as the "stump," we have said all that need be said of the exterior of the edifice.

On Mr Pickwick's presenting himself at the bar, an elderly female emerged from behind a screen therein, and presented herself before him.

"Is Mr Lowten here, ma'am?" inquired Mr Pickwick.

"Yes he is, sir," replied the landlady. "Here, Charley, show the gentleman in, to Mr Lowten."

"The gen'l'm'n can't go in just now," said a shambling pot-boy, with a red head, "'cos Mr Lowten's a singin' a comic song, and he'll put him out. He'll be done d'rectly, sir."

The red-headed pot-boy had scarcely finished speaking, when a most unanimous hammering of tables, and jingling of glasses, announced that the song had that instant terminated; and Mr Pickwick, after desiring Sam to solace himself in the tap, suffered himself to be conducted into the presence of Mr Lowten.

At the announcement of "gentleman to speak to you, sir," a puffy-faced young man, who filled the chair at the head of the table, looked with some surprise in the direction from whence the voice proceeded: and the surprise seemed to be by no means diminished, when his eyes rested on an individual whom he had never seen before.

"I beg your pardon, sir," said Mr Pickwick, "and I am very sorry to disturb the other gentlemen, too, but I come on very particular business; and if you will suffer me to detain you at this end of the room for five minutes, I shall be very much obliged to you."

The puffy-faced young man rose, and drawing a chair close to Mr. Pickwick in an obscure corner of the room, listened attentively to his tale of woe.

"Ah," he said, when Mr Pickwick had concluded, "Dodson and Fogg – sharp practice theirs – capital men of business, Dodson and Fogg, sir."

Mr Pickwick admitted the sharp practice of Dodson and Fogg, and Lowten resumed.

"Perker ain't in town, and he won't be, neither, before the end of next week; but if you want the action defended, and will leave the copy with me, I can do all that's needful till he comes back."

"That's exactly what I came here for," said Mr Pickwick, handing over the document. "If anything particular occurs, you can write to me at the post-office, Ipswich."

"That's all right," replied Mr Perker's clerk; and then seeing Mr Pickwick's eye wandering curiously towards the table, he added, "Will you join us, for half-an-hour or so? We are capital company here to-night. There's Samkin and Green's managing-clerk, and Smithers and Price's chancery, and Pimkin and Thomas's out o' door – sings a capital song, he does – and Jack Bamber, and ever so many more. You're come out of the country, I suppose. Would you like to join us?"

Mr Pickwick could not resist so tempting an opportunity of studying human nature. He suffered himself to be led to the table, where, after having been introduced to the company in due form, he was accommodated with a seat near the chairman, and called for a glass of his favourite beverage.

A profound silence, quite contrary to Mr Pickwick's expectation, succeeded.

"You don't find this sort of thing disagreeable, I hope, sir?" said his right hand neighbour, a gentleman in a checked shirt, and Mosaic studs, with a cigar in his mouth.

"Not in the least," replied Mr Pickwick, "I like it very much, although I am no smoker myself."

"I should be very sorry to say I wasn't," interposed another gentleman on the opposite side of the table. "It's board and lodging to me, is smoke."

Mr Pickwick glanced at the speaker, and thought that if it were washing too, it would be all the better.

Here there was another pause. Mr Pickwick was a stranger, and his coming had evidently cast a damp upon the party.

"Mr Grundy's going to oblige the company with a song," said the chairman.

"No he ain't," said Mr Grundy.

"Why not?" said the chairman.

"Because he can't," said Mr Grundy.

"You had better say he won't," replied the chairman.

"Well, then, he won't," retorted Mr Grundy. Mr Grundy's positive refusal to gratify the company occasioned another silence.

"Won't anybody enliven us?" said the chairman, despondingly.

"Why don't you enliven us yourself, Mr Chairman?" said a young man with a whisker, a squint, and an open shirt collar (dirty), from the bottom of the table.

"Hear! hear!" said the smoking gentleman in the Mosaic jewellery.

"Because I only know one song, and I have sung it already, and it's a fine of 'glasses round' to sing the same song twice in a night," replied the chairman.

This was an unanswerable reply, and silence prevailed again.

"I have been to-night, gentlemen," said Mr Pickwick, hoping to start a subject which all the company could take a part in discussing, "I have been to-night in a place which you all know very well, but which I have not been in before for some years, and know very little of; I mean Gray's Inn, gentlemen. Curious little nooks in a great place, like London, these old Inns are."

"By Jove," said the chairman, whispering across the table to Mr Pickwick, "you have hit upon something that one of us, at least, would talk upon for ever. You'll draw old Jack Bamber out; he was never heard to talk about anything else but the Inns, and he has lived alone in them till he's half crazy."

The individual to whom Lowten alluded, was a little yellow high-shouldered man, whose countenance, from his habit of stooping forward when silent, Mr. Pickwick had not observed before. He wondered though, when the old man raised his shrivelled face, and bent his grey eye upon him, with a keen inquiring look, that such remarkable features could have escaped his attention for a moment. There was a fixed grim smile perpetually on his countenance; he leant his chin on a long skinny hand, with nails of extraordinary length; and as he inclined his head to one side, and looked keenly out from beneath his ragged grey eyebrows, there was a strange, wild slyness in his leer, quite repulsive to behold.

This was the figure that now started forward, and burst into an animated torrent of words. As this chapter has been a long one, however, and as the old man was a remarkable personage, it will be more respectful to him, and more convenient to us, to let him speak for himself in a fresh one.

Pickwickian Inns: The Marquis of Granby

The Marquis of Granby in Mrs Weller's time was quite a model of a road-side public-house of the better class – just large enough to be convenient, and small enough to be snug. On the opposite side of the road was a large sign-board on a high post, representing the head and shoulders of a gentleman with an apoplectic countenance, in a red coat with deep blue facings, and a touch of the same blue over his three-cornered hat, for a sky. Over that again were a pair of flags; beneath the last button of his coat were a couple of cannon; and the whole formed an expressive and undoubted likeness of the Marquis of Granby of glorious memory.

The bar window displayed a choice collection of geranium plants, and a well-dusted row of spirit phials. The open shutters bore a variety of golden inscriptions, eulogistic of good beds and neat wines; and the choice group of countrymen and hostlers lounging about the stable-door and horse-trough, afforded presumptive proof of the excellent quality of the ale and spirits which were sold within. Sam Weller paused, when he dismounted from the coach, to note all these little indications of a thriving business, with the eye of an experienced traveller; and having done so, stepped in at once, highly satisfied with everything he had observed.

━━━━━━

Pickwickian Inns: The White Hart

There are in London several old inns, once the head-quarters of celebrated coaches in the days when coaches performed their journeys in a graver and more solemn manner than they do in these times; but which have now degenerated into little more than the abiding and booking places of country waggons. The reader would look in vain for any of these ancient hostelries, among the Golden Crosses and Bull and Mouths, which rear their stately fronts in the improved streets of London. If he would light upon any of these old places, he must direct his steps to the obscurer quarters of the town; and there in some secluded nooks he will find several, still standing with a kind of gloomy sturdiness, amidst the modern innovations which surround them.

In the Borough especially, there still remain some half dozen old inns, which have preserved their external features unchanged, and which have escaped alike the rage for public improvement, and the encroachments of private speculation. Great, rambling, queer, old places they are, with galleries, and passages, and staircases, wide enough and antiquated enough to furnish materials for a hundred ghost stories, supposing we should ever be reduced to the lamentable necessity of inventing any, and that the world should exist long enough to exhaust the innumerable veracious legends connected with old London Bridge, and its adjacent neighbourhood on the Surrey side.

It was in the yard of one of these inns – of no less celebrated a one than the White Hart – that a man was busily employed in brushing the dirt off a pair of boots, early on the morning succeeding the events narrated in the last chapter. He was habited in a coarse-striped waistcoat, with black calico sleeves, and blue glass buttons; drab breeches and leggings. A bright red handkerchief was wound in a very loose and unstudied style round his neck, and an old white hat was carelessly thrown on one side of his head. There were two rows of boots before him, one cleaned and the other dirty, and at every addition he made to the clean row, he paused from his work, and contemplated its results with evident satisfaction.

The yard presented none of that bustle and activity which are the usual characteristics of a large coach inn. Three or four lumbering waggons, each with a pile of goods beneath its ample canopy, about the height of the second-floor window of an ordinary house, were stowed away beneath a lofty roof which extended over one end of the yard: and another, which was probably to commence its journey that morning, was drawn out into the open space. A double tier of bedroom galleries, with old clumsy balustrades, ran round two sides of the straggling area, and a double row of bells to correspond, sheltered from the weather by a little sloping roof, hung over the door leading to the bar and coffee-room. Two or three gigs and chaise-carts were wheeled up under different little sheds and pent-houses; and the occasional heavy tread of a cart-horse, or rattling of a chain at the further end of the yard, announced to anybody who cared about the matter, that the stable lay in that direction. When we add that a few boys in smock frocks were lying asleep on heavy packages, woolpacks, and other articles that were scattered about on heaps of straw, we have described as fully as need be the general appearance of the yard of the White Hart Inn, High Street, Borough, on the particular morning in question.

A loud ringing of one of the bells, was followed by the appearance of a smart chambermaid in the upper sleeping gallery, who, after tapping at one of the doors, and receiving a request from within, called over the balustrades –

"Sam!"

"Hallo," replied the man with the white hat.

"Number twenty-two wants his boots."

"Ask number twenty-two, whether he'll have 'em now, or wait till he gets 'em," was the reply.

"Come, don't be a fool, Sam," said the girl, coaxingly, "the gentleman wants his boots directly."

"Well, you *are* a nice young 'ooman for a musical party, you are," said the boot-cleaner. "Look at these here boots – eleven pair o' boots; and one shoe as b'longs to number six, with the wooden leg. The eleven boots is to be called at half-past eight and the shoe at nine. Who's number twenty-two, that's to put all the others out? No, no; reg'lar rotation, as Jack Ketch said, wen he tied the men up. Sorry to keep you a waitin', sir, but I'll attend to you directly."

Saying which, the man in the white hat set to work upon a top-boot with increased assiduity.

There was another loud ring; and the bustling old landlady of the White Hart made her appearance in the opposite gallery.

"Sam," cried the landlady, "where's that lazy, idle – why, 'Sam – oh, there you are; why don't you answer?"

"Wouldn't be gen-teel to answer, 'till you'd done talking," replied Sam, gruffly.

"Here, clean them shoes for number seventeen directly, and take 'em to private sitting-room, number five, first floor."

The landlady flung a pair of lady's shoes into the yard, and bustled away.

"Number 5," said Sam, as he picked up the shoes, and taking a piece of chalk from his pocket, made a memorandum of their destination on the soles –

"Lady's shoes and private sittin'-room! I suppose *she* didn't come in the waggin."

"She came in early this morning," cried the girl, who was still leaning over the railing of the gallery, "with a gentleman in a hackney-coach, and it's him as wants his boots, and you'd better do 'em, that's all about it."

"Vy didn't you say so before?" said Sam, with great indignation, singling out the boots in question from the heap before him. "For all I know'd he vas one o' the regular three-pennies. Private room! and a lady too! If he's anything of a gen'lm'n, he's vorth a shillin' a day, let alone the arrands."

Stimulated by this inspiring reflection, Mr Samuel brushed away with such hearty good will, that in a few minutes the boots and shoes, with a polish which would have struck envy to the soul of the amiable Mr Warren (for they used Day and Martin at the White Hart), had arrived at the door of number five.

"Come in," said a man's voice, in reply to Sam's rap at the door.

Sam made his best bow, and stepped into the presence of a lady and gentleman seated at breakfast. Having officiously deposited the gentleman's boots right and left at his feet, and the lady's shoes right and left at hers, he backed towards the door.

"Boots," said the gentleman.

"Sir," said Sam, closing the door, and keeping his hand on the knob of the lock.

"Do you know – what's a-name – Doctors' Commons?"

"Yes, sir."

"Where is it?"

"Paul's Church-yard, sir; low archway on the carriage-side, bookseller's at one corner, hot-el on the other, and two porters in the middle as touts for licenses."

"Touts for licences!" said the gentleman.

"Touts for licences," replied Sam. "Two coves in vhite aprons – touches their hats wen you walk in – 'License, sir, licence?' Queer sort, them, and their mas'rs too, sir – Old Baily Proctors – and no mistake."

"What do they do?" inquired the gentleman.

"Do! *You*, sir! That a'nt the wost on it, neither. They puts things into old gen'lm'n's heads as they never dreamed of. My father, sir, wos a coachman. A widower he wos, and fat enough for anything – uncommon fat, to be sure. His missus dies, and leaves him four hundred pound. Down he goes to the Commons, to see the lawyer and draw the blunt – wery smart – top-boots on – nosegay in his button-hole – broad-brimmed tile – green shawl – quite the gen'lm'n. Goes through the archvay, thinking how he should inwest the money – up comes the touter, touches his hat – 'Licence, sir, license?' – 'What's that?' says my father. – 'Licence, sir,' says he. – 'What licence?' says my father. – 'Marriage licence,' says the touter. – 'Dash my veskit,' says my father, 'I never thought o' that.' – 'I think you wants one, sir,' says the touter. My father pulls up, and thinks abit – 'No,' says he, 'damme, I'm too old, b'sides I'm a many sizes too large,' says he. – 'Not a bit on it, sir,' says the touter. – 'Think not?' says my father. – 'I'm sure not,' says he; 'we married a gen'lm'n twice your size, last Monday.' – 'Did you, though,' said my father. –

'To be sure we did,' says the touter, 'you're a babby to him – this way, sir – this way!' – and sure enough my father walks arter him, like a tame monkey behind a horgan, into a little black office, vere a feller sat among dirty papers and tin boxes, making believe he was busy. 'Pray take a seat, vile I makes out the affidavit, sir,' says the lawyer. 'Thank'ee, sir,' says my father, and down he sat, and stared with all his eyes, and his mouth vide open, at the names on the boxes. 'What's your name, sir,' says the lawyer. – 'Tony Weller,' says my father. – 'Parish?' says the lawyer. – 'Belle Savage,' says my father; for he stopped there wen he drove up, and he know'd nothing about parishes, *he* didn't. – 'And what's the lady's name?' says the lawyer. My father was struck all of a heap. 'Blessed if I know,' says he. – 'Not know!' says the lawyer. – 'No more nor you do,' says my father, 'can't I put that in arterwards?' – 'Impossible!' says the lawyer. – 'Wery well,' says my father, after he'd thought a moment, 'put down Mrs Clarke.' – 'What Clarke?' says the lawyer, dipping his pen in the ink. – 'Susan Clarke, Markis o'Granby, Dorking,' says my father; 'she'll have me, if I ask, I des-say – I never said nothing to her, but she'll have me, I know.' The licence was made out, and she *did* have him, and what's more she's got him now; and *I* never had any of the four hundred pound, worse luck. Beg your pardon, sir," said Sam, when he had concluded, "but wen I gets on this here grievance, I runs on like a new barrow vith the wheel greased." Having said which, and having paused for an instant to see whether he was wanted for anything more, Sam left the room.

Tony Weller at the Marquis of Granby

Other authors

From: The Beaux' Stratagem

SCENE – An Inn at Lichfield.

Enter BONIFACE *and* AIMWELL.

Boniface.   This way, this way, sir.

Aimwell.   You're my landlord, I suppose?

Bon.   Yes, sir, I'm old Will Boniface; pretty well known upon this road, as the saying is.

Aim.   Oh, Mr Boniface, your servant.

Bon.   Oh, Sir, what wilt your honour please to drink, as the saying is?

Aim.   I have heard your town of Lichfield much famed for ale; I think I'll taste that.

Bon.   Sir, I have now in my cellar ten tun of the best ale in Staffordshire: 'tis smooth as oil, sweet as milk, clear as amber, and strong as brandy, and will be just fourteen years old the fifth day of next March, old style.

Aim.   You're very exact, I find, in the age of your ale.

Bon.   As punctual, sir, as I am in the age of my children. I'll show you such ale. Here, tapster, broach number 1706, as the saying is. Sir, you shall taste my "anno domini." I have lived in Lichfield, man and boy, above eight-and-fifty years, and I believe have not consumed eight-and-fifty ounces of meat.

Aim.   At a meal, you mean, if one may guess by your bulk?

Bon.   Not in my life, sir; I have fed purely upon ale. I have ate my ale, drank my ale, and I always sleep upon my ale.

Enter TAPSTER *with a Tankard.*

Now, sir, you shall see . . . Your worship's health. (*Drinks*).

Ha! delicious, delicious: fancy it Burgandy, only fancy it – and 'tis worth ten shillings a quart.

Aim.   (*Drinks.*) 'Tis confounded strong.

Bon.   Strong! it must be so, or how would we be strong that drink it?

Aim.   And have you lived so long upon this ale, landlord?

Bon.   Eight-and-fifty years, upon my credit, sir; but it killed my wife, poor woman, as the saying is.

Aim.   How came that to pass?

Bon.   I don't know how, sir; she would not let the ale take its natural course, sir; she was for qualifying it every now and then with a dram, as the saying is; and an honest gentleman, that came this way from Ireland, made her a present of a dozen bottles of usquebaugh – but the poor woman was never well after; but, however, I was obliged to the gentleman, you know.

Aim.   Why, was it the usquebaugh that killed her?

Bon.   My Lady Bountiful said so. She, good lady, did what could be done: she cured her of three tympanies: but the fourth carried her off; but she's happy, and I'm contented, as the saying is.

Aim. Who's that Lady Bountiful you mentioned?

Bon. Odds my life, sir, we'll drink her health. (*Drinks.*) My Lady Bountiful is one of the best of women. Her last husband, Sir Charles Bountiful, left her worth a thousand pounds a year; and I believe she lays out one-half on't in charitable uses for the good of her neighbours.

Aim. Has the lady any children?

Bon. Yes, sir, she has a daughter by Sir Charles; the finest woman in all our county, and the greatest fortune. She has a son, too, by her first husband, 'Squire Sullen, who married a fine lady from London t'other day; if you please, sir, we'll drink his health. (*Drinks.*)

Aim. What sort of a man is he?

Bon. Why, sir, the man's well enough; says little, thinks less, and does nothing at all, faith; but he's a man of great estate, and values nobody.

Aim. A sportsman, I suppose?

Bon. Yes, he's a man of pleasure; he plays at whist, and smokes his pipe eight-and-forty hours together sometimes.

Aim. A fine sportsman truly! – and married, you say?

Bon. Ay; and to a curious woman, sir. But he's my landlord, and so a man, you know, would not – Sir, my humble service. (*Drinks.*) Though I value not a farthing what he can do to me; I pay him his rent at quarter-day; I have a good running trade; I have but one daughter, and I can give her – But no matter for that.

Aim. You're very happy, Mr Boniface. Pray, what other company have you in town?

Bon. A power of fine ladies; and then we have the French officers.

Aim. Oh, that's all right; you have a good many of those gentlemen. Pray how do you like their company?

Bon. So well, as the saying is, that I could wish we had as many more of 'em. They're full of money, and pay double for everything they have. They know, sir, that we paid good round taxes for the making of 'em; and so they are willing to reimburse us a little; one of 'em lodges in my house. (*Bell rings.*) I beg your Worship's pardon; I'll wait on you in half a minute.

George Farquhar

From: The History of Tom Jones, a Foundling

Mr Jones, and Partridge, or Little Benjamin, (which epithet of Little was perhaps given him ironically, he being in reality near six feet high) having left their last quarters in the manner before described, travelled on to Gloucester, without meeting any adventure worth relating.

Being arrived here, they chose for their house of entertainment the sign of the Bell, an excellent house indeed, and which I do most seriously recommend to every reader who shall visit this ancient city. The master of it is brother to the great preacher Whitefield; but is absolutely untainted with the pernicious principles of Methodism, or of any other heretical sect. He is indeed a very honest plain man, and, in my opinion, not likely to create any disturbance either in Church or State. His wife hath, I believe, had much pretension to beauty, and is still a very fine woman. Her person and deportment might have made a shining figure in the politest assemblies; but tho' she must be conscious of this, and many other perfections, she seems perfectly contented with, and resigned to that state of life to which she is called; and this resignation is entirely owing to the prudence and wisdom of her temper: for she is at present as free from any Methodistical notions as her husband. I say at present: for she freely confesses that her brother's documents made at first some impression upon her, and that she had put herself to the expence of a long hood, in order to attend the extraordinary emotions of the Spirit; but having found, during an experiment of three weeks, no emotions, she says, worth a farthing, she very wisely laid by her hood, and abandoned the sect. To be concise, she is a very friendly, good-natured woman; and so industrious to oblige, that the guests must be of a very morose disposition who are not extremely well satisfied in her house.

Mrs Whitefield happened to be in the yard when Jones and his attendant marched in. Her sagacity soon discovered in the air of our heroe something which distinguished him from the vulgar. She ordered her servants, therefore, immediately to shew him into a room, and presently afterwards invited him to dinner with herself; which invitation he very thankfully accepted: for indeed much less agreeable company than that of Mrs Whitefield, and a much worse entertainment than she had provided, would have been welcome, after so long fasting, and so long a walk.

Besides Mr Jones and the good governess of the mansion, there sat down at table an attorney of Salisbury, indeed the very same who had brought the news of Mrs Blifil's death to Mr Allworthy, and whose name, which, I think, we did not before mention, was Dowling: there was likewise present another person, who stiled himself a lawyer, and who lived somewhere near Lidlinch in Somersetshire. This fellow, I say, stiled himself a lawyer, but was indeed a most vile petty-fogger, without sense or knowledge of any kind; one of those who may be termed train-bearers to the law; a sort of supernumeraries in the profession, who are the hackneys of attornies, and will ride more miles for half a crown than a post-boy.

During the time of dinner, the Somersetshire lawyer recollected the face of Jones, which he had seen at Mr Allworthy's: for he had often visited in that gentleman's kitchen. He therefore took occasion to enquire after the good family there, with that familiarity which would have become an intimate friend or acquaintance of Mr Allworthy; and indeed he did all in his power to insinuate himself to be such, though he had never had the honour of speaking to any person in that family higher than the butler. Jones answered all his questions with much civility, though he never remembered to have seen the petty-fogger before, and though he concluded from the outward appearance and behaviour of the man, that he usurped a freedom with his betters, to which he was by no means intitled.

As the conversation of fellows of this kind, is of all others the most detestable to men of any sense, the cloth was no sooner removed than Mr Jones withdrew, and a little barbarously left poor Mrs Whitefield to do a penance, which I have often heard Mr Timothy Harris, and other publicans of good taste, lament, as the severest lot annexed to their calling, namely, that of being obliged to keep company with their guests.

Jones had no sooner quitted the room, than the petty-fogger, in a whispering tone, asked Mrs Whitefield, 'if she knew who that fine spark was?' She answered, 'she had never seen the gentleman before.' 'The gentleman, indeed!' replied the petty-fogger; 'a pretty gentleman truly! Why, he's the bastard of a fellow who was hanged for horse-stealing. He was dropt at Squire Allworthy's door, where one of the servants found him in a box so full of rain-water, that he would certainly have been drowned, had he not been reserved for another fate.' 'Ay, ay, you need not mention it, I protest; we understand what that fate is very well,' cries Dowling, with a most facetious grin. 'Well,' continued the other, 'the squire ordered him to be taken in: for he is a timbersome man everybody knows, and was afraid of drawing himself into a scrape; and there the bastard was bred up, and fed and cloathified all to the world like any gentleman; and there he got one of the servant maids with child, and persuaded her to swear it to the squire himself; and afterwards he broke the arm of one Mr Thwackum a clergy-man, only because he reprimanded him for following whores; and afterwards he snapt a pistol at Mr Blifil behind his back; and once when Squire Allworthy was sick, he got a drum, and beat it all over the house, to prevent him from sleeping: and twenty other pranks he hath played; for all which, about four or five days ago, just before I left the country, the squire strip'd him stark naked, and turned him out of doors.'

'And very justly too, I protest,' cries Dowling; 'I would turn my own son out of doors, if he was guilty of half as much. And pray what is the name of this pretty gentleman?'

'The name o'un!' answered Petty-fogger, 'why, he is called Thomas Jones.'

'Jones!' answered Dowling, a little eagerly, 'what, Mr Jones that lived at Mr Allworthy's; was that the gentleman that dined with us?' 'The very same,' said the other. 'I have heard of the gentleman,' cries Dowling, 'often; but I never heard any ill character of him' 'And I am sure,' says Mrs Whitefield, 'if half what this gentleman hath said to be true, Mr Jones hath the most deceitful countenance I ever saw; for sure his looks promise something very different; and I must say, for the little I have seen of him, he is as civil a well-bred man as you could wish to converse with.'

Petty-fogger calling to mind that he had not been sworn, as he usually was, before he gave his evidence, now bound what he had declared with so many oaths and imprecations, that the landlady's ears were shocked, and she put a stop to his swearing, by assuring him of her belief. Upon which he said, 'I hope, madam, you imagine I would scorn to tell such things of any man, unless I knew them to be true. What interest have I in taking away the reputation of a man who never injured me? I promise you every syllable of what I have said is fact, and the whole country knows it.'

As Mrs Whitefield had no reason to suspect that the petty-fogger had any motive or temptation to abuse Jones, the reader cannot blame her for believing what he so confidently affirmed with many oaths. She accordingly gave up her skill in physiognomy, and henceforwards conceived so ill an opinion of her guest, that she heartily wished him out of her house.

This dislike was now farther encreased by a report which Mr Whitefield made from the kitchen, where Partridge had informed the company, 'That tho' he carried the knapsack, and contented himself with staying among servants, while Tom Jones (as he called him) was regaling in the parlour, he was not his servant, but only a friend and companion, and as good a gentleman as Mr Jones himself.'

Dowling sat all this while silent, biting his fingers, making faces; grinning, and looking wonderfully arch; at last he opened his lips, and protested that the gentleman looked like another sort of man. He then called for his bill with the utmost haste, declared he must be at Hereford that evening, lamented his great hurry of business, and wished he could divide himself into twenty pieces, in order to be at once in twenty places.

The petty-fogger now likewise departed, and then Jones desired the favour of Mrs Whitefield's company to drink tea with him; but she refused, and with a manner so different from that with which she had received him at dinner, that it a little surprized him. And now he soon perceived her behaviour totally changed; for instead of that natural affability which we have before celebrated, she wore a constrained severity on her countenance, which was so disagreeable to Mr Jones, that he resolved, however late, to quit the house that evening.

He did indeed account somewhat unfairly for this sudden change; for besides some hard and unjust surmises concerning female fickleness and mutability, he began to suspect that he owed this want of civility to his want of horses; a sort of animal which, as they dirty no sheets, are thought, in inns, to pay better for their beds than their riders, and are therefore considered as the more desirable company; but Mrs Whitefield, to do her justice, had a much more liberal way of thinking. She was perfectly well-bred, and could be very civil to a gentleman, tho' he walked on foot: in reality, she looked on our heroe as a sorry scoundrel, and therefore treated him as such, for which not even Jones himself, had he known as much as the reader, could have blamed her; nay, on the contrary, he must have approved her conduct, and have esteemed her the more for the disrespect shewn towards himself. This is indeed a most aggravating circumstance which attends unjustly depriving men of their reputation; for a man who is conscious of having an ill character cannot justly be angry with those who neglect and slight him; but ought rather to despise such as affect his conversation, unless where a perfect intimacy must have convinced them that their friend's character hath been falsely and injuriously aspersed.

This was not, however, the case of Jones; for as he was a perfect stranger to the truth, so he was with good reason offended at the treatment he received. He therefore paid his reckoning and departed, highly against the will of Mr Partridge, who having remonstrated much against it to no purpose, at last condescended to take up his knapsack, and to attend his friend.

Henry Fielding

From: Three Men in a Boat

It was a glorious morning, late spring or early summer, as you care to take it, when the dainty sheen of grass and leaf is blushing to a deeper green; and the year seems like a fair young maid, trembling with strange, wakening pulses on the brink of womanhood.

The quaint back-streets of Kingston, where they came down to the water's edge, looked quite picturesque in the flashing sunlight, the glinting river with its drifting barges, the wooded towpath, the trim-kept villas on the other side, Harris, in a red and orange blazer, grunting away at the sculls, the distant glimpses of the grey old palace of the Tudors, all made a sunny picture, so bright but calm, so full of life, and yet so peaceful, that, early in the day though it was, I felt myself being dreamily lulled off into a musing fit.

I mused on Kingston, or 'Kyningestun', as it was once called in the days when Saxon 'kinges' were crowned there. Great Caesar crossed the river there, and the Roman legions camped upon its sloping uplands. Caesar, like, in later years, Elizabeth, seems to have stopped everywhere: only he was more respectable than good Queen Bess; he didn't put up at the public-houses.

She was nuts on public-houses, was England's Virgin Queen. There's scarcely a pub of any attractions within ten miles of London that she does not seem to have looked in at, or stopped at, or slept at, some time or other. I wonder now, supposing Harris, say, turned over a new leaf, and became a great and good man, and got to be Prime Minister, and died, if they would put up signs over the public-houses that he had patronized: 'Harris had a glass of bitter in this house'; 'Harris had two of Scotch cold here in the summer of '88'; 'Harris was chucked from here in December 1886'.

No, there would be too many of them! It would be the houses that he had never entered that would become famous. 'Only house in South London that Harris never had a drink in!' The people would flock to it to see what could have been the matter with it.

Jerome K Jerome

From: The Diary of a Nobody

April 15, Sunday. At three o'clock Cummings and Gowing called for a good long walk over Hampstead and Finchley, and brought with them a friend named Stillbrook. We walked and chatted together, except Stillbrook, who was always a few yards behind us staring at the ground and cutting at the grass with his stick.

As it was getting on for five, we four held a consultation, and Gowing suggested that we should make for 'The Cow and Hedge' and get some tea. Stillbrook said: 'A brandy-and-soda was good enough for him.' I reminded them that all public-houses were closed till six o'clock. Stillbrook said: 'That's all right – *bona-fide* travellers.'

We arrived; and as I was trying to pass, the man in charge of the gate said: 'Where from?' I replied: 'Holloway.' He immediately put up his arm, and declined to let me pass. I turned back for a moment, when I saw Stillbrook, closely followed by Cummings and Gowing, make for the entrance. I watched them, and thought I would have a good laugh at their expense. I heard the porter say: 'Where from?' When, to my surprise, in fact disgust, Stillbrook replied: 'Blackheath,' and the three were immediately admitted.

Gowing called to me across the gate, and said: 'We shan't be a minute.' I waited for them the best part of an hour. When they appeared they were all in most excellent spirits, and the only one who made an effort to apologize was Mr Stillbrook, who said to me: 'It was very rough on you to be kept waiting, but we had another spin for S. and B.'s.' I walked home in silence; I couldn't speak to them. I felt very dull all the evening, but deemed it advisable *not* to say anything to Carrie about the matter.

George and Weedon Grossmith

At the Chalice, from: The Good Soldier Švejk

There was only one guest sitting at The Chalice. It was the plain-clothes police officer, Bretschneider, who worked for the State Security. The landlord, Palivec, was washing up the glasses and Bretschneider was vainly endeavouring to engage him in serious conversation.

Palivec was notorious for his foul mouth. Every second word of his was 'arse' or 'shit'. But at the same time he was well read and told everyone to read what Victor Hugo wrote on this subject when he described the last answer Napoleon's Old Guard gave to the British at the Battle of Waterloo.

'Well, it's a glorious summer!' said Bretschneider, embarking on his serious conversation.

'Shit on everything!' answered Palivec, putting the glasses away into a cupboard.

'It's a fine thing they've done to us at Sarajevo,' said Bretschneider with a faint hope.

'Which Sarajevo?' asked Palivec. 'Do you mean the wine cellar at Nusle? They're always fighting there, you know. Of course it's Nusle.'

'At Sarajevo in Bosnia, Mr Palivec. They've just shot His Imperial Highness, the Archduke Ferdinand, there. What do you say to that?'

'I don't poke my nose into things like that. They can kiss my arse if I do!' Palivec replied politely, lighting his pipe. 'Nowadays, if anyone got mixed up in a business like that, he'd risk breaking his neck. I'm a tradesman and when anyone comes in here and orders a beer I fill up his glass. But Sarajevo, politics or the late lamented Archduke are nothing for people like us. They lead straight to Pankrác.'

Bretschneider lapsed into silence and looked disappointedly round the empty pub.

'Hallo, there used to be a picture of His Imperial Majesty hanging here once,' he started up again after a while. 'Just where the mirror hangs now.'

'Yes, you're right,' Palivec replied. 'It did hang there, but the flies used to shit on it, so I put it away in the attic. You know, somebody might be so free as to pass a remark about it and then there could be unpleasantness. I don't want that, do I!?'

'In Sarajevo it must have been a pretty ugly business, Mr Palivec.'

This crafty direct question evoked an extremely cautious answer from Palivec: 'At this time of the year it's scorching hot in Bosnia and Herzegovina. When I served there, they had to put ice on our lieutenant's head.'

'Which regiment did you serve in, Mr Palivec?'

'I can't possibly remember anything so unimportant. Bloody nonsense of that sort never interested me and I've never bothered my head about it,' answered Palivec. 'Curiosity killed a cat.'

Bretschneider finally relapsed into silence. His gloomy face only lit up on the arrival of Švejk who came into the pub, ordered a dark black beer and remarked: 'Today they'll be in mourning in Vienna too.'

Bretschneider's eyes gleamed with hope, and he said laconically: 'On Konopiště there are ten black flags.'

'There should be twelve,' said Švejk, after he had taken a swig.

'What makes you think twelve?' asked Bretschneider.

'To make it a round number. A dozen adds up better, and dozens always come cheaper,' answered Švejk.

There was a silence, which Švejk himself broke with a sigh: 'And so he's already lying with God and the angels. Glory be! He didn't even live to be Emperor. When I was serving in the army a general once fell off his horse and killed himself without any fuss. They wanted to help him back onto his horse, to lift him up, but to their surprise he was completely dead. And he was going to be promoted Field Marshal. It happened at a review. These reviews never come to any good. In Sarajevo there was a review too. I remember once at a parade like that I had twenty buttons missing from my uniform and they sent me into solitary confinement for a fortnight, where I lay for two days trussed up like Lazarus. But in the army you must have discipline, otherwise why would anyone bother at all? Our Lieutenant Makovec always used to say: "There's got to be discipline, you bloody fools, otherwise you'd be climbing about on the trees like monkeys, but the army's going to make human beings of you, you god-forsaken idiots." And isn't that true? Just imagine a park, let's say at Charles Square, and on every tree an undisciplined soldier! It's enough to give you a nightmare!'

'At Sarajevo,' Bretschneider resumed, 'it was the Serbs who did it.'

'You're wrong there,' replied Švejk. 'It was the Turks, because of Bosnia and Herzegovina.' And Švejk expounded his views on Austrian foreign policy in the Balkans. In 1912 the Turks lost the war with Serbia, Bulgaria and

Greece. They had wanted Austria to help them, and when this didn't happen, they shot Ferdinand.

'Do you like the Turks?' said Švejk, turning to Palivec. 'Do you like those heathen dogs? You don't, do you?'

'One customer is as good as another,' said Palivec, 'never mind a Turk. For tradesmen like us politics doesn't enter into it. Pay for your beer, sit down in my pub and jabber what you like. That's my principle. It's all the same to me whether our Ferdinand was done in by a Serb or Turk, Catholic or Moslem, anarchist or Young Czech.'

'All right now, Mr Palivec,' resumed Bretschneider, who was again beginning to despair of catching either of them out, 'but all the same you'll admit that it's a great loss for Austria.'

Švejk replied for the landlord: 'Yes, it's a loss indeed, there's no denying it. A shocking loss. You can't replace Ferdinand by any twopenny-halfpenny idiot. Only he ought to have been still fatter.'

'What do you mean?' Bretschneider livened up.

'What do I mean?' Švejk answered happily. 'Just this. If he'd been fatter then of course he'd certainly have had a stroke long ago, when he was chasing those old women at Konopiště when they were collecting firewood and picking mushrooms on his estate, and he wouldn't have had to die such a shameful death. Just imagine, an uncle of His Imperial Majesty and shot! Why, it's a scandal! The newspapers are full of it. Years ago in our Budějovice a cattle-dealer called Břetislav Ludvík was stabbed in the market place in a petty squabble. He had a son called Bohuslav, and wherever that lad came to sell his pigs, no one wanted to buy anything from him and everyone said: "That's the son of that chap who was stabbed. He's probably a first-class bastard too!" There was nothing for him to do but to jump into the Vltava from that bridge at Krumlov, and they had to drag him out, resurrect him, pump water out of him, and of course he had to die in the arms of the doctor just when he was giving him an injection.'

'You do make strange comparisons, I must say,' said Bretschneider significantly. 'First you talk about Ferdinand and then about a cattle-dealer.'

'Oh, no, I don't,' Švejk defended himself. 'God forbid my wanting to compare anyone to anybody else. Mr Palivec knows me very well. I've never compared anyone to anybody else, have I? But I wouldn't for the life of me want to be in the skin of that Archduke's widow. What's she going to do now? The children are orphans and the family estate at Knopиště has no master. Marry a new Archduke? What would she get out of that? She'd only go with him to Sarajevo again and be widowed a second time. You know years ago there was a game-keeper in Zliv near Hluboká. He had a very ugly name – Pind'our. Some poachers shot him, and he left a widow and two little babes. Within a year she married another gamekeeper, Pepík Šavel from Mydlovary. And they shot him too. And then she married a third time, again a gamekeeper, and said: "Third time lucky. If it doesn't succeed this time, then I don't know what I shall do." Well, of course, they shot him too, and with all these gamekeepers she had six children altogether. She even went to the office

At The Chalice

of His Highness the Prince at Hluboká and complained that she'd had trouble with those gamekeepers. And so they recommended her a fellow called Jareš who was a water bailiff in the watch tower at Ražice. And, can you imagine it? He was drowned when they were fishing the lake out. And she had two children by him. And then she took a pig-gelder from Vodňany and one night he hit her over the head with his axe and went and gave himself up voluntarily. And when they hanged him afterwards at the district court at Písek he bit the priest's nose and said he didn't regret anything. And he also said something extremely nasty about His Imperial Majesty.'

'And you don't happen to know what he said?' Bretschneider asked hopefully.

'I can't tell you, because no one dared repeat it. But I'm told that it was something so dreadful and horrible that one of the magistrates went mad, and they keep him to this very day in solitary confinement, so that it shan't get out. It wasn't the usual sort of insulting remark which people make about His Imperial Majesty when they're tight.'

'And what sort of insulting remark do people make about His Imperial Majesty when they're tight?' asked Bretschneider.

'Now come, gentlemen, please change the subject,' said Palivec. 'You know, I don't like it. Somebody might talk out of turn and we'd be sorry for it.'

'What sort of insulting remarks do people make about His Imperial Majesty when they're tight?' Švejk repeated. 'All kinds. Get drunk, have the Austrian national anthem played and you'll see what you start saying! You'll think up such a lot about His Imperial Majesty, that if only half of it were true it would be enough to disgrace him all his life. But the old gentleman really doesn't deserve it. Just think! His son Rudolf – lost in tender years, in full flower of his manhood. His wife Elizabeth – stabbed with a file. And then Jan Orth – also lost. His brother, the Emperor of Mexico – put up against a wall and shot in a fortress somewhere. And now again in his old age they've shot his uncle. A chap needs iron nerves for that. And then some drunken bastard starts to swear at him. If the balloon went up today I'd go as a volunteer and serve His Imperial Majesty to my last drop of blood.'

Švejk took a deep draught of beer and continued:

'Do you really think His Imperial Majesty is going to put up with this sort of thing? If so, you don't know him at all. There'll have to be a war with the Turks. "You killed my uncle and so I'll bash your jaw." War is certain. Serbia and Russia will help us in it. There won't half be a blood bath.'

Švejk looked beautiful in this prophetic moment. His simple face, smiling like a full moon, beamed with enthusiasm. Everything was so clear to him.

'It may be,' he said, continuing his account of Austria's future, 'that if we have war with the Turks the Germans'll attack us, because the Germans and the Turks stick together. You can't find bigger bastards anywhere. But we can ally ourselves with France which has had a down on Germany ever since 1871. And then the balloon'll go up. There'll be war. I won't say any more.'

Bretschneider stood up and said solemnly:

'You don't need to. Just come along with me into the passage. I've got something to say to you there.'

Švejk followed the plain-clothes police officer into the passage where a little surprise awaited him. His drinking companion showed him his eaglet and announced that he was arresting him and would take him at once to police headquarters. Švejk tried to explain that the gentleman must be mistaken, that he was completely innocent and that he had not uttered a single word capable of offending anyone.

However, Bretschneider told him that he had in fact committed several criminal offences, including the crime of high treason.

Then they returned to the pub and Švejk said to Palivec:

'I've had five beers, a couple of frankfurters and a roll. Now give me one more slivovice and I must go, because I'm under arrest.'

Bretschneider showed Palivec his eaglet, stared at him for a moment and then asked:

'Are you married?'

'I am.'

'And can Madame carry on the business for you during your absence?'

'She can.'

'Then it's all right, Mr Palivec,' said Bretschneider gaily. 'Call your wife here, give the business over to her, and in the evening we'll come for you.'

'Take it easy,' Švejk consoled him. 'I'm only going there for high treason.'

'But what am I going for?' moaned Palivec. 'After all, I've been so careful.'

Bretschneider smiled and said triumphantly:

'Because you said the flies shitted on His Imperial Majesty. They'll certainly knock His Imperial Majesty out of your head there.'

And so Švejk left The Chalice under the escort of the plain-clothes police officer. When they went out into the street his face lit up with its good-natured smile and he asked:

'Should I step down from the pavement?'

'What do you mean?'

'I thought as I'm under arrest I've no right to walk on the pavement.'

When they passed through the door of police headquarters Švejk said:

'Well, the time passed very pleasantly for us there. Do you often go to The Chalice?'

And while they were escorting Švejk to the reception office Palivec at The Chalice handed over the running of the pub to his weeping wife, consoling her in his own inimitable way:

'Don't cry, don't howl. What can they do to me because of some shit on a picture of His Imperial Majesty?'

And thus it was that the good soldier Švejk intervened in the great war in his own sweet, charming way. It will interest historians that he saw far into the future. If the situation subsequently developed otherwise than he had expounded it at The Chalice we must bear in mind that he had never had any preparatory training in diplomacy.

Jaroslav Hašek (translated by Cecil Parrott)

A Pint of Plain from: At Swim-Two-Birds

The name or title of the pome I am about to recite, gentlemen, said Shanahan with leisure priest-like in character, is a pome by the name of the 'Workman's Friend'. By God you can't beat it. I've heard it praised by the highest. It's a pome about a thing that's known to all of us. It's about a drink of porter.

Porter!

Porter.

Up on your legs man, said Furriskey. Mr Lamont and myself are waiting and listening. Up you get now.

Come on, off you go, said Lamont.

Now listen, said Shanahan clearing the way with small coughs. Listen now.

He arose holding out his hand and bending his knee beneath him on the chair.

> When things go wrong and will not come right,
> Though you do the best you can,
> When life looks black as the hour of night –
> A PINT OF PLAIN IS YOUR ONLY MAN.

By God there's a lilt in that, said Lamont.

Very good indeed, said Furriskey. Very nice.

I'm telling you it's the business, said Shanahan. Listen now.

> When money's tight and is hard to get
> And your horse has also ran,
> When all you have is a heap of debt –
> A PINT OF PLAIN IS YOUR ONLY MAN.

> When health is bad and your heart feels strange,
> And your face is pale and wan,
> When doctors say that you need a change,
> A PINT OF PLAIN IS YOUR ONLY MAN.

There are things in that pome that make for what you call *permanence*. Do you know what I mean, Mr Furriskey?

There's no doubt about it, it's a grand thing, said Furriskey. Come on, Mr Shanahan, give us another verse. Don't tell me that is the end of it.

Can't you listen? said Shanahan.

> When food is scarce and your larder bare
> And no rashers grease your pan,
> When hunger grows as your meals are rare –
> A PINT OF PLAIN IS YOUR ONLY MAN.

What do you think of that now?

It's a pome that'll live, called Lamont, a pome that'll be heard and clapped when plenty more ...

But wait till you hear the last verse, man, the last polish-off, said Shanahan. He frowned and waved his hand.

Oh it's good, it's good, said Furriskey.

> In time of trouble and lousy strife,
> You have still got a darlint plan,
> You still can turn to a brighter life –
> A PINT OF PLAIN IS YOUR ONLY MAN.

Did you ever hear anything like it in your life, said Furriskey. A pint of plain, by God, what! Oh I'm telling you, Casey was a man in twenty thousand, there's no doubt about that. He knew what he was at, too true he did. If he knew nothing else, he knew how to write a pome. A pint of plain is your only man.

Didn't I tell you he was good? said Shanahan. Oh by Gorrah you can't cod me.

There's one thing in that pome, *permanence*, if you know what I mean. That poem, I mean to say, is a pome that'll be heard wherever the Irish race is wont to gather, it'll live as long as there's a hard root of an Irishman left by the Almighty on this planet, mark my words.

Flann O'Brien

After Hours

At ten o'clock on week nights, at half-nine on Saturday the tide ebbs suddenly, leaving the city high and dry. Unless you are staying at a hotel or visiting a theatre, you may not lawfully consume excisable liquors within the confines of the county borough. The city has entered that solemn hiatus, that almost sublime eclipse known as The Closed Hours. Here the law, as if with true Select Lounge mentality, discriminates sharply against the poor man at the pint counter by allowing those who can command transport and can embark upon a journey to drink elsewhere till morning. The theory is that all travellers still proceed by stage-coach and that those who travel outside become blue with cold after five miles and must be thawed out with hot rum at the first hostelry they encounter by night or day. In practice, people who are in the first twilight of inebriation are transported from the urban to the rural pub so swiftly by the internal combustion engine that they need not necessarily be aware that they have moved at all, still less comprehend that their legal personalities have undergone a mystical transfiguration. Whether this sysem is to be regarded as a scandal or a godsend depends largely on whether one owns a car. At present the city is ringed round with these 'bona-fide' pubs, many of them well-run modern houses, and a considerable amount of the stock-in-trade is transferred to the stomachs of the customers at a time every night when the sensible and just are in their second sleeps.

To go back to the city: it appears that the poor man does not always go straight home at ten o'clock. If his thirst is big enough and he knows the knocking-formula, he may possibly visit some house where the Demand Note of the Corporation has stampeded the owner into a bout of illicit after-hour trading. For trader and customer alike, such a life is one of excitement, tiptoe and hush. The boss's ear, refined to shades of perception far beyond the sensitiveness of any modern aircraft detector, can tell almost the inner thoughts of any policeman in the next street. At the first breath of danger all lights are suddenly doused and conversation toned down, as with a knob, to vanishing point. Drinkers reared in such schools will tell you that in inky blackness stout cannot be distinguished in taste from Bass and that no satisfaction whatever can be extracted from a cigarette unless the smoke is seen. Sometimes the police make a catch. Here is the sort of thing that is continually appearing in the papers:

Guard – said that accompanied by Guard – he visited the premises at 11.45 p.m. and noticed a light at the side door. When he knocked the light was extinguished, but he was not admitted for six minutes. When defendant opened eventually, he appeared to be in an excited condition and used bad language. There was nobody in the bar but there were two empty pint measures containing traces of fresh porter on the counter. He found a man crouching in a small press containing switches and a gas-meter. When he attempted to enter the yard to carry out a search, he was obstructed by the defendant, who used an improper expression. He arrested him, but owing to the illness of his wife, he was later released.

Defendant – Did you give me an unmerciful box in the mouth?

Witness – No.

Defendant – Did you say that you would put me and my gawm of a brother through the back wall with one good haymaker of a clout the next time I didn't open when you knocked?

Witness – No.

Justice – You look a fine block of a man yourself. How old are you?

Defendant – I'm as grey as a badger, but I'm not long past forty. (Laughter.)

Justice – Was the brother there at all?

Defendant – He was away in Kells, your worship, seeing about getting a girl for himself. (Laughter.)

Justice – Well, I think you could give a good account of yourself.

Witness – He was very obstreperous, your worship.

Witness, continuing, said that he found two men standing in the dark in an outhouse. They said they were there 'for a joke.' Witness also found an empty pint measure in an outdoor lavatory and two empty bottles of Cairnes.

Defenant said that two of the men were personal friends and were being treated. There was no question of taking money. He did not know who the man in the press was and did not recall having seen him before. He had given strict instructions to his assistant to allow nobody to remain on after hours. There was nobody in the press the previous day as the gas-man had called to inspect the meter. The two Guards had given him an unmerciful hammering in the hall. His wife was in ill-health, necessitating his doing without sleep for three weeks. A week previously he was compelled to send for the Guards to assist in clearing the house at ten o'clock. He was conducting the house to the best of his ability and was very strict about the hours.

Guard – said that the defendant was a decent hard-working type but was of an excitable nature. The house had a good record.

Remarking that the defendant seemed a decent sort and that the case was distinguished by the absence of perjury, the Justice said he would impose a fine of twenty shillings, the offence not to be endorsed. Were it not for extenuating circumstances he would have no hesitation in sending the defendant to Mountjoy for six months. He commended Guards for smart police work.

Not many publicans, however, will take the risk. If they were as careful of their souls as they are of their licenses, heaven would be packed with those confidential and solicitous profit-takers and, to please them, it might be necessary to provide an inferior annex to paradise to house such porter-drinkers as would make the grade.

Flann O'Brien *The Bell*

Remember what a thrilling experience getting "lates" used to be?

The Porter scene from Macbeth

Enter MACDUFF *and* LENNOX.

Macd. Was it so late, friend, ere you went to bed, that you do lie so late?
Port. Faith, sir, we were carousing till the second cock: and drink, sir, is a great provoker of three things.
Macd. What three things does drink especially provoke?
Port. Marry, sir, nose-painting, sleep, and urine. Lechery, sir, it provokes and it unprovokes; it provokes the desire, but it takes away the performance: therefore, much drink may be said to be an equivocator with lechery: it makes shim, and it mars him; it sets him on, and it takes him off; it persuades him, and disheartens him; makes him stand to, and not stand to: in conclusion, equivocates him in a sleep, and, giving him the lie, leaves him.
Macd. I believe drink gave thee the lie last night.
Port. That it did, sir, i' the very throat o' me: but I requited him for his lie; and, I think, being too strong for him, though he took up my legs sometime, yet I made a shift to cast him.

William Shakespeare

At the Sign of the Spy-Glass

When I had done breakfasting the squire gave me a note addressed to John Silver, at the sign of the 'Spy-glass,' and told me I should easily find the place by following the line of the docks, and keeping a bright look-out for a little tavern with a large brass telescope for sign. I set off, overjoyed at this opportunity to see some more of the ships and seamen, and picked my way among a great crowd of people and carts and bales, for the dock was now at its busiest, until I found the tavern in question.

It was a bright enough little place of entertainment. The sign was newly painted; the windows had neat red curtains; the floor was cleanly sanded. There was a street on either side, and an open door on both, which made the large, low room pretty clear to see in, in spite of clouds of tobacco smoke.

The customers were mostly seafaring men; and they talked so loudly that I hung at the door, almost afraid to enter.

As I was waiting, a man came out of a side room, and, at a glance, I was sure he must be Long John. His left leg was cut off close by the hip, and under the left shoulder he carried a crutch, which he managed with wonderful dexterity, hopping about upon it like a bird. He was very tall and strong, with a face as big as a ham – plain and pale, but intelligent and smiling. Indeed, he seemed in the most cheerful spirits, whistling as he moved about among the tables, with a merry word or a slap on the shoulder for the more favoured of his guests.

Now, to tell you the truth, from the very first mention of Long John in Squire Trelawney's letter, I had taken a fear in my mind that he might prove to be the very one-legged sailor whom I had watched for so long at the old 'Benbow.' But one look at the man before me was enough. I had seen the captain, and Black Dog, and the blind man Pew, and I thought I knew what a buccaneer was like – a very different creature, according to me, from this clean and pleasant-tempered landlord.

I plucked up courage at once, crossed the threshold, and walked right up to the man where he stood, propped on his crutch, talking to a customer.

'Mr Silver, sir?' I asked, holding out the note.

'Yes, my lad,' said he; 'such is my name, to be sure. And who may you be?' And then as he saw the squire's letter, he seemed to me to give something almost like a start.

'Oh!' said he, quite loud, and offering his hand, 'I see. You are our new cabin-boy; pleased I am to see you.'

And he took my hand in his large firm grasp.

Just then one of the customers at the far side rose suddenly and made for the door. It was close by him, and he was out in the street in a moment. But his hurry had attracted my notice, and I recognised him at a glance. It was the tallow-faced man, wanting two fingers, who had come first to the 'Admiral Benbow.'

'Oh,' I cried, 'stop him! it's Black Dog!'

'I don't care two coppers who he is,' cried Silver. 'But he hasn't paid his score. Harry, run and catch him.'

One of the others who was nearest the door leaped up, and started in pursuit.

'If he were Admiral Hawke he shall pay his score,' cried Silver; and then, relinquishing my hand – 'Who did you say he was?' he asked. 'Black what?'

'Dog, sir,' said I. 'Has Mr Trelawney not told you of the buccaneers? He was one of them.'

'So?' cried Silver. 'In my house! Ben, run and help Harry. One of those swabs, was he? Was that you drinking with him, Morgan? Step up here.'

The man whom he called Morgan – an old, grey-haired, mahogany-faced sailor – came forward pretty sheepishly, rolling his quid.

'Now, Morgan,' said Long John, very sternly; 'you never clapped your eyes on that Black – Black Dog before, did you, now?'

'Not I, sir,' said Morgan, with a salute.

'You didn't know his name, did you?'

'No, sir.'

'By the powers, Tom Morgan, it's as good for you!' exclaimed the landlord. 'If you had been mixed up with the like of that, you would never have put another foot in my house, you may lay to that. And what was he saying to you?'

'I don't rightly know, sir,' answered Morgan.

'Do you call that a head on your shoulders, or a blessed dead-eye?' cried Long John. 'Don't rightly know, don't you! Perhaps you don't happen to rightly know who you was speaking to, perhaps? Come, now, what was he jawing – v'yages, cap'ns, ships? Pipe up! What was it?'

'We was a-talkin' of keelhauling,' answered Morgan.

'Keelhauling, was you? – and a mighty suitable thing, too, and you may lay to that. Get back to your place for a lubber, Tom.'

And then, as Morgan rolled back to his seat, Silver added to me in a confidential whisper, that was very flattering, as I thought: –

'He's quite an honest man, Tom Morgan, on'y stupid. And now,' he ran on again, aloud, 'let's see – Black Dog? No, I don't know the name, not I. Yet I kind of think I've – yes, I've seen the swab. He used to come here with a blind beggar, he used.'

'That he did, you may be sure,' said I. 'I knew that blind man, too. His name was Pew.'

'It was!' cried Silver, now quite excited. 'Pew! That were his name for certain. Ah, he looked a shark, he did! If we run down this Black Dog, now, there'll be news for Cap'n Trelawney! Ben's a good runner; few seamen run better than Ben. He should run him down, hand over hand, by the powers! He talked o' keelhauling, did he? I'll keelhaul him!'

All the time he was jerking out these phrases he was stumping up and down the tavern on his crutch, slapping tables with his hand, and giving such a show of excitement as would have convinced an Old Bailey judge or a Bow Street runner. My suspicions had been thoroughly reawakened on finding Black Dog at the 'Spy-glass,' and I watched the cook narrowly. But he was too deep, and too ready, and too clever for me, and by the time the two men had come back out of breath, and confessed that they had lost the track in a crowd, and been scolded like thieves, I would have gone bail for the innocence of Long John Silver.

'See here, now, Hawkins,' said he, 'here's a blessed hard thing on a man like me now, ain't it? There's Cap'n Trelawney – what's he to think? Here I have this confounded son of a Dutchman sitting in my own house, drinking of my own rum! Here you comes and tells me of it plain; and here I let him give us all the slip before my blessed dead-lights! Now, Hawkins, you do me justice with the cap'n. You're a lad, you are, but you're as smart as paint. I see that when you first came in. Now, here it is: What could I do, with this old timber I hobble on? When I was an A.B. master mariner I'd have come up alongside of him, hand over hand, and broached him to in a brace of old shakes, I would; but now – '

And then, all of a sudden, he stopped, and his jaw dropped as though he had remembered something.

'The score!' he burst out. 'Three goes o'rum! Why shiver my timbers, if I hadn't forgotten my score!'

And, falling on a bench, he laughed until the tears ran down his cheeks. I could not help joining; and we laughed together, peal after peal, until the tavern rang again.

'Why, what a precious old seal-calf I am!' he said, at last, wiping his cheeks. 'You and me should get on well, Hawkins, for I'll take my davy I should be rated ship's boy. But, come, now, stand by to go about. This won't do. Dooty is dooty, messmates. I'll put on my old cocked hat, and step along of you to Cap'n Trelawney, and report this here affair. For, mind you, it's serious, young Hawkins; and neither you nor me's come out of it with what I should make so bold as to call credit. Nor you neither, says you; not smart – none of the pair of us smart. But, dash my buttons! that was a good 'un about my score.'

And he began to laugh again, and that so heartily, that though I did not see the joke as he did, I was again obliged to join him in his mirth.

On our little walk along the quays, he made himself the most interesting companion, telling me about the different ships that we passed by, their rig, tonnage, and nationality, explaining the work that was going forward – how one was discharging, another taking in cargo, and a third making ready for sea; and every now and then telling me some little anecdote of ships or seamen, or repeating a nautical phrase till I had learned it perfectly. I began to see that here was one of the best of possible shipmates.

When we got to the inn, the squire and Dr Livesey were seated together, finishing a quart of ale with a toast in it, before they should go aboard the schooner on a visit of inspection.

Long John told the story from first to last, with a great deal of spirit and the most perfect truth. 'That was how it were, now, weren't it, Hawkins?' he would say, now and again, and I could always bear him entirely out.

The two gentlemen regretted that Black Dog had got away; but we all agreed there was nothing to be done, and after he had been complimented, Long John took up his crutch and departed.

'All hands aboard by four this afternoon,' shouted the squire after him.

'Ay, ay, sir,' cried the cook, in the passage.

'Well, squire,' said Dr Livesey, 'I don't put much faith in your discoveries, as a general thing; but I will say this, John Silver suits me.'

'The man's a perfect trump,' declared the squire.

'And now,' added the doctor, 'Jim may come on board with us, may he not?'

'To be sure he may,' says squire. – 'Take your hat, Hawkins, and we'll see the ship.'

Robert Louis Stevenson *Treasure Island*

The Cittie of Yorke, Holborn, London: a veritable palace

CHAPTER 4

INNS, PUBS AND TAVERNS

Palaces of Refreshment

I regard the pub as a valuable institution.

Sir A P Herbert ... election address 1935

There is nothing which has yet been contrived by man, by which so much happiness is produced as by a good tavern or inn.

Dr Samuel Johnson

He goes not out of his way that goes to a good inn.

Anon

Do you remember an inn, Miranda?

Hillaire Belloc *The South Country*

I rose politely in the club
And said 'I feel a little bored;
Will someone take me to a pub?'

G K Chesterton *Ballade of an Anti-Puritan*

The incognito of an inn is one of its striking privileges.

William Hazlitt *On Going a Journey*

When you have lost your inns drown your empty selves, for you will have lost the last of England.

Hillaire Belloc

When I die I want to decompose in a barrel of porter and have it served in all the pubs in Dublin. I wonder would they know it was me?

J P Donleavy *The Ginger Man*

Two inches to the north-west is written a word full of meaning – the most purposeful word that can be written on a map. 'Inn.'

A A Milne *An Ordnance Map*

It was a swing door. You can't bang a pub door. The pubs know a lot, almost as much as the churches. They've got a tradition.

Joyce Cary *The Horse's Mouth*

A tavern is a degree or (if you will) a pair of stairs above an ale-house . . . it is the busy man's recreation, the idle man's business, the melancholy man's sanctuary, the stranger's welcome, the Inns of Court man's entertainment, the scholar's kindness, and the citizen's courtesy.

John Earle, 1628

A village inn is not simply a place where one goes for food and drink and lodging, as one goes to an hotel in the city. It is an integral part of the village, and the dale in which it stands. It has a character of its own, which it has acquired through years – and sometimes through centuries – of its existence. The old innkeepers appreciated and treasured this tradition; they became part and parcel of the inn itself. They were proud of their heritage and jealous of their reputations. The inn to them was a sacred trust.

Alfred J Brown *Broad Acres*

How fine it is to enter some old town, walled and turreted, just at approach of nightfall, or to come to some straggling village, with the lights streaming through the surrounding gloom; and then, after inquiring for the best entertainment that the place affords, to 'take one's ease at one's inn!'

William Hazlitt *On Going a Journey*

We dined at an excellent inn at Chapel-house, where he expatiated on the felicity of England in its taverns and inns, and triumphed over the French for not having, in any perfection, the tavern life. 'There is no private house, (said he), in which people can enjoy themselves so well, as at a capital tavern' . . . He then repeated, with great emotion, Shenstone's lines:

Whoe'er has travell'd life's dull round,
Where'er his stages may have been,
May sigh to think he still has found
The warmest welcome at an inn.

James Boswell *The Life of Samuel Johnson*

For on this my heart is set:
When the hour is nigh me,
Let me in the tavern die,
With a tankard by me,
While the angels looking down
Joyously sing o'er me,
Deus sit propitius
Huic potatori.

Anon (12th century)

Pubs in Dublin

Near by is O'Meara's pub – the 'Irish House,' though why it should be called that in Ireland, I don't know. I used to know the man that owned it – it has changed hands since; and I remember him principally for a few lines of poetry that he recited to me:

'Then Hoolihan hit Hannaghan and Hannaghan hit McGilligan
And everyone hit anyone of whom he had a spite,
And Larry Dwyer, the cripple, who was sitting doing nothing
Got a kick that broke his jawbone for not indulging in the fight.'

A friend of mine painted that pub one time – Dinny Bowles, a very famous man – a signwriter he was and a very good one at that.

Pubs are dull enough places at any time though not so dull in Ireland as they are in England. I suppose I know most of them in Dublin and I'd rather have them than the pubs in London. I remember being in the 'Blue Lion' in Parnell Street one day and the owner said to me: 'You owe me ten shillings,' he said, 'you broke a glass the last time you were here.' 'God bless us and save us,' I said, 'it must have been a very dear glass if it cost ten shillings. Tell us, was it a Waterford glass or something?' I discovered in double-quick time that it wasn't a glass that you'd drink out of he meant – it was a pane of glass and I'd stuck somebody's head through it.

It was about the Blue Lion also that I remember my grandmother, Christina, getting into a bit of embarrassment. It's more or less at the back of what was Joyce's Night-town, near Montgomery Street, which was one of the streets in the red light district. My grandmother had me by the hand and as we were walking down the street, we met a friend of hers who said: 'Come on, Christina, and have one,' meaning come in for a glass of porter. So my grandmother said all right but she didn't want to go into the 'Blue Lion' because, she says: 'All those characters go in there' – meaning whores; but her friend says: 'Ah, they won't take any notice of us.' So in they went. 'We'll go in the private part,' she says and: 'All right,' says my grandmother. So when they went into the private part all the 'characters' roll up and say: 'Ah, hello, Christina, come on in, we didn't see you these years.'

There's a pub up near Guinness's Brewery on the Liffey Quay – it must be the nearest pub to Guinness's – known as 'The Shaky Man.' I don't know if it's there now or not because it's a long time since I was in it, but I think it was there I heard one of my friends – a man named Crippen – refer to 'Evelyn Warr.' 'Aye,' he said, 'Evelyn Warr was a tough woman.' I don't know what we had been talking about but I sang him a bar or two:

'They told me, Francis Hazley, they told me you were hung
    With red protruding eyeballs and black protruding tongue.'

And says he, 'Aye, Evelyn Warr,' he said, 'she was a great soldier and a great warrior. And she was called Evelyn because that was her name and she was called Warr because she was all for war.'

I was in 'The Shaky Man' one evening when a prostitute, who combined shoplifting with prostitution, came in and discovered that a pair of nylon knickers which she had carefully stolen from a Grafton Street shop that day, had disappeared during one of her absences on business. There was hell to pay, but all I remember of the row was her voice roaring again and again, in tones of the bitterest indignation: 'There's no honest whores left. There's no honest whores left.'

Or you'd have some old one sitting in the snug, where ladies who were ladies could have their jorums without the rude gazes of the men, and they'd remember Johnny going off in his pill-box cap to fight Kruger, or going off to do the Kaiser in, in the war after that. Like the time they were drawing the ring-money for their husbands away in the wars, one old one says to another:

'Anything in the paper this morning, Julia?'

'Nothing, Mary, only the Pope is trying to make peace.'

'God forgive him, it's a wonder he wouldn't mind his own interference. It's enough to make you turn Protestant.'   Brendan Behan

The Coaching Inns of Doncaster

One of the oldest inns on the road was the Old Angel at Doncaster, which was connected with coaching from its introduction to its fall, and when stage coaching fell this celebrated old posting house fell with it. Royalty on several occasions honoured it with their presence. In 1603 James I stayed within its walls, while in 1778 His Royal Highness the Duke of York remained at least one night, and a week later the Prince of Wales was an occupant of the state rooms; both rested here on their return journey in the same month, and the Duke of York again slept here in 1795, whilst noblemen and gentlemen innumerable availed themselves of its excellent accommodation.

In its earlier days the Old Angel was known by the sign of the Bear, though the names of any of the landlords in those early days do not transpire; but long before post-chaises were known we find that the mails were conveyed on horseback from this place, and we likewise find that the postmastership at Doncaster was in one family from 1588 to 1725, and on the 2nd of February, 1623, there died a member of this family, William Hayford, innkeeper and postmaster at Doncaster, so that it is quite possible that he was landlord of the Old Angel or the Bear, as it would then be called.

At the beginning of the last century Richard Whitaker kept this famous hostelry, which was undoubtedly the chief house of entertainment at that time. At assize time it was customary for the mayor and corporation to receive the judges at the boundary of the borough and conduct them with all due ceremony as far as Rossington Bridge, at the completion of the law business. The corporation voted £12 out of the funds to be paid to Whitaker at each assize for brisket and sack when the judges, aldermen and twenty-four men were entertained by the host of the Angel, except such of the councillors as failed to put in an appearance at the ceremony of attending on the judges. Richard Whitaker seems to have been a man of considerable moment in his time (but the innkeepers of that day were altogether of superior calibre), and he was elected mayor of Doncaster in 1728. He was succeeded at the Angel by his son James Whitaker, who was likewise elected mayor in 1760 or 1761.

Mr Woodcock was the next landlord of the Angel, and he was at the house and had charge of mails when the first Mail coach came along the road in 1786. This coach, nevertheless, was worked from the Red Lion, in Scot Lane, which at that time was a coaching house. The mayor and corporation seem to have 'kept it up' pretty considerably in those days, as we find their names and the Angel in constant collision, and some of our municipal ratepayers would open their eyes if they found such items paid out of the rates as: the ringers when the Marquess of Rockingham dined at the Angel, £1; the waits playing at the Angel, 5s; to extra music at the Angel during Alderman Whitaker's year of office, £6 6s; to say nothing of the various sums voted for sack and brisket, and we can now easily understand the source of inspiration which prompted the following:-

> The Doncaster mayor sits in his chair,
> His mills they merrily go,
> His nose doth shine with drinking wine,
> And the gout is in his great toe.

In Mr Woodcock's time the Leeds and London Diligence, and the Paul Jones (the forerunners of the Rockingham), and the old York and London coach were all worked from the Old Angel. Towards the end of last century Mr Woodcock was succeeded by a Mr Day, who remained for a few years, when the house was purchased by Robert Belcher, who came to Doncaster from the Sun Inn, Bradford, and prior to his going to the Old Angel kept the Red Lion Inn, in Scot Lane. Mr Belcher, like his predecessors, was also an alderman, but the inn had seen its best days, and the bulk of the coaching and posting business had gone over to the New Angel, on the opposite side of the way, which was opened in 1810. In 1842 railways had completely sealed the doom of the road, and the old hostelry that had seen so much in its time was at last without an occupant. For four years it remained empty, when it was purchased by the corporation and pulled down to make room for the Guildhall, which now stands on the old site.

The New Angel, now called the Royal, was a busy house from its opening to the demise of coaching, and the house as it stands at present is but little altered since those times, a remark which equally applies to the other coaching inns in Doncaster: the Reindeer, the Ram, the Red Lion, the Black Boy, and the Salutation. The coach offices at the New Angel were kept by Mr Dunhill, and the principal coaches starting from that inn were the Royal Mails, which left for London every forenoon at eleven o'clock and half-past respectively, the former going by way of Bawtry, Tuxford, Newark, Huntingdon, Ware, and Waltham Cross; the latter pursuing the same route to Alconbury Hill, thence by way of Biggleswade, Hatfield, and Barnett; and the Wellington, which left the New Angel every evening at six o'clock, and arrived in London early the following afternoon. The Leeds Union was still worked from the Old Angel across the way. Mr Dunhill was succeeded at the New Angel by Thomas Pye, who remained at the house long after the coaches had gone off the road. He used to drive the Edinbro' Mail between Doncaster and Stamford, and being a good-sized well-made man, when he donned his brown great-coat he looked the very type of an old stage coachman. His father was a coachman before him, and although he appenticed his son to a joiner, his inclinations were always with the horses. Breed will tell, so the jack-plane was ultimately exchanged for the box seat. He still continued to drive the Mail after he became the landlord of the New Angel; in fact, he and George Leach, another Doncaster coachman of steady habits, who succeeded in saving £2,000, were the two last men to drive the Edinbro' Mail between Doncaster and Stamford. Pye's family carried on the New Angel long after he was dead, and it was not until 1851, when the Queen stopped at this house, that its name was changed to the Royal.

Two other well-known posting houses in Doncaster which lay in close proximity to each other were the Reindeer and the Ram, at both of which places Mr Richard Wood had his coach offices, and when stage coaching was at its height and there was an increasing demand for accommodation, Mr Wood also stood some of his horses and horsed some of the coaches from the Black Boy Inn, in Frenchgate, the Highflyer amongst others. He was succeeded at the Black Boy by Mr Wilkinson, who remained until the coaches went off the road. 'Dickey' Wood as he was familiarly called, was the principal coach proprietor in Doncaster, and worked many of the stages both on the main and the cross roads. He horsed the Rockingham and the Highflyer, and had over two hundred horses engaged in the business. He likewise horsed several pair-horse coaches which ran between Doncaster and Sheffield, Nottingham, Wakefield, Thorne, Hull, Lincoln, Stamford, Gainsborough, etc. Some of the heavy luggage waggons and post-chaises were also under his control, and his whole business was of a very extensive character.

Mr Wood lived at the top of Hall Gate, and was one of the best known and most popular men in Doncaster. He was a rather stout, fresh-looking, good-natured fellow, wearing a top hat and a high white choker, and was never so happy as when he was entertaining his friends during the race week at the Red House Farm on the race-course. He farmed the land connected with this well-known house, and it was here that he used to turn out his horses to graze. At one time he sold his coaching interests to a Mr Booth, who failed in business, and Mr Wood was obliged to take them back again.

On the St Leger and Cup days it was customary for the London coaches to make a stay in Doncaster until those races were over, when they proceeded on their journey.

The London coaches that were on the road in Mr Wood's time were the Rockingham, the Highflyer, the Royal Mails (two), the Wellington, the Express, and the Leeds Union, which were all four-horse coaches, leaving Doncaster daily for London, as their duplicates likewise did to their several destinations further North, making in all fourteen four-horse coaches on the main road, besides about forty other coaches, chiefly pair-horse, running on the cross roads. Besides these there were from fifteen to twenty heavy luggage waggons passing in and out of Doncaster daily, and an innumerable number of post-chaises and gentlemen's private carriages travelling post. Some idea may be gathered from the above of the busy times and the daily whirl of excitement to which the old town would be subjected in the earlier part of the century.

In reviving recollections of the old coaching days you cannot long remain in Doncaster without learning something of one of the old stage coachmen who left an indelible mark on the coaching history of this town. Mr Wood had in his employ a man who divided his time between driving the Highflyer, elaborating the panels of the various coaches, and painting the signs of many of the inns with pictorial representations of their names. This man was John Frederic Herring, the artist who in after life acquired such a fame as a painter of horses and coaching scenes as to give him the highest place of honour in his profession in his especial line. He was born in London in the year 1795, and was brought up as a fringe maker, which business was carried on by his father in Newgate Street, but his heart was with his pencil and brush, so he was sent by his father to one Mr Phelps, an artist, to receive instruction, who sent him back after a few lessons, saying that the pupil knew more than the master. At the age of nineteen he fell madly in love with a young and charming girl, and taking advantage of a brief business absence of his father in Holland, they eloped and were married. Being without means and fearing a father's anger, they determined to fly, but not knowing whither to go they stuck a pin at random into an old gazetteer, which distinctly pointed to Doncaster, so to Doncaster they wended their way poor and penniless. With respect to Herring's life at Doncaster we cannot do better than give an extract from an excellent work on 'Ancient and Modern Doncaster,' by John Tomlinson.

'Herring arrived at Doncaster 'during the races of 1814, and saw William win the St Leger. The main consideration to an entire stranger was how to live after he had arrived at Doncaster. Local tradition says that as he passed a coach-builder's premises he observed a workman with pencil and palette striving to portray the Duke of Wellington on his charger, which representation was intended for the panel of a new coach to be called the "Commander-in-Chief." To delineate the horse evidently puzzled the painter, when noticing his perplexity young Herring offered to sketch the animal for him. So satisfied was the workman by this outline that he begged the stranger to complete the whole, and while thus engaged the proprietor came in. "This is clever," said he, and after a few other questions inquired if Herring was engaged as an art painter. Not long after the quondam artist asked the coach proprietor to let him drive, when Mr Wood observed, "I acknowledge your abilities as a painter, but to drive four-in-hand is quite another matter." "Trust me with the ribbons as a trial," said the young man, "and accompany me on the box-seat." After some pressing, consent was given, and the trial proving eminently successful, Herring was soon installed on the Highflyer.

'For several years while driving coaches he employed his leisure in painting animals, chiefly on signs of public-houses, the best remembered being the Coach and Horses in Scot Lane, the Brown Cow in Frenchgate, the White Lion in St George Gate, the Stag in the Holmes, and the Salutation, near Hall Cross. With one solitary exception, the Stag, painted on plaster, all have been removed. There are local reminiscences of keen competition to possess those faded relics. It is said that a gentleman travelling north was so struck with the painted cow that he ordered the postboy to stop there while he tried to bargain for the sign. He began by offering twice as much as had been paid for it. "Not for twenty times as much," replied the landlady, so the gentleman in the post-chaise had to depart without obtaining what he coveted. I remember that the 'Salutation' (which was a picture of angels, and not of men) was in its place about twenty years ago. The Coach and Horses, after being restored, if not entirely repainted by another hand, was purchased and removed to Beverley. Herring's career as a coachman at length gave place to a higher if not a more remunerative career. Numerous Yorkshire gentlemen, including Mr Stanhope, of Cannon Hall; Mr Frank Hawksworth, of Hickleton; Mr Christopher Wilson, of Ledstone; the Hon. E. Petre, of

Stapleton; Sir Bellingham Graham, of Norton Conyers; and others showered commissions upon him, chiefly for representations of their favourite horses. But it was as a painter of racehorses that Herring achieved his highest renown, and for upwards of thirty years in succession he pictured winners of the St. Leger. At length not only noblemen with turf proclivities, but even royalty honoured him with commissions.'

It was in 1821, after being seven years at Doncaster, that Herring threw up the ribbons to follow that which ultimately proved a more lucrative calling. During his stay in Doncaster things could not have been in too flourishing a condition for the young coachman-artist. Reduced to the necessity of sign painting, the prices obtained were incompatible with the quality of work given, and hampered as he was with a young wife, he knew something of the struggle of life, and was at times obliged to fall back on some of his other accomplishments. He sang a good song and played the clarionet most excellently, and we find among many other things that he did he was engaged at the Doncaster Theatre for a short period.

When he left Doncaster to go in for the higher branches of art he took up his abode near to the head-quarters of the Turf at Fulbourn, between Cambridge and Newmarket, and finally, when he had become famous, went to reside at Meopham Park, a short distance from Tonbridge, where he died in 1865.

In the latter part of his time he suffered very much from asthma, and was at times quite unable to leave home to execute the commissions of his royal and noble patrons. During one of these indispositions Her Majesty sent down three of her horses for him to paint. These were Bagdad, a powerful black charger which belonged to the late Prince Albert, a white Arab called Korseed, and the Arab Said, the horse on which the royal children were taught to ride. Doncaster may well be proud of its connection with the man who began life by driving the Highflyer, and rose to so exalted a position as painter to the Queen.

Before leaving Doncaster it would perhaps be as well to say a word or two about the old postboys, the father of whom, so to speak, belonged to that town. Of the genus postboy that in the pre-railway days swarmed along that great head line of posting, the Great North Road, little or nothing is known. There are men still living in whose minds memories of the old posting days are still green, who can recall certain individual members of this quaint old class of men; and then comes the oft-repeated question: 'I wonder what became of him?' a question that remains unanswered except in a very few cases, for history has left no record of where they went or how they ended their days. Whether they drove off to another world, one postboy to a pair, as the versatile Sam Weller suggested, or they vanished into thin air, certain it is that when the railways superseded the road, this numerous class disappeared so completely as to leave but little trace of their after life.

The regular down-the-road old postboy was a rum-looking customer to gaze upon, many of them being of very diminutive stature, with shrivelled-up figures, quaint, wrinkled faces, and a quiet, knowing eye, the body stooping forward, and a constant drooping at the knee, as though they were continuously in the saddle. The old postboys' jackets were red and blue in colour in Yorkshire, although yellow jackets were much in vogue in the south. These short jackets were trimmed at the collar and wrists in some cases with silver braid, and had down each side two wondrous rows of closely-fitting buttons. The blue jackets were made of superfine cloth, and though not containing much material cost as much as two guineas each, an extra guinea being sometimes added to that sum for silver braid. These jackets were worn on state occasions and in winter; the red jackets, which were for common use, being made of a cheaper and thinner material. The waistcoat, which was also profusely ornamented with buttons, was of red or blue stripes or buff, according to the place to which the wearer belonged; for instance, the Doncaster lads wore blue stripes, the Ferrybridge and Wetherby lads red stripes. The cravat was a mystery of folds and wraps, for the manufacture of which the old postboy used to purchase two yards of fine linen, and slitting this lengthwise down the middle, joined two of the ends and wound its long length in many folds round his throat, and high up under his chin. White cords, and boots with yellow tops completed his lower attire, except the false leg, which was made of iron and leather, and was worn on the off-side leg as a protection against the carriage pole. For winter and wet weather he had a buff-coloured great-coat with long laps reaching to his heels, and a double row of large pearl buttons. In wet weather when riding he would pull these long laps forward and wrap them round his legs as a protection. To crown all, he wore a long straight black or white stove-pipe hat with a square brim. The black hats were considered better form, and were usually worn by the lads connected with the head posting houses, and the colour of the hat was also a distinguishing feature where opposition posting houses were established; thus the lads at the Angel at Ferrybridge wore black hats and those at the Greyhound wore white.

The regular postboy did not receive any wages from the post-master who employed him, and besides this he was obliged to provide his own clothing. He depended for his source of emolument entirely on tips, his only receipts from his master being his board and lodging. Nevertheless, he did not fare badly, and some of them made as much as five pounds a week with little difficulty in busy times such as Doncaster races. Each postboy had four horses under his charge, and the *modus operandi* was as follows: gentlemen travelling post would, in many instances, send forward an outrider to the next posting station to order the next relay, in order to have them in readiness on the arrival of the carriage, each successive establishment sending on the outrider. The postboys took their regular turns, the first and second pair out held themselves in readiness, so that even when no outrider had been sent on in advance there was very little time lost. After a change a ticket was handed to the postboy from the posting office before starting, which he gave up to the gate-keeper of the toll-bar that happened to be on his stage, not stopping to pay the fees, as he did this on his return journey with the loose horses or empty chaise as the case might be. Arrived at the end of the stage the traveller, whilst the next pair were being put to, settled up with the postboy for the post-horses, the toll-bar fees, and his own douceur. The postboy, before starting out on his return journey, was regaled at the expense of the house to which he had posted. The nature of the entertainment varied according to the amount of opposition afforded by rival establishments. At a place like Doncaster, where there were plenty of posting establishments, the lads were very well treated at some of the places, who were desirous of encouraging them to stop at their houses instead of going over to the opposition inn. The New Angel at Doncaster always gave incoming postboys a square meal along with a quart of ale and a glass of spirits; whilst on the other hand the Swan at Aberford, where there was no opposition, had a bad name for its hospitality, as the 'Ferrybridge gentleman' can attest.

The first of the old Yorkshire postboys may be said to have been Tommy Adkin, who was postboy at the Old Angel Inn, Doncaster. For sixty years he carried the mail bags on horseback, and was engaged at the work long before the advent of post-chaises. The first post-chaise was put upon the road for general purposes in 1753, and in this year old Tommy drove the first of its kind in and out of Doncaster. He died at the age of seventy-nine years, and the fact of his leaving £1,000 shows that there were worse things than being a postboy.

Another Doncaster postboy was Samuel Briggs, who began life at the Sun Bridge Inn, Bradford, which was a well-known posting house in that town. He afterwards entered the employ of Mr Belcher, at the Red Lion Inn, Scott Lane, to which house the first Mail ran that entered Doncaster. After leaving the Red Lion he went to the Old Angel, in Frenchgate, where he did so well that he entered the Marquis of Granby, at Bawtry, as landlord, where he remained for thirty-seven years. He died at Sheffield on the 27th of August, 1862, aged seventy-nine years. Two other well-known Doncaster postboys were the Yates', father and son, but record does not say what became of them, save that the elder died at Doncaster; whilst another, called Major, died in that town only a year ago, at the age of eighty; and there is still living in Doncaster, in his seventy-ninth year, James Smith, who was postboy with Mr Wood, and subsequently with Mr Pye, at the New Angel.

Tom Bradley *The Old Coaching Days in Yorkshire*

The Country Pub

The Kirkstyle and Sportsman's Rest is very small and does not welcome strangers. It is hard to find and, when you have found it, it is as blank and forbidding and anonymous as a St James's Street club. Indeed, it has much more in common with a gentleman's club than with the brash roadhouses that most country pubs have now become. But if you are brave enough, or thirsty enough, to open the door you find yourself in an interior rarer than that of a church untouched by the 19th century restorer and as valuable as a social document as a cottage parlour by an 18th century journeyman painter or a Surrey garden by Helen Allingham. I found it because I was on foot. Had I been in a car, I would not have noticed it, let alone been tempted to stop.

The little village of Slaggyford consists of a few houses round a green, a substantial farmstead and a stone-built terrace of railwaymen's cottages, tucked under the eastern flank of the Pennines. In front of these, short steep gardens run down to the road, neatly cultivated with vegetables. The right hand cottage is distinguished from the others by a dilapidated wooden board over the door; with faded lettering telling that it is the Kirkstyle and Sportsman's Rest and that the proprietor, Mr George Brogdon, is licensed to sell beer and spirits. The evening I arrived it was getting dark, there was a light in the ground floor window, but no sound. Inside the front door was a tiny lobby and another door on the right, beyond that a small room crowded with people who stopped talking as I entered. There was no bar at which to seek sanctuary from the blank stares. I squeezed in on a bench against the wall and the spell cast by my arrival was broken. The room was about 10 feet by 8. It was brilliantly lit by a sodium strip, though gas fittings still hung from the ceiling. Walls and ceiling were stained by tobacco smoke rich and varied shades of brown. It was July but a fire smouldered in the grate. Round the walls on wooden benches, bursting leather settles and a variety of modern chairs and stools sat fourteen people, men of all ages, a veteran asleep by the fire, boys of 18 or so talking loudly and unintelligibly and four women cackling in a row behind a table against the wall. There was a heavy pall of smoke and in the centre of the room a pile of black and white sheep dogs. After a while someone shouted for George and an old man carrying tankards of beer emerged from an open doorway in the corner.

Through the door was what appeared to be a barn, cavernous and dark, with rows of barrels on trestles and hundreds of empty bottles standing on the floor. George was harassed and petulant, teased and chivvied to fill glasses and bring me mine. I did not stay long, but have remembered the place clearly, a glimpse of what the country pub used to be like when it served only the local people as an extension of home and had no need to provide for car-born travellers. I was there nearly twenty years ago. Today, no doubt, George is dead and, if the little terrace house is still a pub, it will have a car park, a swinging sign and, inside, two bars and banks of upturned bottles, which in the trade are mysteriously known as optics.

To the south of the road from Eastbourne to Lewes are a series of little villages approached by lanes that peter out at the foot of the South Downs. In one of these near the church and overlooking the green was until recently another survivor. Like the inn at Slaggyford, The Cricketers was the end cottage of an attached row. It had a long front garden, no longer cultivated but full of straggling old roses. A straight path led to the door, which always stood open. Above the door was a signboard, the only indication that it was not a private house. The parlour was bright and sunny with a long low window to the south and a view of the Downs. There was brown linoleum on the floor and match-boarding on the walls up to four feet. The ceiling was low and every surface was painted the colour of Jersey cream. There were wooden benches fixed to the walls, a dart board, a framed print or two, a notice board, to which were pinned announcements of flower shows and dart matches and across one corner a small three-sided bar with a door behind it. Through this door could be seen the sitting room of the owner, a smiling lady in a flowery overall, and through it she would disappear to fetch the beer and, if she was not busy, a sandwich. It may have been possible to order other things to drink but beer, but I had never seen anyone do so. At midday there were never more than two customers. It was a quiet, simple place. When I was last there, the lady licensee had gone, there was pine furniture in the bar parlour and ranks of bottles behind the bar. Drains were being laid for lavatories in the front garden. I have no doubt, though I do not remember, there was rustic furniture too and the possibility of two kinds of ploughman's lunch.

Soon it will be fashionable to reconstruct pub parlours such as these, with bare boards in place of carpet and paint in place of stripped oak, but the pub in which you cannot buy tomato juice or something to eat is already an anachronism. And who ever heard of a pub without a bar? You might as well say that there was a time when no church had an altar.

Martin Drury *Time Gentlemen Please!*

The Northern Urban Pub

The best-known pub in Northern England has no beer – and no customers, though its fictional customers are watched by up to 16 million television viewers every week. The 'Rovers Return' is the centre of social life in 'Coronation Street.' So potent is the appeal of the long-running series that Granada TV has constructed a section of the street, complete with pub, adjacent to its Manchester studios and tourists will soon be able to visit 'the street.' It is likely to become one of the most popular tourist attractions in the North West yet, if the 'Rover's Return' had been a genuine pub in Manchester or Salford, there is a good chance that it would by now have been demolished. Here, as elsewhere, countless street corner pubs have succumbed to road schemes, wholesale clearance and the rationalising policies of the breweries. The 'New House', 'an enormous drinking barracks' with 'a windy rubber-tiled hallway' and a concert room where the hero of Keith

Waterhouse's *Billy Liar* tried hard to be a comedian, is perhaps more typical of the urban North today. The last century has seen a steady reduction in the number of licensed premises. The 1853 directory for Leeds lists no fewer than 309 'hotels, inns and taverns,' with an equal number of beerhouses. (Until 1869 it was possible for virtually any house to be used for the sale of beer and no proper licensing system operated). Even after the introduction of more stringent licensing Salford had 657 licensed houses, producing 'appalling disorder and terrible immorality.' Frederick Engels was one of the most radical of the many critics of the drinks trade. His picture of a typical Saturday evening in Manchester is a vivid one: 'I have rarely come out of Manchester on such an evening without meeting numbers of people staggering and seeing others lying in the gutter'. It was hardly surprising that the temperance movement grew up in the industrial towns in response to the drunkenness all around – the Band of Hope was founded in Leeds in 1847.

The English pub, as both building type and social institution, is very largely a 19th century creation. Every town had its ancient inns – though few were as architecturally distinguished as the 'Angel and Royal' at Grantham (illustrated in Pugin's *Contrasts* as a symbol of Old English hospitality). The 'Bull's Head' in Bradford was one of the chief meeting places of merchants and manufacturers and the headquarters of the town's choral society, while the 'New Inn' staged the first Bradford flower show (in 1827). The new hotels and gentlemen's clubs, combined with the impact of the temperance movement and a rising mood of middle class respectability, made the inns of Bradford (as of other towns) 'a thing of the past.' Most were quickly swept away for the exchanges, banks, and large retail premises so typical of Victorian cities. In the smaller market towns and county towns inns survived as important institutions. The 'dramshops' were left to the working class and the more raffish elements amongst the wealthy. Most of these buildings were domestic in style and in scale, mere converted cottages. A high proportion of the old inns and taverns had been built as houses. The 'Bear and Billet' in Chester and the 'White Swan' in York are notable examples, whilst it is uncertain exactly when such ancient establishments as the 'Sun' or the 'White Horse' at Beverley became inns. Hull's 'Old White Hart' was built as a grand town house, but its present use dates from the mid 18th century. Humbler pubs dating from before the mid-Victorian period are comparatively rare. The 'Trip to Jerusalem' in Nottingham (claimed as 'the oldest inn in England') has cellars and bars excavated from the Castle rock many centuries ago, but the bulk of the present building seems to be of early 18th century date. (Both the 'Bell' and the 'Salutation' in Nottingham incorporate medieval timber framing.) The famous 'Whitelock's' off Briggate in Leeds, is externally typical of late Georgian courtyard housing in the city and several other pubs in central Leeds represent survivals from the pre-Victorian town. The 'Palace,' next to the city's Parish Church, is a Georgian house, comparatively little altered to the rear. Bradford's 'Jacob's Well' is a simple, stone-slated building of early Victorian date, surviving amidst aggressive modern office blocks.

The development of a specific style of pub architecture (and of an associated approach to planning) has been traced in London by Mark Girouard. Amongst provincial cities, only Birmingham has been studied with any thoroughness. Girouard has described the pubs of Liverpool as 'very much a world of their own,' with a distinctive character of plan and design unique to that city. Some are justifiably renowned: the 'Vines,' Lime Street, and the staggering 'Philharmonic,' Hope Street, both palatial works by the great pub architect Walter Thomas, the 'Lion' Tithebarn Street, the 'Central' and the 'Midland,' both in Ranelagh Street and 'Peter Kavanagh's' in Egerton Street, Toxteth. Most of these buildings date from the very end of the 19th century (the 'Vines' is as late as 1907). They represent an expression of the confident wealth of a world port. The 'Baltic Fleet', close to the South Docks, is older, a stuccoed *palazzo* with an amazing glazed 'stern' like that of an ocean liner. The opulence of late Victorian Liverpool is reflected, albeit less strikingly, in other cities. In Leeds, several large 'gin palaces' (in fact, a misleading term) were designed by Thomas Winn, including the 'Jubilee,' a riot of red brick and terracotta opposite the Town Hall, and the 'Adelphi,' with largely intact interiors. The 'Garden Gate,' Hunslet, a splendid faience covered survivor in an arid area of clearance, is similarly of c1900. Its plan is unusual, with a long corridor running through from front to back and various bars opening off it. The same period saw the remodelling of the interior at 'Whitelock's' with plenty of copper, brass, stained glass and tiles. The 'Crown Posada' in The Side, Newcastle-upon-Tyne, is perhaps the best

surviving interior in that city. Manchester is perhaps less rich in fine Victorian pubs than might be expected from so rich a city. One of the best, the 'Oxford,' was a serious recent loss, but the 'Crown and Kettle,' Oldham Road, survives. The interior of this pub is striking. The fan vaulted ceilings include pendentives housing ventilators and (formerly) gaslights.

The 'progressive' architects of the Edwardian period were rarely involved with pub design. The 'Rising Sun' at Whitwood, near Normanton (West Yorks.), is a distinctive work by C. F. A. Voysey, though built as a miners' institute intended to counter the influence of local ale-houses! Edgar Wood, the notable Manchester architect of this era, designed the 'George and Dragon' at Rochdale in 1897. The Government take-over of pubs in and around Carlisle (a major centre of armaments manufacture) in 1916 was a landmark in the development of the reformed public house. Many pubs were totally closed and others rebuilt by the Central Control Board's architects, headed by Harry Redfern (assisted at various times by both C. F. A. Voysey and George Walton). The new pubs were noted for 'cleanliness and good order,' offering tea-rooms, gardens and bowling greens alongside facilities for the sale of alcohol. The prevalent styles were a dignified Jacobean (exhibited strikingly in the 'Apple Tree,' Lowther Street, Carlisle,) or a sober neo Georgian. The tea-room of the 'Rose and Crown,' Carlisle, furnished in a tasteful manner, with furnishings designed by Redfern, seems a world away from the somewhat risqué glitter of the 'Vines'. In Liverpool and other cities great rehousing schemes were moving people from the old working class districts to new suburbs. The new pubs serving these estates were designed on the best 'reformed' lines. Some of those done in and around Liverpool for Higson's brewery by H. Hinchcliffe Davies reflect the refined Georgian taste of C. H. Reilly (albeit with marked 'Moderne' touches). The spreading road houses of the South East are largely absent from the Northern towns and cities, though there are the usual large suburban pubs of the inter war years. The scheme for the 'Dicken Green' at Rochdale was one of the most elaborate conceived by J. W. Lees and Co.'s brewery and included not only the normal facilities associated with a large 'reformed' pub but extensive grounds, including a 'wild garden' and bird sanctuary! Deferred by the outbreak of the war, the project was subsequently abandoned. Too much of the neo-Tudor of these years was mechanical and unimaginative, but there are exceptions. The 'Royal Oak' at Halifax is a most elaborate specimen of half timbering, complete with carvings showing the history of the town. (The interior here has been totally wrecked.)

The post-war years have seen a continuing steady decline in the total number of pubs, and in many areas this has been accelerated by the massive clearance of old housing. J. W. Lees, one of the small independent brewers in the Manchester area, had over 200 tied houses in 1950. They now have 130, virtually all the others having been demolished. The 'Hanky Park' area of Salford once had over fifty pubs, the majority surviving until the whole district was cleared in the 1960s and replaced by a modern high-rise housing estate. Only three of the old pubs survived. The same sort of process could be documented in Everton or Hunslet, Attercliffe or Gateshead. Many areas once densely populated have been given over to new factories, warehouses and roads. Road 'improvements' have claimed many pubs. A number in the Sheepscar area of Leeds were recently demolished for such a scheme, including the much loved 'Roscoe', an intact ale-house of the mid-19th century.

Local campaigns (with CAMRA often in the fore) have saved many pubs, though very few have been listed as of architectural interest. The Department of the Environment refused to list the 'Griffin' at Heaton Mersey, Stockport, one of the best Victorian pubs in the area, when it was recently threatened with demolition. (At the time of writing, the pub is still standing.) City centre redevelopment has engulfed pubs along with other buildings. The 'Black Boy' at Nottingham, a splendid Victorian rebuilding by Watson Fothergill of an ancient coaching inn, was demolished c1970 for a new chain store. The proposed redevelopment of the area around Cases Street and Clayton Square in Liverpool will destroy a number of pubs. The best known, the 'Villiers,' has recently been listed but the developers have refused to consider its retention.

The vast sums of money spent by the brewing industry on refurbishing pubs reflect a belief that the public is no longer satisfied with the traditional pub. The 'Lowther Hotel' on York's riverside was a well-preserved local institution. Virtually gutted, it has become the 'Le Dijon Bar.' Even Yates's Wine Lodges, familiar sights in much of the North, are now being rapidly brought up to date with the aid of plastic laminate and stainless steel. (The finest example, that in Nottingham, remains intact, a fine galleried interior of the 1870s.) Even listing cannot protect all the interior fittings of a pub. The 'Harrington Arms' at Gawsworth, Cheshire, is (or was) a remarkably unaltered village pub of Georgian date. Internal alterations were recently done without listed building consent, though the local authority has insisted that some of the fittings be reinstated.

It is, fortunately, no longer the case that all the brewers are set on a course of insensitive modernisation. Tetley Walker of Liverpool and Joshua Tetley of Leeds have nominated a number of their pubs as 'Heritage Inns' and a genuine attempt has been made to safeguard the character of these buildings. External plaques and notices in the bars draw attention to their historic interest. A number of companies have abandoned the policy of attaching standard fascias to all their pubs (the yellow plastic strip formerly used by Allied Breweries was as unpleasant as the omnipresent blue of Barclay's Bank). Individual gilt letters or painted sign boards are becoming increasingly common and in many cases the names of now defunct breweries in carved stone or glazed tiles have been once more revealed. The practice is a logical corollary of the revival of the old company names for newly introduced real ales.

Ironically, the drive towards standardisation is now more typical of the smaller companies. Nottingham's Home Brewery has pursued an energetic modernisation programme and fine faience facades such as those of the 'Lion' in Clumber Street or the 'Blue Bell' in Upper Parliament Street mask completely renewed interiors. Local protests failed to prevent the destruction of a fine tiled bar in Hull's 'New White Hart,' though the owners, North Country Breweries, now generally take a more enlightened view of their properties. Indeed, they have been responsible for some interesting conversions of redundant buildings to pubs. The 'High Farm,' the sole interesting feature of a new housing estate at Holt Park, Leeds, incorporates the former farmhouse and barn (both rescued from total dereliction). Most of the larger companies at least are now conscious of the fact that they have responsibility for some remarkable historic buildings. William Stones of Sheffield own the 'Green Dragon' at Dronfield, said to incorporate part of the medieval manor house. Aware of claims that the pub was to be ruined by alterations, the brewery made sure that 'local historical society members were in constant attendance' while the work was being carried out. Few historic pubs have been deemed worthy of the attentions of the National Trust, though it does own the Crown Liquor Saloon in Belfast (described by Mark Girouard as 'the crown of Victorian pubs in Ireland and many would say in the British Isles'). The Trust preserves and runs the 'Tower Bank Arms' at Near Sawrey, Cumbria, on account of its close association with Beatrix Potter (who lived in the village for many years). Associations with famous writers are good for business and many of James Herriot's readers now visit the 'Wheatsheaf Inn' at Carperby (North Yorks), where the author spent his honeymoon. All too many of the simple, vernacular village inns of the Yorkshire Dales and the Lake District have been radically modernised in the last quarter century.

In the same way that the remote moorland inn (such as the Barrel Inn at Bretton in Derbyshire) is still a refuge for travellers, the surviving pubs of redeveloped city centres and inner-city areas remain as anchors in a shattered environment. Many people travel miles to the pubs in such districts from the new housing estates. J. M. Richards declared (in 1950) that 'the art of the pub is one of the few living arts which is still popular in a spontaneous, unselfconscious way.' The pub is supposedly a national institution, yet we have spent three decades demolishing pubs and refashioning those that remain. The 'Rover's Return,' and the many surviving 'locals' which it epitomises, stands for civilised social values in a world of change. That must surely be the argument for saving it.

Ken Powell *Time Gentlemen Please!*

The Black Lion on the Great North Road

It was on the great northern road from York to London, about the beginning of October, and about the hour of eight in the evening, that four travellers were, by a violent shower of rain, driven for shelter into a little public-house on the side of the highway, distinguished by a sign which was said to exhibit the figure of a black lion. The kitchen, in which they were assembled, was the only room for entertainment in the house, paved with red bricks, remarkably clean, furnished with three or four Windsor chairs, adorned with shining plates of pewter, and copper saucepans nicely scoured, that even dazzled the eyes of the beholder; while a cheerful fire of seacoal blazed in the chimney.

Tobias Smollett *Sir Lancelot Greaves*

Comber's Bar, Lahinch

Look out from Comber's, that's all you need to do,
And you'll see the rest of the world pass by.
Up and down and round and about, people and machines;
Rain, hail or shine; they'll be there. You see.

Watch out from the back bar, keep your eyes open,
And you'll see everyone you've ever known,
Wandering hither and thither, whither and which;
Morning, noon and night and other times. You see.

When darkness comes with wraps, keep watching.
You can still see them, everyone of them.
They're moving in rotation to and from the bar,
Until the early hours and even later. You see.

There's a time when you can close your eyes. But listen,
And you'll hear the rest of the world pass by.
Bass, baritone, soprano, croaker, chorus and all;
In the Grand Opera House of Combers Bar, Lahinch. You see.

Wilf Lowe

Four Views on The Fleece at Bretforton

Medieval farmhouse in the centre of the village; became a licensed house in 1848, and remains largely unaltered; family collection of furniture.

The National Trust Handbook, 1989

Famous old inn, owned by the National Trust (no outside signs allowed). Interior has remained untouched for many years; inglenook and antiques. Darts and Evesham quoits. Guest beers.

The Good Beer Guide, 1990

Readers who've driven right across the country just to find this glorious antique tell us they're really glad they've made the trip. It is the character of the building and what's in it that delights people so. A farm and then a farm-pub, it's been preserved as carefully by the National Trust and its tenants for the last dozen years – original furnishings and all – as it had for the preceding centuries by the family that had owned it for nearly 500 years. Mid-week or on a winter's day, it's usually quiet and roomy enough for you to see all the treasures inside. But the present licensees have also coped splendidly with its huge popularity in summer, making the most of the extensive orchard behind, by the beautifully restored thatched and timbered barn. Out here, besides an adventure playground, a display of farm engines, barbecues and

goats cropping the grass, you may find anything from morris dancing, a vintage car rally or a sheep-shearing, spinning and weaving demonstration, to the merriment of their Friday to Sunday festival on the first weekend in July, with up to thirty real ales, bands and pony-rides. Inside, there are massive beams and exposed timbers, huge inglenooks with log fires, worn and crazed flagstones (scored with marks to keep out demons), and loads of striking antiques – from a rocking-chair and ancient kitchen chairs to curved high-backed oak settles, from the great cheese press and set of cheese moulds to the rare dough-proving table, from the fine grandfather clock to the dresser filled with Stuart pewter which is the pub's particular pride. Yet this 'museum' is still very much alive, with local regulars still playing darts, dominoes, cribbage, shove-ha'penny or quoits. Well kept Hook Norton Best, M&B Brew XI, Uley Pigs Ear and a guest beer on handpump are backed up by a choice of farm ciders and country wines, with mulled wine or hot toddy in winter, and a chilled summer punch. Food is appropriately simple, freshly prepared and good value, including sandwiches (from 80p), ploughman's (from £2), chilli con carne (£2.20), Gloucester sausages (£2.40), home-cured ham (£2.80), steak and kidney pie (£3.10) and locally cured gammon (£4). Service is pleasant and normally quick, though they warn of delays at busy times.

The Good Pub Guide 1990

Bretforton is three miles east of Evesham, just off the B4035, and the pub we are travelling to is the Fleece.

There is a noble tradition in British pubs of indomitable women licensees, who rule over their pubs with a rod of iron, reigning supreme for decades, and who are remembered with respect and, more remarkably, with great affection. One of the most indomitable of all was Lola Taplin. Her family had owned the Fleece Inn at Bretforton for over 500 years and she ran it single-handed for the last thirty years of her long life, until her death in 1977 at the age of eighty-three.

It is said that she never let her customers forget that they were drinking in her family home and not just any old public house, and any who forgot their manners would be out on their ears in very quick time.

On her death, Lola Taplin left the inn, its magnificent contents and its gardens to the National Trust on condition that it continued to be run as an unspoilt country pub.

Originally a medieval farmhouse, the Fleece was converted to an inn in 1848 by Henry Byrd, Ms Taplin's great-grandfather. The interior and the furniture and ornaments used by the family remain as they were in the nineteenth century. The farm dairy became the brewhouse, producing beer and cider for the inn, and reminders of both these uses can be seen in the room still known as The Brewhouse, though the last home-produced beer was brewed over fifty years ago.

Off this room is the 'Dugout,' once the farmhouse pantry, and still containing the coffin-like table in which dough was placed to 'prove,' free from draughts. The pub's other room, once the farm kitchen, contains a stunning, and world famous, collection of pewter. Legend has it that the collection was left by Oliver Cromwell in return for gold and silver plate taken to pay the parliamentary armies during the Civil War.

In this room and the Brewhouse, 'witch-marks' can still be seen. To ward of evil spirits, charms were hung over doors and windows, while circles (chosen because they have no corners in which spirits can hide) were chalked on hearths to prevent entry through the chimney. The marks in the Brewhouse are indented into the stone through centuries of daily chalking.

You can find furniture and artefacts that are as interesting in a museum, but you will not find a family home preserved over centuries, where you can eat, drink good beer, or sit outside in the shade of an old thatched barn, anywhere but at the Fleece. Before you travel on, drink a toast to Henry Byrd for making the Fleece into one of the finest pubs in Britain and to Lola Taplin and the National Trust for keeping it that way.

Neil Hanson *Classic Country Pubs*

The Haycock at Wansford

On a haycock sleeping soundly
The river rose, and took me roundly
Down the current, people cried,
As along the stream I hied,
'Where away?' quoth they, 'From Greenland?'
'No; from Wansford Bridge in England.'

John Taylor (the Water Poet)

The Maid's Head, Norwich

It was rumoured that when Mr Webster (who and whose wife had been rather the personal friends of his guests than ordinary innkeepers) left the Maid's Head, the whole scope of the old house – the nearest approach to the typical old hostel that I ever saw – was going to be changed; that it was to be let to a big brewer, and be turned into a commercial inn, with a coloured glass bar, a billiard-room, and the rest of it; and, in fact, that the whole place was to be spoiled, and no longer be a refuge for those who like peace and quiet and old surroundings.

Walter Rye

The Seven Day Licence of Joseph McHugh

Come all you young fellows who travel the land
In search of the crack with guitar in your hand.
Go down to Liscannor in the County of Clare,
You'll find a pub in it that's ever so rare.
Go into McHugh's shop the centre of town
You'll get a warm welcome from Joe, chalk it down.
The one-legg'd canary will sing 'How de do'
In the seven day licence of Joseph McHugh.

You'll meet men from Moher, Lisdoon and Rineen
Judges from Lahinch and an off-duty queen.
A tinker from Kerry drops in for a glass
A box of rat poison and oats for his ass.
Joe strolls up the bar like a Captain on deck,
He don't tip his cap and he don't give a reck.
If you're Irish or Spanish or Russian or Jew
You'll get a warm welcome from Joseph McHugh.
Diddly-de-di diddly-dar-dar di-dar-diddly-doo
Fill 'em up round the house again, Joseph McHugh.

The shop is well stocked for allcomers to see
With brushes and buckets, balloons and whiskey,
Bulleyes, licorice allsorts displayed in glass jars
And an out of space suit just imported from Mars.
There's onion sets stacked in the bar and some rope,
A picture of Joe shaking hands with the Pope
He's our Parish Priest that's the truth I tell you
Declares the Clare publican, Joseph McHugh.

He sells streaky bacon all covered with salt
To ward off blue bottles from making a halt,
He has cups from coursing, some say that's not fair
But Liscannor is famous for chasing the hare.
He's a bachelor gay on the market I hear
He may make a move by the end of the year.
But if the greyhound has pups you can say toodleoo
For he'll never get married then Joseph McHugh.

So there you have it, the song I declare
About the small pub in the sweet County Clare.
Where time has stopped still and the auld life remains
To laugh at computers and mad college brains.
So if you're in trouble, find yourself in a jam
Want a wife or a greyhound or a half pound of ham,
You can do a lot worse that's the truth I tell you
Than call on that publican, Joseph McHugh
Diddly-de-di etc.,   Dermot Kelly

Joe McHugh's is the smallest emporium in the world. It's the only pub I know that is about 20 feet deep and three feet wide and yet never seems to be uncomfortable to be in. There are brushes and hams and galvanised buckets and spades at one end and loaves of bread at the other and in between those there are fellows playing fiddles and fellows drinking pints and there's an atmosphere there I haven't met anywhere else and a lot of it is attributable to the man himself, to Joe McHugh. He stands there and runs proceedings like the Chairman of a County Council or even the President of a country, wearing a cap and saying things like 'Mighty fine' and 'Don't get upset.' So you take your time and you get your drink in good order in due course and it will be well served and reasonably priced and its just an unbelievable place.

I got a card after a television series in which I played a parish priest, wishing me well from 'my flock.' I knew very well it from Joe McHugh's. It's a place where you can have fun or serious conversation in and music too and, as I've said, what is a small place that never seems to be too uncomfortable. It's wonderful.

Donal Farmer

The Moon Under Water

My favourite public house, 'The Moon under Water,' is only two minutes from a bus stop, but it is on a side-street, and drunks and rowdies never seem to find their way there, even on Saturday nights.

Its clientele, though fairly large, consists mostly of 'regulars' who occupy the same chair every evening and go there for conversation as much as for the beer.

If you are asked why you favour a particular public house, it would seem natural to put the beer first, but the thing that most appeals to me about 'The Moon under Water' is what people call its 'atmosphere.'

To begin with, its whole architecture and fittings are uncompromisingly Victorian. It has no glass-topped tables or other modern miseries, and, on the other hand, no sham roof-beams, ingle-nooks or plastic panels masquerading as oak. The grained woodwork, the ornamental mirrors behind the bar, the cast-iron fireplaces, the florid ceiling stained dark yellow by tobacco-smoke, the stuffed bull's head over the mantelpiece – everything has the solid comfortable ugliness of the nineteenth century.

In winter there is generally a good fire burning in at least two of the bars, and the Victorian lay-out of the place gives one plenty of elbow-room. There is a public bar, a saloon bar, a ladies' bar, a bottle-and-jug for those who are too bashful to buy their supper beer publicly, and upstairs, a dining-room.

Games are only played in the public, so that in the other bars you can walk about without constantly ducking to avoid flying darts.

In 'The Moon under Water' it is always quiet enough to talk. The house posesses neither a radio nor a piano, and even on Christmas Eve and such occasions the singing that happens is of a decorous kind.

The barmaids know most of their customers by name, and take a personal interest in everyone. They are all middle-aged women – two of them have their hair dyed in quite surprising shades – and they call everyone 'Dear,' irrespective of age or sex. ('Dear,' not 'Ducky': pubs were the barmaid calls you 'Ducky' always have a disagreeable raffish atmosphere.)

Unlike most pubs, 'The Moon under Water' sells tobacco as well as cigarettes, and it also sells aspirins and stamps, and is obliging about letting you use the telephone.

You cannot get dinner at 'The Moon under Water,' but there is always the snack counter where you can get liver-sausage sandwiches, mussels (a speciality of the house), cheese, pickles and those large biscuits with caraway seeds in them which only seem to exist in public houses.

Upstairs, six days a week, you can get a good, solid lunch – for example, a cut off the joint, two vegetables and boiled jam roll – for about three shillings.

The special pleasure of this lunch is that you can have draught stout with it. I doubt whether as many as ten per cent of London pubs serve draught stout, but 'The Moon under Water' is one of them. It is a soft, creamy sort of stout, and it goes better in a pewter pot.

They are particular about their drinking vessels at 'The Moon under Water' and never, for example, make the mistake of serving a pint of beer in a handleless glass. Apart from glass and pewter mugs, they have some of those pleasant strawberry-pink china ones which are now seldom seen in London. China mugs went out about thirty years ago, because most people like their drink to be transparent, but in my opinion beer tastes better out of china.

The great surprise of 'The Moon under Water' is its garden. You go through a narrow passage leading out of the saloon, and find yourself in a fairly large garden with plane trees under which there are little green tables with iron chairs round them. Up at one end of the garden there are swings and a chute for the children.

On summer evenings there are family parties, and you sit under the plane trees having beer or draught cider to the tune of delighted squeals from children going down the chute. The prams with the younger children are parked near the gate.

Many as are the virtues of 'The Moon under Water' I think that the garden is its best feature, because it allows whole families to go there instead of Mum having to stay at home and mind the baby while Dad goes out alone.

And though, strictly speaking, they are only allowed in the garden, the children tend to seep into the pub and even to fetch drinks for their parents. This, I believe, is against the law, but it is a law that deserves to be broken, for it is the puritanical nonsense of excluding children – and therefore to some extent, women – from pubs that has turned these places into mere boozing-shops instead of the family gathering-places that they ought to be.

'The Moon under Water' is my ideal of what a pub should be – at any rate, in the London area. (The qualities one expects of a country pub are slightly different.)

But now is the time to reveal something which the discerning and disillusioned reader will probably have guessed already. There is no such place as 'The Moon under Water.'

That is to say, there may well be a pub of that name, but I don't know of it, nor do I know any pub with just that combination of qualities.

I know pubs where the beer is good but you can't get meals, others where you can get meals but which are noisy and crowded, and others which are quiet but where the beer is generally sour. As for gardens, offhand I can only think of three London pubs that possess them.

But, to be fair, I do know of a few pubs that almost come up to 'The Moon under Water.' I have mentioned above ten qualities that the perfect pub should have, and I know one pub that has eight of them. Even there, however, there is no draught stout and no china mugs.

And if anyone knows of a pub that has draught stout, open fires, cheap meals, a garden, motherly barmaids and no radio, I should be glad to hear of it, even though its name were something as prosaic as 'The Red Lion' or 'The Railway Arms'.

George Orwell *Evening Standard, 9th February 1946*

The Sailors Arms, Llaregyb

Up the street, in the Sailors Arms, Sinbad Sailors, grandson of Mary Ann Sailors, draws a pint in the sunlit bar. The ship's clock in the bar says half past eleven. Half past eleven is opening time. The hands of the clock have stayed still at half past eleven for fifty years. It is always opening time in the Sailors Arms.

Dylan Thomas *Under Milk Wood*

Tan Hill Inn, England's Highest Inn

Whichever way you travel, north or south, there is one pub right on the roof of England – the Pennines – that you should not miss. The Tan Hill Inn, at 1,732 feet above sea level, is the highest inn in England. It is situated about four miles south of the summit of the notorious Stainmore Pass on the A66, invariably one of the first roads to be blocked by the winter snows, but to reach it requires a round trip of several miles to the east or the west.

One way to approach Tan Hill is from the east through Richmond, up Swaledale to Reeth; then fork right into Arkengarthdale and keep going. It can also be reached from the A66 just west of Stainmore Summit (take the Barras/South Stainmore turning; Tan Hill is signed off that road); from the

A685 Brough-Kirkby Stephen road (follow the Kaber or South Stainmore signs); or from just west of Keld in Upper Swaledale. There is also a (very) rough road from Bowes across Sleightholme Moore; use it only if you have every confidence in your suspension . . . or if you are driving someone else's car! From whatever direction you approach, you will think that you must have missed Tan Hill and that no one could possibly have built a pub in such a desolate spot – but you have not, and someone did!

Tan Hill sits right on the Pennine Way, at the crossroads of tracks that were ancient when the Romans invaded Britain. Drovers, pack-horse traders and the coal miners who worked the numerous fell-top pits all once used the inn. There is nothing luxurious about Tan Hill's thick stone walls, flagged floors and wooden benches, but countless lost and weary travellers down the centuries have been grateful for the shelter offered by this lonely inn, and for the warmth from its blazing open fire. Now it sits in splendid isolation, its nearest neighbour almost four miles away, the only sounds the bleating of sheep, the call of grouse and curlew and the wind keening across the moor.

The wind blows so strongly here that many incautious motorists have lost their car doors to it – one famous landlady declared that it blew hard enough to 'blow the horns off a tup' (the local word for a ram) – and in winter it can whip the snow up into huge drifts that block the inn off from the outside world for weeks at a time.

A tale is told of the landlord who wished a shepherd 'Happy New Year' on 16 April because he was the first person he had seen that year. In another winter it was so cold that the whisky froze in the optics behind the bar! The Swaledale breed of sheep, with their distinctive black faces and white noses, was developed in the area around Tan Hill, and they are so hardy that they live up on 'the tops' in all but the wildest weather and can survive on a diet that would starve almost any other breed. If buried under the snow they have been known to survive for weeks, even eating their own fleeces to do so.

Tan Hill's isolation is lessened by the annual influx of summer tourists, and on the last Thursday in May every year it plays host to the Swaledale sheep world championships – the Tan Hill Show. On that day, a thousand people will be there to look at the sheep or just to share in the atmosphere of a unique event – there is no other country show like it. The judging of the sheep is deadly serious – a champion tup can command a price of well into five figures – and the judges' decisions will be discussed and disputed far into the night. The uninvolved can simply sit outside on a warm spring evening and listen as the sound of a silver band playing the local anthem 'Beautiful Swaledale' drifts over the fells.

Tan Hill is absolutely unique. See it in summer, surrounded by ten thousand acres of wild moorland. In winter snows it is best to leave it to the sheep and the shepherds who have learned to live with its wild weather – if you are lucky you may be stranded in the inn for some weeks and will have some tales to tell your friends; but if you are not so lucky, you may be dead from exposure before help can reach you.

Neil Hanson *Classic Country Pubs*

The Waggon and Horses, Lancaster

When I first became involved with starting the theatre in Lancaster I shared a hope with Peter Oyston that it would make the old town into a centre for new plays and ideas, but those aspirations have been over-taken by the sturdier stride of practical life – Lancaster, has remained itself, and my ambitions have been diverted elsewhere. Only down on the quay at the Waggon and Horses do I keep bumping into these past romances of mind. It is the pub where we started two theatres and the regulars remain as cheerfully unconscious of that as they are of any difference between writing for your living and selling fantasies. The people down there are coal-men, plasterers, drivers, process operators, booksellers, bookmakers, and they have a knack of letting all men through the net at the door providing they leave their pretensions behind.

In six years I have never seen a punch-up in the Waggon and Horses, nor have I seen the Christmas decorations ever taken down until August when the summer light insists on picking them out against the tobacco-brown ceiling of the room as they turn in the breeze from the river because the windows have been dragged open. On the floor is the world's most extraordinary carpet, made up of off-cuts from the warehouse next door and sewn into a tapestry of diabolical colours. The omnipresent television is perpetually screening green as if all characters suffered from seasickness, and the Ladies' toilet is always full of men who can't get through the crowd round the dart-board to the Gents. One room is full of whippets on Mondays and Tuesdays when the races are held at the field at the back, and I have seen someone playing Chopin on the piano in there surrounded by panting winners and losers in tartan waistcoats wearing wire muzzles. The oldest inhabitant has a pipe with a bowl the size of a hand-basin, and he can sing songs that were presumed forgotten on the morning after Bonnie Prince Charlie left the town. He was declared unfit for military service in the 1914–18 War and now sits by the fire which is built up to the mantelshelf summer and winter by the pyromaniac publican, and drinks pints of mild with navy rum chasers for a couple of hours each night, cap on, huge pipe smouldering.

The Waggon and Horses is the only pub where I have seen a man served a pint in his dressing-gown, with no questions asked. You are allowed to sing, stand on your head, fall over, talk backwards, take umbrage or give outrage. Les, the publican, an ex-jockey, has a gentle talent for governing excited men when they horse around. It is a wonderful place and it is about to be changed. It may be better after the improvements. I may walk in there with an even greater sense of good-nature and generosity waiting to greet me. The publican will be the same, but the carpet will have gone and the route through to the Gents will be better determined. When a place you have come to love undergoes a change, it is doubtful if it can actually improve because your trust is always working off memories. On the day the Old Waggon and Horses gets its face-lift I think I will get drunk and lie down in the gutter for a while.

Drinking has been a part of this landscape for me and it would be one-sided to consider the relationship which I have to the town and the land without it. To stand outside on a July night with a glass of beer and watch the early moon coming up over Lancaster is a warmer pleasure if it is the sixth or seventh you have had. Being on the quayside the better for drink when the bore comes floating white under the railway bridge, flying over the mud like a front-line of feathers, is a moment you will not repeat by waiting. On a Sunday afternoon in spring when the customers pile out into the street and board their shrimping boats to spend the next hour going round in circles on the tide, shouting and acting the goat, you will enjoy it more if you are as inspired as they are. Walking a fell with your lungs and legs firing off drink, your sweat reeking of it, is a bountiful feeling. As you come down from the alcohol and the air takes over and the eye clears, there is a loss. Pubs do not exist outside the need to celebrate each day. No one will deny the danger, but without unloosening, the mind gets into a worse fix. Alcohol is perhaps the most land-based, land-themed stimulant. With it inside you there is a stronger connexion with the scene. The grass smells sweeter and the river rushes more musically. A tree under your hand grows into it and the passing bird slows to show its beauty.

I fished in a blizzard two years ago, trying to spin for trout as the snow poured out of the north across the face of the water. I was wrapped up to the eyeballs and determined to catch something, having come a long way to do so. Standing up to my knees in the icy water I shot the spinner out into the snow in a regular rhythm, casting up-stream and bringing it back in a half-moon across the current. I made contact with a trout which danced over the running surface on the hook only to throw it when I was a yard away. Back into the air went the spinner and I took a pull at a half-jack of whisky to keep warm. An hour later the friend I was fishing with returned from down-stream with my son and found me deeper into the water, rod flailing in the snowflakes, with no fish but a song on my lips and an empty bottle in my pocket. The blizzard could not touch me and the haunting flow of white across the grey water, the arc of the silver spinner, the shapes of the two figures on the opposite bank holding up a big trout *they* had caught, is a scene I can conjure up now. It had been a perfect hour.

Travelling through different landscapes, different peoples and different times seems to be part of the atmosphere and use of this pub; usually someone is fresh back from Africa or South America or France. Behind the bar are postcards from far-off places, plus the battered straw sombrero worn by Les, the publican, on the trip to Menorca which he took with me and Ed, the bookseller. It was the first time he had ever been abroad, and he marked the first night by being so uplifted by the Mediterranean moonlight that he had to be brought home by the Guarda Civile in a jeep at half-past three in the morning. Maybe it is the moving river outside that conveys a sense of endless journeying, or the two centuries of talk about wars in every continent and the soldiering done by men from this town that creates this focus of motion.

David Pownall *Between Ribble and Lune*

The Pubs of Pepys

16 January, 1660. To the Greene Dragon on Lambeth Hill, both the Mr
Pinknys, Smith, Harrison, Morrice that sang the bass, Sheply and I, and
there we sang of all sorts of things and I ventured with good success upon
things at first sight and after that played on my flagelette; and stayed there till
9 a'clock, very merry and drawn on with one song after another till it came to
be so late. After that, Sheply, Harrison and myself, we went towards
Westminster on foot, and at the Golden Lion, near Charing Cross, we went in
and drank a pint of wine, and so parted; and thence home, where I found my
wife and maid a'washing. I sat up till the bell-man came by with his bell, just
under my window as I was writing of this very line, and cried, 'Past one of the
clock, and a cold, frosty, windy morning.' I then went to bed and left my wife
and the maid a'washing still.

22 March, 1660. I went forth about my own business to buy a pair of riding
gray serge stockings, a sword, and belt and shoes. And after that took Wotton
and Bridgen to the Popes Head tavern in Chancery Lane, where Gilb.
Holland and Shelston was; and we dined and drank a great deal of wine, and
they paid all. Strange how these people do now promise me anything; one a
rapier, the other a vessel of wine or a gown, and offered me his silver hatband
to [do] him a courtesy. I pray God keep me from being proud or too much
lifted up hereby.

30 December, 1661. I at the Miter, whither I had invited all my old
acquaintance of the Exchequer to a good chine of beefe – which, with three
barrels of oysters and three pullets and plenty of wine and mirth, was our
dinner. There was about twelve of us. And here I made them a foolish
promise to give them one this day twelvemonth, and so for ever while I live.
But I do not entend it.

2 February, 1664. Thence to the Change again, and thence off to the Sun
taverne with Sir W. Warren and with him discoursed long and had good
advice and hints from him; and among [other] things, he did give me a pair of
gloves for my wife, wrapped up in paper; which I would not open, feeling it
hard, but did tell him my wife should thank him, and so went on in discourse.
When I came home, Lord, in what pain I was to get my wife out of the room
without bidding her go, that I might see what these gloves were; and by and
by, she being gone, it proves a pair of white gloves for her and 40 pieces in
good gold: which did so cheer my heart that I could eat no victuals almost for
dinner for joy to think how God doth bless us every day more and more – and
more yet I hope he will upon the encrease of my duty and endeavours. I was
at great loss what to do, whether tell my wife of it or no; which I could hardly
forbear, but yet I did and will think of it first before I do, for fear of making
her think me to be in a better condition or in a better way of getting money
then yet I am.

5 March, 1668. To Westminster; where I found myself come time enough, and my brethren all ready. But I full of thoughts and trouble touching the issue of this day: and to comfort myself did go to the Dog and drink half-a-pint of mulled sack, and in the hall did drink a dram of brandy at Mrs Hewlett's; and with the warmth of this did find myself in better order as to courage, truly.

Early June, 1668. Come about ten at night to a little inn (George, Salisbury), where we were fain to go into a room where a pedlar was in bed, and made him rise, and there wife and I lay, and in a truckle-bed Betty Turner and Willett. Good beds, and the master of the house a sober, understanding man, and I had good discourse with him about this country's matters, as wool and corn and other things. And he also merry, and made us mighty merry at supper, about manning the new ship at Bristol with none but men whose wives do master them. Up, finding our beds good, but lousy, which made us merry. We set out, the reckoning and servants coming to 9s. 6d.

Samuel Pepys

The Sign above the Door

> O, Mortal man, that lives by bread,
> What is it makes thy nose so red?
> Thou silly fool, that looks so pale,
> 'Tis drinking Sally Birkett's ale,

Sign of The Mortal Man at Troutbeck

> Who does not know the famous *Swan,*
> Object uncouth, and yet our boast,
> For it was painted by the host.
> His own conceit the figure planned,
> 'Twas coloured all by his own hand.

Lines by William Wordsworth after the Landlord of the Swan at Grasmere
painted his own sign

In this tavern you may find
Everything to suit your mind –
Good wine, good fish, and flesh in courses;
Coaches, chaises, harness, horses.

Advertisement used during coaching days

In this hive we are all alive,
Good liquor makes us funny!
If you be dry, step in and try
The value of our honey.

Sign of the Beehive, Birmingham

Stop! Traveller, this wondrous sign explore,
And say when thou has viewed it o'er and o'er,
Grantham, now, two rarities are thine,
A lofty steeple, and a *living sign*,

Sign of the Beehive at Grantham (an actual hive)

Good malt makes good beer,
Walk in, and you'll find it here.

Malt Shovel Inn, Chatham

I HAM A CUNNING FOX
YOU SEE THER HIS
NO HARME ATCHED
TO ME, IT IS MY MRS. (Master's)
WISH TO PLACE ME
HERE TO LET YOU NO
HE SELLS GOOD BEERE.

Sign of the Fox Beerhouse, Folkesworth near Stilton

Ye gentlemen and yeomen good,
Come in and drink with Robin Hood.
If Robin Hood is not at home,
Then stop and drink with Little John.

Sign of the Robin Hood, Castleton near Whitby

Faith and Grace this house doth keep,
An Angel guards the door.
Faith is dead, the Angel fled,
And Grace is now no more.

Sign of the Angel Inn, Silkstone near Barnsley

The worthy boniface of a small inn in the neighbourhood of Liverpool, not less known by its sign of the "Gray Ass" than by the virtues of its home-brewed ale, having taken it into his head that his symbol was scarcely commensurate with the dignity and importance of his establishment, resolved to change it the first fitting opportunity. The result of the battle of Waterloo, so exhilarating to all loyal Englishmen, afforded him an excellent excuse for carrying his intentions into effect. He accordingly employed an itinerant artist to paint him a portrait of the Duke of Wellington, which he substituted for the effigy of poor Neddy. In the meantime, a shrewd rival, who knew the value of a name, took a house immediately opposite mine host of the 'Wellington,' and adopted his discarded sign. The country people, who knew more of the character of the 'Gray Ass' than of the qualifications of the great captain of the age, all flocked to the inn designated by their favourite appellative, until at length the elder publican had little or no custom left. Finding that his friends were ebbing from him like a spring tide with a breeze from the shore, he bethought him of an expedient to put a stop to the desertion. This *dernier ressort* was to attach to the portrait of his Grace of Wellington a supplemental panel, containing, in large and legible characters, the following pithy inscription: '*This is the Original Gray Ass!*' It is scarcely necessary to add that the intimation had the desired effect.

Anon

I'm amused at the signs
   As I pass through the town,
To see the odd mixture –
   A Magpie and Crown
The Whale and the Crow
   The Razor and Hen
The Leg and Seven Stars
   The Scissors and Pen
The Axe and the Bottle
   The Tun and the Lute
The Eagle and Child
   The Shovel and Boot.

From: *The British Apollo, 1707*

The Mail Coach Guard

At each inn on the road I a welcome could find:
At the Fleece I'd my skin full of ale;
The Two Jolly Brewers were just to my mind,
At the Dolphin I drank like a whale.
Tom Tun at the Hogshead sold pretty good stuff;
They'd capital flipp at the Boar;
And when at the Angel I'd tippled enough,
I went to the Devil for more.
Then I'd always a sweetheart so snug at the Car;
At the Rose I'd a lily so white;
Few planets could equal sweet Nan at the Star,
No eyes ever twinkled so bright.
I've had many a hug at the sign of the Bear,
In the Sun courted morning and noon;
And when night put an end to my happiness there,
I'd a sweet little girl in the Moon.
To sweethearts and ale I at length bid adieu,
Of wedlock to set up the sign,
Hand in Hand the Good Woman I look for in you,
And the Horns I hope ne'er will be mine.
Once guard to the mail, I'm now guard to the fair;
But though my commission's laid down,
Yet while the King's Arms I'm permitted to bear,
Like a Lion I'll fight for the Crown.

Anon

Inside the Inn

Tomorrow we give credit, but not today.

Call frequently
Drink moderately
Part friendly
Pay today – trust tomorrow

All you, who stand before this fire,
I pray sit down – it's my desire
That other folks, as well as you,
May see the fire and feel it too.

NB – My liquor's good
My measure's just
Excuse me, Sirs,
I cannot trust.

"If you ask me it's a con-
'spiracy."

They also serve

God I thank thee, that I am not as other men are, extortioners, unjust, adulterers, or even as this publican.

St Luke 18 v 11

'My wife keeps a public-house, and as my parish is so wide that some of my parishoners have to come from ten to fifteen miles to church, you will readily allow that some refreshment before they return must occasionally be necessary; and when can they have it more properly than when their journey is half performed?

'. . . to divert their attention from foibles over their cups, I take down my violin and play them a few tunes, which gives me an opportunity of seeing that they get no more liquor than is necessary for refreshment; and if the young people propose a dance I seldom answer in the negative. . . . Thus my parishoners enjoy a triple advantage of being instructed, fed, and amused at the same time.'

Letter from Reverend Jerimiah Carter, Curate of Lastingham in the North Riding of Yorkshire and husband of the licensee of the Blacksmith's Arms, to the Archdeacon of York after being reprimanded. He was acquitted of clerical impropriety.

A publican stood at the Golden Gate,
His head was bent and low,
He meekly asked the man of Fate,
Which way he had to go;
'What have you done?' St Peter said,
'To seek admission here':
'I kept a public house below,
For many and many a year.'
So Peter opened wide the gate
And gently pressed the bell;
'Come inside and choose your harp,
You've had your share of Hell.'

Anon

He must be genial, not easily discouraged, firm and sure of himself, watchful as a cat over himself, as well as over his staff and his customers. He must have a broad outlook, must be a ready speaker, and still readier listener. He must be house-proud, with an eye trained to notice small detail, and student of human nature. He must be active, methodical, and good-tempered under trying conditions; retentive of memory for a fact or a face, and his character, both in public and private, must be above reproach. He must try to emulate the example of a man of whom I have heard, who was a churchwarden for seventeen years, and still remained a Christian. His patience must be beyond that of the ass. He must be a handy man, and a sportsman in the widest sense of the words. He is expected to know a great deal of law; to be a good accountant, a born caterer, an expert chef, a good housekeeper, a good buyer and seller, and an encyclopaedia of general information. The man who combines all these qualities will, even then, fail to be successful if he does not care for the business – in other words, unless he really loves playing the part of host. I care not how primitive your accommodation is ... it is your welcome, and your air, that count most. Think of your guests by name and characteristics, not by numbers.

Alexander Port *The Art and Practice of Inn-Keeping*

To Peggy – a Barmaid

See her as she moves,
Scarce the ground she touches,
Airy as a fay,
Graceful as a duchess.
Bare her rounded arm is
Bare her little leg is.
Vestris never showed
Ankles like to Peggy's
Braided is her hair,
Soft her look and modest
Slim her little waist,
Comfortably bodiced.

William Makepeace Thackeray

The Landlady of the Swan at Thames Ditton

The Swan, snug inn, good fare affords,
    As table e'er was put on,
And worthier quite of loftier boards,
    Its poultry, fish, and mutton;
And while sound wine mine host supplies
    With beer of Meux or Tritton.
Mine hostess with her bright blue eyes,
    Invites to stay at Ditton.

Theodore Hook

Closing Time

Keats once bought a small pub in London and one day he was visited by Dr Watson, confrère of the famous Baker Street sleuth. Watson came late in the evening accompanied by a friend and the pair of them took to hard drinking in the back snug. When closing time came, Keats shouted out the usual slogans of urgent valediction such as 'Time now please!', 'Time gents!', 'The Licence gents!' 'Fresh air now gents!' and 'Come on now all together!' But Dr Watson and his friend took no notice. Eventually Keats put his head into the snug and roared 'Come on now gents, have yez no Holmes to go to!'

The two topers then left in that lofty vehicle, high dudgeon.

Flann O'Brien *Irish Times*

Cockney Arrest

A police-sergeant knows the history of hundreds of criminals in his district. He knows how much 'time' they have behind them, the houses they 'use,' and, as a rule, where to lay his hand upon them at any hour of the night and day.

When a young man was arrested on suspicion of being concerned with his brother in the murder of an old couple in High Street, Deptford, the police-officer just looked into a public-house and said, 'Alf, I want you.'

George Robert Sims

Epitaphs

IN MEMORY OF
SUSAN PEACOCK
WHO DIED 24 MAY 1937
LIVED HERE FROM 1902

Outside the Tan Hill Inn, North Yorkshire

Here lies the landlord of the Lion
His soul is on the way to Zion;
His widow carries on the business still
Resigned unto the Master's will.

Upton churchyard (there are at least 23 places of this name)

Hic jacet Walter Gunn
Sometime landlord of the 'Sun'.
He drank hard on Friday,
That being a high day.
Then took to his bed and died on Sunday
Sic transit gloria Mundi.

Northallerton churchyard.

Poor John Scott lies buried here
Though once he was both hale and stout,
Death laid him on his bitter bier.
In another world he hops about.

Oh! poor Joe Neale
Who loved good ale!
For lack of good ale
Here lies poor Joe Neale!

Here lies Johnnie Pigeon;
What was his religion,
    Wh'er desires to ken,
To some other warl
Maun follow the carl,
    For here Johnnie Pigeon had nane.

Strong ale was ablution,
Small beer persecution,
    A dram was *memento mori*;
But a full flowing bowl
Was the saving his soul,
    And port was celestial glory.

Line by Robert Burns on an Innkeeper friend

HERE LIES THE BODY
OF
JOHN WIGGLESWORTH

More than fifty years he was the perpetual innkeeper in this Town. Notwith-standing the temptations of that dangerous calling, he maintained good order in his House, kept the Sabbath Day Holy, frequented the Public Worship with his family, induced his guests to do the same, and regularly partook of the Holy Communion. He was also bountiful to the poor, in private, as well as in public, and by the blessings of Providence on a life so spent, died possessed of competent Wealth.

Whalley Churchyard

Here John Randal lies
Who counting of his Tale
Lived threescore years and Ten,
Such vertue was in ale.
    Ale was his meat,
    Ale was his drink.
    Ale did his heart revive,
    And if he could have drunk his ale
    He still had been alive.

SUSANNA WELLS
COOK OF THE *Three Swans*
IN MARKET HARBOROUGH
FOR 41 YEARS.

Market Harborough Churchyard

'One 'undred ... Kerrect.

(*Loud applause.*) One 'undred ... Kerrect. (*Loud applause.*) Twenty ...
Kerrect. ('*Quiet, please.*') Twenty-five ... Kerrect. ('*Keep a little order,
please.*') Kerrect ... sorry, mate ... Fifty ... Ker–' and pandemonium broke
loose.

The visitors from 'The Star of Asia' had lost, which meant that the
Chinese team throwing their darts in the bar of 'The Three Clippers,' had
won the championship of Limehouse.

The landlord was one of the players, the only Englishman in the Chinese
team, and the occasion did not permit that he should immediately retire
behind his bar to serve his customers. But his lady and the barman, and a
friend called in specially for the occasion, were soon hard at work drawing
pints of beer for all.

'Bumpy couldn't frow straight.'
'Yer can't touch these Chinese.'
'How you play in China?'
'We not play in China.'
'Why for you not let us win?'
'Can't help. We try let you win.'
'I don't fink! Not 'arf!'
'In China, little boy play dart.'

Such were some scraps of the conversation in the bar of 'The Three
Clippers.' The beer flowed freely and after a while the captain of the losing
team proposed a vote of thanks to the Chinese victors.

'A very good match it were. They beat us fair and they give us a good
match. Three cheers for the Chinese team – the only Chinese dart players in
Limehouse – or in London for that matter.'

They all cheered – all except Common* with the small hands, who
refused, as he put it, 'to be beat by a bloomin' Chink.'

''E beat yer fair enough,' said the captain, 'and their team beat our team –
the best we could get together, and a better lot than last year. Maybe if you
and old Stoney keeps off the beer till the match is over, we'll beat 'em next
time and have a medal to show.'

'Yer can't beat bloomin' Chinks,' replied the disgruntled one. 'Look 'ow
they frows their bloomin' darts – not like a Christian. Look at old Slinky, the
way he does it.'

Low Wai, he who was referred to as Slinky, rose from his seat.

'What you say about me?' he asked. 'I play you fair, don't I? Don't we all
play fair? You teach us how play. If we no play fair then you no play fair. We
play only what you show us. Dart game no Chinese game.'

'Yus, but we didn't show you how you should frow the bloomin' dart. We
didn't teach you to frow it backways and make it turn round. Why, that ain't
dart frowing; that's blooming conjurin'.'

'No, you not show like that, because you no can do, but we can do because
we more clever.'

'Clever, yer calls it. I calls it a bloomin' China trick.'

'No trick,' Low Wai quietly replied. 'Only more clever. I throw you how you like – for any number.'

'Fro at my little finger, then. Just you try and get my finger,' said Common as he spread a hand across the dart board. 'If yer hits my finger I pays yer five pound, and if yer hits anywhere else, you pays me five pound. Fair enough, ain't it?'

The crowd of stevedores and Chinese pressed round the challenger. The presence of the Chinese was felt rather than seen or heard. The turmoil was of Limehouse, with a feeling of some ghostly spirit hovering near: the sense of an age-old civilisation insulted and on trial.

As for Low Wai, he felt that he could not well avoid such a direct challenge, particularly as everyone present knew something of his prowess at throwing a dart. He looked at his friends, whose faces were as inscrutable as his own.

Meantime, Common, leaning against the end wall, kept his hand spread out across the board.

Low Wai glanced first at the figure of the stevedore and then at his outstretched hand. Slowly he picked up the chalk from the marking board and carefully outlined the hand upon the dart board.

'Put your hand in your pocket,' he said. 'I no want hurt you and I no want you hurt me.'

Common withdrew his hand, and Low Wai filled it in with chalk, just enough of the fourth finger to denote the nail.

'Keep back,' cried the stevedores. 'Keep back for Slinky, the sport.'

Low Wai held his dart by the point, looked with half-closed eyes at the chalked outline on the board and, with a movement quicker than anyone could remember having seen before, shot his dart into the centre of the white nail.

They forgot to cheer. It was as if uncertain lights trembled in the air while a memory of the legend of the ancient civilisation of the Middle Kingdom, with all its insufficiencies but with all its rich beauty, glided quietly out of the past.

* Stevedore's back-slang. Small hands = Common lands = Common.

PUBS, journal of the Pub Users' Protection Society, June 1946

In the 1930s there was a lot of hustling going on in the pit town of Ashington, deep in the mining heart of Geordieland. You name it, the lads gambled on it. Men running, dogs running, frogs jumping, billiards, snooker, cards . . . and darts. Ashington, the biggest pit town in the world, had 33 working men's clubs: rich pickings for a darts hustler if he played it right.

It was a crisp and stormy night as the stranger approached the West End, or High Market, district of Ashington. He entered the Top Club, and a beery throng gazed at this lean, white-mufflered man in an expensive blue serge suit but wearing no tie. He stood menacingly by the dartboard, chalked a game, then began to practise. He was good. Suddenly an old man gasped out:

'It's Neasham of Byker – the greatest darter in Geordieland. He's come to take your money.'

Up stepped the young bucks, darts at the ready. One asked: 'Are you really Lol Neasham?'

'Yes, son – and I'm playing for a pound a game.'

Neasham won a couple. Then he lost one – some said deliberately. The club filled up quickly; the word spread like wildfire:

'Neasham of Byker's playing all-comers at the Top Club!'

At the East End of Ashington a man the spitting image of 'Neasham' took to the oche at the Premier Club. He said his name was Joe Smith of Newcastle. He would play anyone at darts for five pounds and he would cover all side bets. The mugs obliged. Before closing time 'Joe Smith' took the best in the East End to the cleaners for over £100. Somebody did say: 'Hell, he doesn't half look like Neasham of Byker.' The reply came: 'No, Neasham's playing at the Top Club.'

Later that night 'Lol Neasham' and 'Joe Smith' met up in a car behind the greyhound stadium. 'Lol' said: 'How'd it go, Lol?' 'Joe' said: 'Skinned 'em.'

They then began planning their next Sting.

Sid Waddell *Bedside Darts*

The only reason I come here is to get away from all the violence on television...

Licensing (Abolition of State Management)

A
BILL

To remove the restriction on the sale and supply, otherwise than by the Secretary of State, of intoxicating liquor in the Carlisle district or of exciseable liquor in the State management districts in Scotland; to provide for the disposal of property held by the Secretary of State for the purposes of Part V of the Licensing Act 1964 or Part V of the Licensing (Scotland) Act 1959 and for the repeal of those provisions.

Presented by Mr. Secretary Maudling,
supported by
Mr. Secretary Campbell, Mr. Patrick Jenkin
and Mr. Mark Carlisle.

Ordered, by The House of Commons,
to be Printed, 2 *February* 1971

LONDON
Printed and Published by
Her Majesty's Stationery Office
Printed in England at St. Stephen's
Parliamentary Press
1s. 6d. [7½p] net

[Bill 100]   (379824)   45/1

CHAPTER 5
ALE, BEER AND BREWING

Beer at its best is a reflection of a golden field of barley, a reminder of the rich aroma of a hop garden. Scientists can argue endlessly about the merits of the man-made concoctions which go into much of today's beer but the proof of the pint is in the drinking ... the best of British beer is produced from the gifts that nature gave us and by methods which have been proudly handed down over the centuries. The story of beer is a story of nature and of craftsmanship; a story of farmers and brewers who join forces to create beer naturally.

Michael Hardman *Beer Naturally*

A fine beer may be judged with only one sip, but it is better to be thoroughly sure.

Czech proverb

He that buys land buys many stones;
He that buys flesh buys many bones;
He that buys eggs buys many shells;
He that buys good ale buys nothing else.

Anon

Good ale will make a cat speak.

Anon

Good ale is meat drink and cloth.

Anon

The Origin of Beer

The origin of beer is lost in what speculative writers conveniently call the mist of ages. At any rate, that wonderful people, the ancient Egyptians, from whom we seem to have inherited a very large proportion of our knowledge, are said to have been acquainted with it. Herodotus, the 'father of History,' whom at one time it was thought pertinent to dub the 'father of lies,' but whose character for veracity has of late years been pretty satisfactorily whitewashed, and who wrote about 450 B.C., distinctly states that they made wine out of barley; and even goes so far as to attribute its invention to Isis, and to fix the seat of its first manufacture at Pelusium, an island of the Nile. Without going so far as this, Sir G. Wilkinson has found some confirmatory evidence of their acquaintance with the art of brewing, amongst the paintings and sculpture of this enlightened nation; so that after all there is a possibility of Pharaoh's chief butler having been versed in the mysteries of the mash tun, and in Potiphar having been the possessor of a cellar of old October. The ancient Greeks, who borrowed or, it might just as well be written stole, the bulk of their knowledge from the Egyptians, were also acquainted with the merits of a barley wine, as is shown by passages of Eschylus and Sophocles; whilst Xenophon and Diodorus Siculus respectively describe the Armenians and Galatians as consuming a similar beverage. Tacitus, writing in the first century of our era, shows that the Germans of that day could make malt and brew beer; and Pliny makes out that the Gauls and Spaniards of his time were also consistent consumers of this noble liquor.

The art of malting and the use of beer seem actually to have been introduced into England by the Romans. The soldiers of Julius Caesar fought and marched on beer and vinegar, whilst prior to their arrival the only beverages of the Britons were water, milk, and mead. The new drink, at any rate, was speedily recognised as one above all others suited to our tastes and climate; and from that time forward 'John Barleycorn was Old England's King,' though Dioscorides, writing in the first century, mentions that beer was also made here from wheat. Isidorus and Orosius describe the making of ale in England during the Roman domination; and whether or not the Saxons, as is alleged, obtained their knowledge of its manufacture from the Britons they subdued, there can be no doubt of their appreciation of, and fondness for it. Amongst numerous other instances ale is mentioned in the laws of Ino, King of Wessex, and is described as figuring at the banquets of Edward the Confessor.

Ale continued to be the national beverage during the Middle Ages – the principal and most famous brewers being the monks. Already, in the twelfth century, according to William of Malmesbury, many monasteries were renowned for the strength and quality of their brew. To the monks, too, in the following century, is due the credit of having discovered the especial virtues of the waters of Burton-on-Trent. It must not, however, be supposed that the ale of this epoch was anything like the clear, sparkling fluid now known by that name. The 'mighty ale' celebrated by Chaucer appears to have been a dull, clammy liquid, brewed for immediate consumption, unhopped, and devoid of keeping properties. The distinction between ale and beer, as understood in the 15th century, is plainly pointed out in the 'Promptuarium Parvulum,' a manuscript of about the year 1440. The former is described as being drunk new as 'gyylde,' or gile, whilst the latter was brewed for keeping, and preserved by the addition of hops. This seems to be the first mention of hops being used for this purpose in England, though ale-hoof or ground ivy and kindred berries had been employed. Hops had, strange to say, to fight a severe battle for public favour. Fuller mentions a petition to Henry VI, in which they were denounced as a wicked weed. In 1528 a number of physicians protested against their importation from abroad, which had commenced four years previously, and had given rise to the oft quoted but generally misunderstood distich:

'Turkeys, hops, carp, piccarel and beer,
Came into England all in one year.'

The lines plainly refer to the first arrival in quantities from beyond the sea of articles of which several were already produced at home, since hops are also mentioned as being used for brewing in the Northumberland Household Book of 1512. Henry VIII shared the prejudice noted, for in 1530 he wrote to his brewer from Eltham, telling him not to put hops or brimstone in the ale intended for the royal consumption. Gradually, but steadily, however, the 'wicked weed' won its way, and by the commencement of the seventeenth century; as appears from the writings of Gervase Markham, hops were used in both ale and beer. From this time forward the history of brewing is little more than a chronicle of successive technical developments.

A few words as to the relative import of the terms 'ale' and 'beer.' Our word 'ale' is plainly derived from 'öl,' the liquor quaffed by the pailful, by the Norse worshippers of Thor and Odin, and originally brewed not from malt, but from a large red berry, growing wild in most parts of Scandinavia. As to 'beer,' the primary source of this word seems to be a very vexed question to philologists, who have consumed a great deal of ink and paper, and presumably of the beverage under notice, in their attempts to elucidate the matter. At any rate, it appears to have been immediately derived from the German 'bier,' for which at least half-a-dozen distinct roots have been found by different investigators, and to have been introduced into our vocabulary at a later date than 'ale.' Modern usage, however, has generally adopted it as the generic term for the fermented infusion of malt and hops in all its varieties of ale, stout, porter, etc., and as such it is employed in the title of this little pamphlet. As already pointed out, there was anciently a clear distinction between the unhopped ale and the hopped beer, the art of brewing the latter, like its title, being most probably derived from Germany or the Netherlands. Since the abolition of this marked difference by the general employment of hops, a certain amount of confusion has prevailed. The usual published definition is that ale contains less hops than beer. But whilst in some parts of England, including London, 'ale' is used to imply the stronger drink of the two, in others, on the contrary, 'beer' is the title given to denote pre-eminence both in potency and keeping powers.

How Beer is Made (Stansfield & Co., Swan Brewery, Fulham)

Brewing Beer

As to using barley in the making of beer, I have given it a full and fair trial twice over, and I would recommend it to neither rich nor poor. The barley produces strength, though nothing like the malt; but the beer is flat, even though you use half malt and half barley; and flat beer lies heavy on the stomach, and of course, besides the bad taste, is unwholesome. To pay 4s. 6d. tax upon every bushel of our own barley turned into malt, when the barley itself is not worth 3s. a bushel, is a horrid thing; but, as long as the owners of the land shall be so dastardly as to suffer themselves to be thus deprived of the use of their estates to favour the slave-drivers and plunderers of the East and West Indies, we must submit to the thing, incomprehensible to foreigners, and even to ourselves, as the submission may be.

With regard to hops, the quality is very various. At times when some sell for 5s. a pound, others sell for sixpence. Provided the purchaser understands the article, the quality is, of course, in proportion to the price. There are two things to be considered in hops; the power of preserving beer, and that of giving it a pleasant flavour. Hops may be strong, and yet not good. They should be bright, have no leaves or bits of branches amongst them. The hop is the husk, or seed-pod, of the hop-vine, as the cone is that of the fir-tree; and the seeds themselves are deposited, like those of the fir, round a little soft stalk, enveloped by the several folds of this pod or cone. If, in the gathering, leaves of the vine or bits of the branches are mixed with the hops, these not only help to make up the weight, but they give a bad taste to the beer; and, indeed, if they abound much, they spoil the beer. Great attention is therefore necessary in this respect. There are, too, numerous sorts of hops, varying in size, form, and quality, quite as much as apples. However, when they are in a

The hop-bine: quality is paramount

state to be used in brewing, the marks of goodness are, an absence of brown colour (for that indicates perished hops); a colour between green and yellow; a great quantity of the yellow farina; seeds not too large nor too hard; a clammy feel when rubbed between the fingers; and a lively, pleasant smell. As to the age of hops, they retain for twenty years, probably, their power of preserving beer; but not of giving it a pleasant flavour. I have used them at ten years old, and should have no fear of using them at twenty. They lose none of their bitterness; none of their power of preserving beer; but they lose the other quality; and therefore, in the making of fine ale, or beer, new hops are to be preferred. As to the quantity of hops, it is clear, from what has been said, that that must, in some degree, depend upon their quality; but, supposing them to be good in quality, a pound of hops to a bushel of malt is about the quantity. A good deal, however, depends upon the length of time that the beer is intended to be kept, and upon the season of the year in which it is brewed. Beer intended to be kept a long while should have the full pound, also beer brewed in warmer weather, though for present use: half the quantity may do under an opposite state of circumstances.

The water should be soft by all means. That of brooks, or rivers, is best. That of a pond, fed by a rivulet, or spring, will do very well. Rainwater, if just fallen, may do; but stale rain-water, or stagnant pond-water, makes the beer flat and difficult to keep; and hard water, from wells, is very bad: it does not get the sweetness out of the malt, nor the bitterness out of the hops like soft water; and the wort of it does not ferment well, which is a certain proof of its unfitness for the purpose.

William Cobbett *Cottage Economy*

The Meaux Porter Vat

To the Meaux family goes the dubious honour of having built the largest porter vat of the eighteenth century. The Times of the 7th of April, 1785, reported the construction: 'There is a cask now building at Messrs Meaux and Co's brewery in Lickapond Street, Grays Inn Lane, the size of which exceeds all credibility, being designed to hold 20,000 barrels of porter. The whole expense attending the same will be upwards of £10,000.'

In October, 1814, owing to the defective state of its hoops, it burst and the results were most disastrous. The brewery in Tottenham Court Road was at that time hemmed in by miserable tenements which were crowded by people of the poorer classes. Some of these houses were simply flooded with porter; two or three collapsed and no less than eight persons met their death either in the ruins, or from drowning, the fumes of the porter or by drunkenness. At the inquest the jury returned the verdict; death by casualty.

John Bickerdyke *The Curiosities of Ale and Beer*

Chiswell Street, 1802

Mr Whitbread's brewery in Chiswell Street, near Moorfields, is the greatest in London. The commodity produced in it is also esteemed to be of the best quality of any brewed in the metropolis. The quantity of porter brewed in the year in this house is generally about 200,000 barrels.

There is one stone cistern that contains 3,600 barrels, and there are 49 large oak vats, some of which contain 3,500 barrels ... There are three boilers, each of which holds about 500 barrels ... In the upper part of the building are cooling cisterns, that would cover about five acres of land, only six inches deep, but made quite tight, and kept very clean ...

Great improvements are daily making, and particularly in the boilers, two of which are covered so as to collect the steam, and use it instead of cold water, which saves a great deal of fuel.

The barrels or casks, of ordinary dimensions, are in number about 20,000; 200 workmen are employed, and 80 horses of a very large size. One was lately killed, being diseased, whose four shoes weighed 24 lb ...

In the course of the operations, the beer is forced by a pump, in pipes under the street, to a large building on the other side, to be put in casks.

In the mash-tubs which are about 20 ft. deep, there is a machine to stir up the malt, that constantly turns round, and is very ingeniously managed so by means of a screw, as to rise and fall alternately, so as to move alternately at the top, the middle and the bottom.

Whether the great size, or ingenuity of contrivance is considered, this brewery is one of the greatest curiosities that is to be seen anywhere, and certainly little less than half a million sterling is employed in machinery, buildings and materials.

We must not omit here to mention, in contradiction to a long but ill-founded belief, that Thames water alone would make good porter, that in this large brewery the water used *is not from the Thames*, but from the New River.

The Union Magazine and Imperial Register

A Visit to Burton

One no sooner enters the town of Burton than he begins to be oppressed by a sense of brewery on the brain. There is no escape from the brewery incubus. There are breweries to right, to left, in front, and in rear. Huge piles of casks, arranged as we see shot and shell in an arsenal, rise high above the walls flanking the streets. You meet a locomotive coming serenely down the street drawing a long tail of trucks loaded with barrels full of beer, or with grains on their way to the dairies. A scent of brewing ever floats upon the air. Through the open-work iron-gates burly men are seen crossing the yards, carrying cans and pails of foaming beer from the 'allowance store,' and you envy their lot in being favoured to draw thus at the very fountain head. Walk whither you will, the breweries are interminable. Bass, left behind half a mile on the left, springs into sudden being again on the right front; and when you are looking from the Town-hall you find a few more acres of Bass right in the centre of the town.

It is impossible to realize that Burton is a town with breweries in it; the inevitable impression is that Burton consists of a congeries of breweries, in the interstices between which and around their edges a town has diffidently grown up, and exists on sufferance, while the ground on which it stands is not required for brewery purposes.

There grows up within me, as I wander through the maze of breweries of which Burton is composed, a keen desire to visit the interior of one of the great beer-producing establishments. To the lover of beer – and who need blush to own a love for beer? – it is natural that pleasant associations should weave themselves around the place of its nativity. The utilitarian may be content with results; so long as the glass for which he calls and pays is of fine flavour and in good condition, he may accept the existing, and care not a jot for sentiment. Such a man would not go a yard out of his way to gaze on the birthplace of a hero, and would think his time wasted on a visit to the nursery in which his bosom friend had spent his childhood's happy hours. I don't profess to be a utilitarian, and for me the process of beer-making has a real tenderness of interest. Look at the crystal water in the great well, waiting till the time comes for it to form an alliance with the malt, and to spend a couple of days with the hops and the yeast, and ultimately to become beer. Tell me, cynic, is that water, with its proud future, to be looked upon without interest – I had almost said without emotion? Can it be to the least imaginative as the ignoble futureless water in which we wash our hands, and which thenceforth sinks into the miserable abyss of 'slops?'

As I approached the portals of Bass, I did not exactly pause owing to my tread being on an Empire's dust, but I moved with reverential interest, by reason that I was within the confines of the birthplace of a world's beer. Before reaching the office it became apparent to me that 'Bass' is not Bass alone, but is 'Bass, Ratcliff, & Gretton.' I pictured to myself Ratcliff & Gretton as soured misanthropists – passing gloomily through this vale of sorrows in the bitter realization of being unknown to fame, although partners in the firm producing the fluid with which the world identifies solely the name of Bass. But this was only a momentary fancy; although there is much truth in the poet's statement that 'fame to generous minds is dear,' dearer still to most people are satisfactory partnership profits; and I unhesitatingly express my readiness to become a partner in the firm of Bass, even although my name should not so much as appear above the door of a malthouse or on the plate of a waggon.

Saturday is washing-day at Bass's, and on learning this, knowing to the full the dread significance of 'washing-day' when it occurs in the domestic circle, my first impulse was to withdraw and present myself at a more convenient season. But Bass is superior to the trial of temper and general 'aggravations' which washing-day entails on the domestic matron. I was bidden welcome by a gentleman with an unclouded brow, and handed over to a guide who possessed a thorough knowledge of his profession as a practical and scientific brewer, along with a considerate courtesy, for which my warmest acknowledgments are due, and are hereby tendered.

Time did not permit of an exploration of Bass in all his multifarious ramifications. Of the three great breweries of the concern in Burton – the Old Brewery, the Middle Brewery, and the New Brewery (otherwise called the Red, White, or Blue Breweries) – the last was the one selected for inspection, and on the way thither my companion gave me some details, the statistics of which may interest the reader. So far as Burton is concerned, Bass stands upon a little over 140 acres of ground. Bass used last year 267,000 quarters of malt for brewing purposes; if it be reckoned that an acre grows four quarters of barley, 66,750 acres were occupied in growing the malt which Bass used. Of hops his consumption was 36,000 cwt, which engrossed about 5,000 acres of hop-growing country. In malt-tax and licence-duty Bass paid last year £300,000. The total brew of Bass during the past year amounted to 837,000 barrels – each barrel containing 36 gallons; so that Bass could have served more than half the estimated number of the human race with a glass of beer per head from his brewing of one year. Throughout his Burton premises Bass owns over twelve miles of private railway, runs nine private locomotives, and uses 32 steam-engines, with a collective horse-power of 610. Bass employs in Burton over 2,000 persons, and pays more than £2,500 in weekly wages. Bass used last year 40,000 tons of coal. Bass has in use 47,000 butts, 160,000 hogsheads, 140,000 barrels, and 200,000 kilderkins; a stock of casks in all, in store and scattered over the country, exceeding half a million.

Our arrival at the New Brewery opportunely occurs to avert from me the abject imbecility which an attempt to realize figures so stupendous is calculated to produce. We begin methodically by visiting the great well from which is drawn the water that makes the beer. Most people are aware that it is to the quality of its water that Burton-on-Trent owes its eligibility as a beer-making centre. It stands in a basin surrounded by hills which largely contain marl and gypsum. The water impregnated with these substances percolates into the basin, there to pick up an infusion of sulphate of lime, which is of so great importance in brightening beers and saving the use of finings. In the early days of Burton-beer brewing it was only necessary to sink a shaft-well some 30 feet deep, but there is now so large a consumption of water that it is necessary to bore for it to a depth of from 100 to 200 feet. One shudders at a possibility that some day the water may be wholly exhausted. The possibility of the exhaustion of our coal measures is to be contemplated with equanimity in comparison with such a misfortune as this. Meanwhile the well is full, and the great pumps are at work elevating the water to the large service reservoir on the top of the brewery. The malting is done outside the brewery, and the sacks of malt are brought thither in railway trucks.

We ascend to a floor on which, in long perspective, the sacks stand ready for their contents to be used. A certain given number are being emptied into a large hopper fitted with a wire netting to prevent the intrusion of any extraneous substances which may have become mixed with the malt. This is next acted upon by a screen for the removal of particles of dust, and then it passes between two iron rollers, revolving at the rate of 160 revolutions per minute. This is the malt-mill, where the malt is crushed, but not ground. When so crushed it is picked up by a 'Jacob's ladder,' fitted with a series of small pockets or receptacles. The action of this 'Jacob's ladder' is exactly like that of the endless belt fitted with buckets, which may be seen at work any day on a dredging-machine in the Thames. Its shell is of iron, to resist explosions. Occasionally, notwithstanding every precaution, a particle of grit gets up, and a spark struck from it may suddenly ignite the highly-desiccated malt dust gathered about the interstices of the ladder and its sheath. With the latter of strong iron, no lateral explosion results: there is a bang, and then a momentary tongue of flame shoots harmlessly into the air. From the 'Jacob's ladder' the malt is taken in hand by an Archimedean screw working in a trough, and is so propelled into the respective hoppers, which are receptacles placed over the mash-tubs. Upwards of 5,000 bushels per day may be so forwarded, small as is the quantity elevated in each pocket of the 'Jacob's ladder.'

While as yet it is in the hopper the malt is dry, and unsuggestive of beer to the most fertile imagination; but the auspicious moment approaches for the celebration of the nuptials between it and the water, the arena of the ceremony being the mash-tub, and the officiating high priest being a ferocious instrument known as the 'Porcupine.' We are on a floor in which there are 9 mash-tubs all of a row, each one capable of mashing 60 quarters of malt. The mash-tub is a great oaken vat with a false bottom, perforated by a number of small holes. The 'Porcupine,' in its interior, is a particularly lively instrument. It revolves at once round the mash-tub from a pivot in the centre, and has a rotatory motion around its own axis; it is armed with long wooden teeth, which have a peculiarly searching manner of their own, the contemplation of which is most eligible at a little distance.

The first process in a mash is to admit into the mash-tub, until it is about half full, water heated to the proper temperature. By the turn of a lever the malt comes streaming down out of the hopper above through six separate orifices, and simultaneously the 'Porcupine' is set in motion. It rotates around the mash-tub, blending the water and the malt, until finally the twain are mixed into a smooth pasty mass. The amalgam is then allowed to stand for a few hours, to admit of the necessary chemical assimilations and changes; and these effected, the solution of malt, which by this time is of a beautiful transparent amber colour, is undermost, the emasculated malt floating on the top.

This solution, now called 'wort,' is run off through the false bottom, and the malt left is 'sparged' by a shower-bath of hot water to extract from it the last remains of saccharine matter, before it finally lapses into the ignoble condition of 'grains,' and is shovelled out into trucks for cattle-feeding. The earth is strewn with the bones of those who have fallen that others might rise. We turn from the spent grains – thrown away like a squeezed orange – to follow the onward course of the wort, which has flowed downwards into the 'underback.' Hence it is pumped up into a great tank on the upper floor of the brewery. All round this floor are set large coppers, each capable of containing a hundred barrels. Spotlessly brilliant is the metal of these coppers, scrubbed and polished as they are weekly by gangs of men who work with nothing on them but a pair of canvas trousers. Into them the wort passes through copper pipes, and now comes the blending of the wort with the hops. The latter, in bags, line the edge of the coppers. The bags are upended, and the hops fall down into the wort. Below each copper is a big furnace. In it a roaring fire is made, and soon the contents of the copper are boiling furiously. The hops on the surface swell and upheave themselves high above the margin of the copper, so that constant care is needed to flatten them down, and to prevent boiling over. When the copper has boiled long enough for the wort to have extracted most of their essence out of the hops, the hops and wort together – now called 'boiled wort,' and of a curious sweetish-bitter taste – pass from the copper through large taps into a receptacle called the 'hop back,' whence the fluid is strained off through a false bottom, leaving the hops behind, to be sent down below for a final squeeze in the hydraulic presses, and afterwards to be sold for manure or as cattle bedding. Paper has been made of spent hops, but they are not generally used for this purpose.

The 'hop back' is in the corner of a large open floor, the area of which consists almost wholly of great shallow trays. These are the 'coolers.' On to them flows from the 'hop back' the boiled wort, but it remains there only a short time. The natural cooling is a slow and uncertain process, dependent in its conditions on the temperature of the air, which for a great part of the year is too high to produce the desired effect. While 'coolers' only were used brewing was possible only in the cold season; now, with the use of 'refrigerators,' beer may be made the summer through. The 'coolers' are now merely a convenient ante-chamber to the 'refrigerators,' which are on the floor below. It is difficult to make these out to be anything else than huge flat boxes; but by climbing up and peeping over the edge, we see a shallow lake, laced by successive long straight coils of copper piping. In each refrigerator there is of this piping about 3,000 yards. The boiled wort is flowing slowly from the coolers through this mighty submerged snake, while the cold water that covers it has given to it a slow steady motion at right angles to the flow of the wort, so as to intensify the refrigerating power.

Thus cooled, the wort quits the refrigerators and passes into the 'squares,' to undergo the process of fermentation. One gets some faint conception of the brewing power of the place, when it is told that on this one floor there are 160 of these 'squares,' each one holding fifty barrels. Hitherto the wort has been a dull phlegmatic fluid, seemingly incapable of being stirred into animation. But the yeast (which is added to it in the 'squares') soon alters its temperament. We see the process of active fermentation in a variety of different stages. In one square the wort is sulking – the yeast has not yet stimulated it into briskness, and has only evolved on the surface a whity-brownish froth. The contents of another square have thrown up a 'head' that resembles a dingy iceberg; the surface of another is like snow that has lain a couple of days in a city churchyard. There is a pungent sweetish smell, not unpleasant as we have it here with plenty of ventilation, but not a happy thing to encounter in the bottom of a well or in the far interior of a coal mine. It is the carbonic acid gas we smell, evolved in the destruction of the sugar and the formation of the alcohol. A lighted candle held close to the surface of the fermentation burns blue for a second, and then goes out. I hold my face where the candle had been, and am right fain to withdraw it while as yet consciousness remains. In the 'squares' for the first time we recognise beer. It would be possible for a man to get drunk upon this mawkish loaded fluid, if he could bring himself to undergo the preliminary ordeal of swallowing what tastes so remarkably nasty. But let the fermentation be finished, and the cleansing be accomplished, and nastiness will no longer be the characteristic of the fluid. There is nothing very complicated in the process. From taps in the squares, the beer runs away by a trough into the 'Union-room' – so called because the rows of barrels which are marshalled on its floor are all linked together, or 'united,' by one pipe.

What a ball-room would this Union-room make if its floor were clear, for it is 125 yards long by as many wide. But instead of dancers it holds 2,500 casks, each one containing 160 gallons. These are ranged in double rows, and above each row is a long shallow trough, called the 'barm trough.' Into it flows the beer, and from it, by the removal of plugs, into the casks. It is in these casks, which are fixtures, that the process of fermentation is completed. From each rises an inverted syphon, whose orifice overhangs the 'barm trough.' Drip, drip, drip, the yeast – the product of fermentation – comes in frothy clots and glutinous gouts out from the orifice into the barm trough, while the loss is compensated in the cask by letting in beer from the 'union pipe,' whence the room takes its name. The desiderated coolness is main-

The Burton Union system of fermentation

tained while the fermentation is working itself out by cold water contained in a tube which passes through each cask. When all fermentation has ceased – generally the beer is in the 'union casks' from two to three days – it is run off into the racking-room below, where the service or 'trade' casks are at once filled.

The racking-room is a busy scene, for men cannot well stand idle in a place where 2,000 barrels of beer are filled as a day's work. As each empty cask comes in, a man, whose duty it is to do nothing but exercise his sense of smell, takes a long exhaustive sniff at its bunghole, to be certain that its interior is thoroughly sweet. Two have done this before him, but he makes security trebly sure. As soon as filled each cask has placed in its bunghole a handful of the very finest hops, a practice which is found to add to the tone and flavour. Care being taken that the cask is as full as it can hold, it is finally bunged down, and in an hour's time it is on a railway truck on its way to an agency.

Of each brew a simple cask is retained as a standard for reference, and the sample-store is a bower of bliss to the beer-lover. Life is too short, and no head is sufficiently strong, for the most conscientiously-inclined visitor to taste right through the samples, from the thin sparkling T beer sold in the neighbourhood at 4d. a gallon, to the potent old nectar laid down when an heir was born to Bass. Over against the sample-cellar is the great store, which, large as it is, can contain little more than a month's brew. There are three floors, the two upper supported on iron pillars, of which there are long bewildering vistas. Each floor has an area of two acres, and the six acres of stowage room can contain in all about 60,000 barrels, and 20,000 pockets of hops. At St Pancras, Bass has a store of equal dimensions. From the ale-store we then look in upon the "lowance store,' where are served with their day's drink the employés of Bass. Not a man on the premises but has his stated allowance of beer – some a quart of ale; others a quart of ale and three pints of light beer, according to the nature of their work. Beer is a thing by itself. It has been asserted on reputable authority that a dog may be choked with pudding, and it is certain that raisins, treacle, and figs very soon cloy on the grocer's apprentice, no matter how keen his original appetite for those extremely sticky dainties. But beer cloyeth not, and as men who work among beer would help themselves, spite of every precaution, if they were debarred from beer, it is judged wiser to allowance them on a moderate sufficiency. There is more beer in this "lowance store' than in the cellar of a big public-house. It flows from a barrel into a great tub, over which presides a burly man armed with a quart measure on a long handle. By his side is a receptacle for the tokens upon the authorization of which he serves. A man walks in, wheeling before him a metal tank. He presents a token on which are the words, 'Stable Department, 20 quarts.' With the nimbleness of legerdemain 20 quarts are measured out into his tank, which he rolls away for the refreshment of the 'Stable Department' in an outlying portion of the brewery.

Daily News, 22nd October, 1872

Davy Jones Brewery

A recent enquiry to the Society about a Davy Jones Brewery has brought to light a fascinating story. At first it seemed like a joke, it certainly does not appear in any available directories but the brewery did exist, albeit briefly, and although British built to produce draught Mild it was never actually in this country as such!

The story starts in 1944 when two 'kits' of brewing plant were ordered from Messrs George Adlam Ltd, of Bristol, for export to Vancouver, Canada. The reason for this unusual export in times of war was that the Board of Admiralty had decided that, in order to ensure adequate supplies of beer for the troops engaged in the Pacific theatre of war, they would install floating breweries in their two proposed 'amenity ships.' The vessels concerned were two ex-Blue Funnel cargo liners which had been engaged in mine-laying duties. They were sent to Vancouver for refitting with such varied facilities as theatres, cinemas, dance halls, barber and tailors shops, bars and their own breweries! Only one vessel however was completed and brewed at sea – T.S.M.V. Menestheus.

The Director of Victualling of the Admiralty, after consulting many eminent brewers, decided to adopt Clarke's pressure fermentation system. The system had been perfected at Cooper's brewery in Southampton after the destruction of their fermenting room by enemy action in 1943. By Clarke's method brewing was enabled to continue by using enclosed conditioning tanks as fermenters – a sort of halfway house between the 'Burton Union'-type plant and the modern continuous fermentation systems much used today. Mashing would be done in the UK, malt extract in 70lb tins and hop concentrate would be shipped out to the bases from which the floating breweries would operate.

Lt Cmdr George Brown A.R.I.C., R.N.V.R. was appointed Head Brewer and travelled to Canada in September 1945 to supervise the fitting up of the plant in the cramped forward hold of each ship. He found upon arrival however that many of the small components shipped from Adlams had gone astray and it was only possible to get one set of plant functional by cannibalising the other plant from T.S.M.V. Agememnon. The first trial brew was carried out on 31st December 1945 with some of the plant still 'jury-rigged' and, following some rectification work, another brew was put through on 8th January 1946. The yeast had been prepared from a streak culture at the University of British Columbia Faculty of Agriculture – it had originally been supplied from Guinness's Park Royal Brewery. The beer produced in these trial brews was an English-style Mild Ale of 1037° original gravity and it proved immediately popular when served at the ship's commissioning party. It was still on stillage when the Menestheus reached Tokyo Bay on her maiden voyage – this cruise, her last as well as first, took her to Yokohama, Kure, Shanghai and Hong Kong.

The first three ports of call proved disappointing in terms of over-the-side sales but Hong Kong was to prove a great success. This was due largely to the fact that the ship was berthed at a convenient wharf, where the crews from other ships would set up their own temporary canteens at their own berth, and to the fact that there were a great many Royal Marines barracked in the Dockyard. The China Fleet Club also displayed great enterprise in being up the gangplank almost before it touched the quay and carrying off an average of 400 gallons daily! However, with the war now at an end the ship was really surplus to requirements and she sailed for the UK calling at Saletar, Trincomalee, Aden, Malta, Gibraltar and Portsmouth before finally being de-commissioned at Hebburn-on-Tyne in September 1946.

Distilled water was used for brewing, being heated by steam from the ship's boilers. One ton of malt extract was dissolved in a purpose-designed vessel with a live steam outlet before transfer to a 55 barrel capacity pressure wort copper where it was made up to 50 barrels with hot liquor. During the boil the wort was passed continuously through a cylinder containing seven pounds of hop concentrate. The hopped wort then passed through a standard A.P.V. Paraflow against sea water until passing (at 62°f) into one of six glass-lined fermenting tanks where it was pitched with 30lbs of top yeast. Surplus yeast was forced by CO_2 pressure up a swan neck into a sealed yeast back where careful control of relative pressures allowed the barm ale to run back. Pressure in the fermenter was held at 7psi and surplus CO_2 was collected, scrubbed and stored for re-use. This collection system was efficient enough to make the plant independent of outside supplies being used for carbonation and beer-raising from the bright beer tanks in the cold room up to two 50 gallon measured tanks in each bar, each of which served ten counter taps. Fermentation took six days when isinglass finings, made on board, was added. After two days settling the beer was chilled to 32°f and carbonated before passing to the bright beer tanks. As well as being sent to the ship's bars by counter pressure the beer was also racked into five gallon stainless steel casks (1,200 were carried) fitted with Barnes Patent valves. Normal practice was to brew five days a week giving a capacity of 250 barrels per week.

From the brewer's report to the Board of Admiralty it is clear that, despite minor teething problems, the plant worked admirably, producing a popular product with a long stability period. Had the plan been conceived earlier or, heaven forbid, the war lasted longer then no doubt Davy Jones' Brewery would have done great service slaking the thirsts of British and Allied troops overseas and bringing them, to quote a contemporary handbill, – 'Something from the OLD COUNTRY . . . a breath from BRITAIN!'.

Peter Moynihan *The Brewery History Society Journal*

Advertisement for the short-lived 'floating brewery'

THE ROYAL NAVY AMENITY SHIP

"MENESTHEUS"

· · ·   # BEER   · · ·

ENGLISH MILD ALE

brewed in

DAVY JONES BREWERY

"THE WORLD'S ONLY
FLOATING BREWERY"

On Sale at all BARS of the AMENITY SHIP

9d. per pint   Supplies Unlimited

Operated by

NAVY, ARMY & AIR FORCE INSTITUTES

Sponsored by Board of Admiralty

Supplies of " DAVY JONES " ALE are available in Bulk to R.N. Wardrooms and Shore Establishments.

Terms—30s. (Sterling) per 5-gallon container. Deposit on container, which must be returned within four days—£6 Sterling.

Enquiries to " NAAFI " Officer—M.V. MENESTHEUS.

Use of " DAVY JONES " containers :

Set up the container as an upright cylinder (NOT on side as with a usual cask).

With tool provided, remove tinfoil seal from both outlets.

Insert tap with tail into lower outlet, pressing in, then give a quarter turn to the left (*i.e.*, counter-clockwise) to lock. Keep tap turned off during this operation.

Likewise, insert tap without tail in top outlet.

Draw beer from the lower tap, and open top tap as vent when the first couple of pints have been drawn.

When not serving keep top tap closed.

Withdraw taps when container is empty by rotating clockwise a quarter turn.

Please rinse taps before returning.

The beer is despatched at about 40 F. and is best served at about 52° F.

IMPORTANT :

Prompt return of empty containers to " DAVY JONES " Brewery will ensure continued supply.

Brewing in Bohemia

Yes, dear friends, an effervescent and foaming glass of beer is the result of the patient endeavours and experience of innumerable generations of many nations who since ancient times have improved and developed beer production up to the standard in which we know beer today. Bohemia has had the honour of contributing in a significant way to the development of beer production and particularly of good beer. In the remote past beer was often the object of the interest of even the highest offices in Bohemia – even of the kings themselves – which granted towns the privilege of brewing beer and issued regulations governing its production and sale. The advantageous position of the Czech Lands in the centre of Europe affords very favourable natural conditions for growing high-quality raw materials – spring malt barley and hops. Diligent journeymen and brewers spread the renown of Bohemian beer even in distant foreign countries. In Bohemia itself, especially in certain towns, beer-brewing has in the past few decades reached a very high standard on the basis of this country's long standing tradition. One of these towns is České Budějovice.

In 1265 the Czech king, Přemysl Otakar II, founded the royal town of České Budějovice in the forested countryside of South Bohemia, interwoven with a dense network of rivers, choosing for its site the confluence of the Rivers Vltava and Malše. Thanks to the privileges which it was granted, the town soon overcame its difficult beginnings and became a busy crossroad of trade routes running to neighbouring Bavaria and other South European countries. As early as at the turn of the 13th and 14th centuries the municipal archives contained the names of Budějovice brewers and thus it can be said in all truth that beer has been brewed for at least seven centuries at České Budějovice. Right from the very beginning this long path of Budějovice beer-brewing has been accompanied by great endeavour and care and 'Budějovice' beer soon found its way beyond the boundaries of the town and won renown and recognition. As early as in 1531 Budějovice beer won favour with King Ferdinand and beer began to be supplied to the royal court. Since then it has been called the 'Beer of Kings' by some people.

On the basis of the beer-brewing right, beer was brewed in individual beer-brewing citizens' houses of which there were, for example, fifty-two in České Budějovice in the mid-16th century. Later beer-brewing in the town was concentrated in the so-called Small and Big Breweries. Although these breweries disappeared in the course of time in the growing residential part of the town, the production of the two modern breweries – the Budweiser Budvar and Samson Breweries – is based on their tradition.

Budweiser Budvar

Beer has been brewed at Plzeň ever since the town was founded in 1295. The founder of Plzeň, the Czech King Václav II, endowed his new royal town with numerous privileges which included the exclusive right to brew and sell beer – the so-called brewing right – on the periphery of the town fortifications. In the course of development, the originally personal right of burghers was changed into a real right connected with the burghers' houses inside the fortification walls. For over five hundred years, the citizens of Plzeň exploited their profitable right, i.e., they brewed beer which fermented in the cellars of their houses until their turn came to tap beer in their home. The quality of the brewed beer was the concern of inspectors appointed by the Town Council. These inspectors decided whether the brew in question was wholly of the prescribed quality and could, therefore, be normally tapped and sold. Beer of low quality could be sold at a lower price only to the poor of the town, while completely unsuccessful brews, if they occurred at all, were publicly poured away in front of the Town Hall, this being the greatest disgrace which a burgher-brewer could suffer.

Handed down by word of mouth throughout the centuries has also been a description of how the quality of beer is tested. It is alleged that the beer to be tested was poured on to an oak bench and the inspectors then sat on it in their leather trousers. After a while they rose from the bench and if the latter stuck to their leather trousers as they did so, the beer was of the required density and, put simply, honestly brewed. If this did not prove to be the case, the brewer could be punished on the same bench for his lack of proficiency or dishonesty. However, it seems that such tests rank in the sphere of historical anecdotes rather than in the field of reality.

Thus the people of Plzeň brewed and drunk their beer throughout long centuries until one day, the cleverest of them began to realize that time was advancing and that new production methods giving better results had been discovered. And so in 1842, on the initiative of these burghers, a new, common brewery of citizens holding the beer-brewing right was founded. As time passed, the individual brewers ceased to brew beer separately and all beer-brewing activity in Plzeň was concentrated exclusively in the new brewery. And this also brought to an end the long period of scattered medieval manual production and the opening of the period of industrial enterprise with beer-brewing concentrated in one place. The historical houses with the beer-brewing right in the old part of the town continued, however, to be the bearers of the beer-brewing tradition of Plzeň. All that happened was that the ancient institution acquired new contents. The 'beer-brewing burghers' became a closed economic and legal corporation with a permanent number of 250 shares, since after 1842 the number of beer-brewing houses had become stabilized at that number. However, these 250 houses continued to own the medieval monopoly right to brew beer in the town (new rights did not originate after an end had been put to individual brewing activity) and represented 250 property shares and 250 votes when decisions had to be taken regarding the management of the brewery of the new organization.

And an interesting curiosity came about. Certain houses beyond the boundaries of the medieval streets lost their original economic and dwelling functions, their owners preferring to live in newer districts and letting their old houses fall into ruin. However, since the beer-brewing right was still of great value and would have died out together with the disappearance of a house which owned it, the house-owner left the old Gothic entrance with a piece of wall, which continued to be inscribed in the register of beer-brewing rights, and kept in a good state of repair. Thus instead of the former house its 'brewing-right-bearing gate' bore a share in the property and management of the brewery.

Introduced at the new brewery was also the modern production technology based on the so-called 'bottom fermentation' method which, combined with the local natural conditions and the old production tradition at Plzeň, brought a surprising result. The new kind of beer was lighter and had a greater sparkle. It had a rich, dense foam and a specific flavour, a strange, inimitable bitter, vigorous flavour which, after some beer had been drunk, turned sweet and incited the drinker to take another draught. Moreover, the new beer was more digestible and even fostered the digestive process. In brief, the new beer possessed right from the moment of its first appearance on the market all the qualities and success which accompanied it on its later journey to the world.

Pilsner Urquell

Manx Purity

No brewer shall use in the brewing, making, mixing with, recovering or colouring, any beer or any liquid made to resemble beer, or have in his possession any copperas, coculus Indicus, nux vomica, grains of paradise, Guinea pepper, or opium, or any article, ingredient or preparation whatever, for, or as a substitute for, malt or sugar or hops. For any offence against this section, the person offending shall incur a penalty of three hundred pounds. And all such beer, or other liquid brewed, made, or mixed as aforesaid, and also all the beer grounds and stale beer brewed, made or mixed as aforesaid and all copperas, coculus Indicus, nux vomica, grains of paradise, Guinea pepper, opium, and every other article, ingredient, or preparation as aforesaid (other than malt and sugar) in the custody or possession of such brewer, together with every copper, cooler, tun, vat or other vessel or utensil whatsoever, in which any such beer, liquid, material, article, ingredient, or preparation shall be contained, or which shall have been made use of or employed for or in the brewing, making, mixing with, recovering, or colouring such beer or liquid, shall be forfeited to Her Majesty, her heirs and successors.

Paragraph 18 of The Brewers' Act, 1874, promulgated 'At a Tynwald Court holden at Saint John's Chapel, the 11th day of September, 1874.'

Andrew Boord on Ale and Beer

Ale is made of malt and water and they which do put any other thing to ale than is rehearsed except yeast, barm or godisgood, doth sophistical their ale. Ale for an Englishman is a natural drink. Ale must have these properties: it must be fresh and clear; it must not be ropey or smokey nor it must have no weft nor tail. Ale should not be drunk under five days old; new ale is unwholesome for all men and sour ale and dead ale that which doth stand the tilt is good for no man. Barley malt maketh better ale than oaten malt or any other corn duff. It doth engender gross humours but yet it maketh a man strong.

Beer is made of malt, of hops and water. It is the natural drink for a Dutchman. And now of late days it is much used in England to the detriment of many English people. Specially it killeth them which be troubled with colic and a stone and a strangulion for the drink is a cold drink yet it doth make a man fat and doth inflate the belly as it doth appear by the Dutchman's faces and bellies. If the beer be well served and be fined, and not new it doth qualify heat of the liver.

Dyetary of Health

The Ale-Wife

Her ale, if new, looks like a misty morning, all thick; well if her ale be strong, her reckoning right, her house clean, her fire good, her face fair, and the town great or rich, she shall seldom or never sit without chirping birds to bear her company.

Donald Lupton 1632

Ale, Glorious Ale

Then to the spicy nut-brown ale.

John Milton

And malt does more than Milton can
To justify God's ways to man.
Ale, man, ale's the stuff to drink
For fellows whom it hurts to think.

A E Housman *A Shropshire Lad*

Beneath our feet the roads wind by,
The pleasant fields unfold;
The larks are singing in the sky
Of cloudless blue and gold,
And though our thirst's incredible,
An inn will soon appear,
Then won't our cup indeed be full –
And full of what? Of beer!

1930s advertisement aimed at hikers

Down the Ancestral Throat

'*Hek*,' said the Ancient Egyptian petulantly.

Immediately his retainer brought him a beaker of beer.

This drink would not have tasted like any kind of modern beer, for there were no hops in Egypt to give the fermented barley the distinctive bitter taste of beer. It would have been more like sweet ale, also made from barley but without the addition of hops. But the method used five thousand years ago, of moulding barley into a kind of malt and then fermenting it, has not basically changed since. The means of brewing, not brewing itself, has become more sophisticated.

Hek, even then, was a very popular drink. *Hek* shops were to be found everywhere in Egypt. They became so numerous, indeed, that about four thousand years ago the authorities came to the conclusion that there were too many of them and tried to close them down, making the drinking of *hek* illegal.

This is the first recorded example of prohibition.

Hek was also used as a medicine, a tonic for those whose strength needed building up, or so a medical manual of the time would indicate. It is mentioned in the *Book of the Dead*, and there was even a god, Osiris, allocated to the drink, according to Herodotus, that not very reliable historian. He added that Osiris taught the Egyptians how to brew *hek* because they had no vineyards, and thus could not make wine.

But the Ancient Egyptians knew how to make wine long before Herodotus wrote his controversial history. Both *hek* and wine were probably made simultaneously. According to Aeschylus, it was not considered a very good drink. The Pharaohs would drink wine, their subjects *hek*.

Hek continued to be drunk in Egypt for centuries, and existed until comparatively modern times, under the slightly altered name of *hemki*. Even at the end of the last century, a traveller on the Nile recorded that he saw the crew of a ship make an intoxicating liquor from barley bread and water. The name of this concoction was, the traveller declared, *boozer*.

The Jews of the Old Testament also knew how to make a drink from barley. They probably brought the recipe out of Egypt with them at the time of the Exodus. Some historians believe that the Hebrew word *sicera* covers the brewing of all non-grape alcohol whether from corn, barley or honey, although in Tyndale's Bible the word is translated as 'sydyr' or cider. *Sicera* was also supposed to protect its drinkers from leprosy. The Jews remained free from the disease during their captivity in Babylon because, it is said, they drank *sicera*.

The Ancient Greeks, who made the first and best of wines, did not think much of the various brews made from barley. Only the Thracians to the north seem to have preferred their home-brewed drinks to wine. Xenophon mentions a malt drink brewed by villagers in Armenia in 401 B.C. Despite the responsibility of leading his ten thousand Greeks through hostile territory from Mesopotamia to the Black Sea where safety lay with the Greek ships, he had time to observe the customs of many of the places he traversed during the extraordinary march that followed Cyrus's disastrous defeat.

This particular village was situated deep in snow-covered mountains. All the dwellings were underground, their entrances being holes in the ground that resembled wells. Ladders led down to the living quarters. In every home there was always a large bowl of brewed malt, filled to the brim. Hollow reeds of various lengths lay beside the bowl, and when anyone wanted a drink they picked up a reed, dipped it into the bowl and sucked vigorously. The liquor, Xenophon records, was very strong but not unpleasant, once one got used to it. People in the Khanns district of Armenia still live in the same kind of underground houses today, but the art of brewing seems to have been lost.

It was not however until barley found its way to northern Europe, probably by way of the inquisitive trading Phoenicians, the first to send their ships out of the Mediterranean, that the drink began to be brewed in greater quantities. It has always been more popular in northern than in southern countries.

It was the Danes who first called the drink they brewed from barley, ale, or *öl*, meaning oil. The name slowly took over from all the various local names along the north German coast and in Britain.

The Ancient Britons drank *metheglin* and cider. *Metheglin* was not, as its name seems to indicate, a kind of tranquilliser, but mead. It was made from wild honey found in hollow trees and was drunk by the more primitive nomadic tribesmen. The honey could be scooped up during hunting trips and brewed immediately around the camp fire. It was essentially an 'instant' drink, needing no special preparation or preservation.

Cider was also a drink that suited the needs of wandering tribes. The small hard apples grew abundantly on the stunted crab-apple trees. Again, it was just a question, when the men were out hunting, of picking the quantities they needed.

Ale had been introduced into the British Isles just before the Roman Conquest. But even so, it was restricted to the more advanced tribes of the South-East. They had ceased to be nomadic and had settled down on the land as cultivators, thus being able to sow the barley that was needed for making the new, fashionable drink from northern Europe. The Romans did not think much of ale, and even less of the *metheglin* they found as they pushed northwards. They considered that all British home-grown brews were undrinkable. It seems that only the local oysters received Roman approval; empty British oyster shells from sumptuous Roman feasts can still be found wherever Romans lived.

Ale seems to have reached Ireland about the same time as St Patrick for 'suppers with ale' are mentioned in the *Senchus Mor*, the ancient law book of Ireland composed about AD 430. An Irish chief was expected to have in his house three sacks and two casks. The sacks contained malt, salt and charcoal; the casks, milk and ale. It is not revealed who was to drink the milk and who the ale, but it is not too difficult to guess.

In Wales, ale was a luxury. Mead was the common drink for centuries both before and after the Roman Conquest. The ale was kept in casks that, according to an old ruling, must be 'so capacious as to serve the King and one of his counsellors for a bathing tub.' There were two kinds of ale in Wales. One was common ale, the other spiced. Spiced ale was twice as expensive as common ale and four times as expensive as mead. Wine was completely unknown to the Welsh, although there is mention of a vineyard at Maenarper, near Pembroke in South Wales, about a century after the Roman Conquest, but this was probably planted by an exiled Roman, homesick for his native land.

There is no record of ale having reached Scotland at the time of the Roman Conquest, or in the subsequent years of Roman occupation. But then neither did the Romans. They were content to build Hadrian's Wall and let the Picts and Scots sit on the other side, drinking their own peculiar mixtures.

By the time the Roman Empire ended, and the legions were recalled to the defence of Rome itself, ale was a fairly well-established drink, particularly along the northern coastline of Europe and the wilder islands out to sea. There are occasional mentions of it being drunk even as far south as Spain, but on the whole wherever the grape could grow it ousted barley as the basis of a country's ordinary drink.

The grape frontier runs along the River Loire in France, then to the north of the Champagne country, over the Vosges and thus into Germany. This 'line' divided the wine drinkers from the ale drinkers even at the time of the Roman Empire. There were incursions on both sides. The Romans marched north with their casks of wine, merchants headed south with samples of barbaric ales; but, at least as far as drink was concerned, the grape line divided Europe more effectively than any geographical frontiers.

John Watney *Beer is Best*

Who comes here?
   A Grenadier.
What does he want?
   A pot of beer.

Charles Dickens *Our Mutual Friend*

They who drink beer will think beer.

Washington Irving *Sketch-book*

Champagne certainly gives one werry gentlemenly ideas, but for a continuance, I don't know but I should prefer mild hale.

R S Surtees *Jorrock's Jaunts and Jollities No 9*

What two ideas are more inseparable than Beer and Britannia?

Reverend Sydney Smith

Hermit hoar, in solemn cell,
Wearing out life's evening gray;
Strike thy bosom, sage! and tell
What is bliss and which the way?
Thus I spoke, and speaking sighed
Scarce repressed the starting tear,
When the hoary sage replied
'Come, my lad and drink some beer.'

Dr Samuel Johnson

I will make it a felony to drink small beer.

William Shakespeare *Henry VI part 2*

St George he was for England,
And before he killed the dragon
He drank a pint of English ale
Out of an English flagon.

G K Chesterton *The Englishman*

For he by geometric scale
Could take the size of pots of ale.

Samuel Butler *Hudibras*

Beer drinking don't do half the harm of lovemaking.

Eden Philpotts *The Farmer's Wife*

Upon my faith beer is a heavenly gift.

Karel Sabiňa *The Bartered Bride*

Wine: I, generous Wine am for the Court.
Beer: The Citie call for Beere.
Ale: But Ale, bonnie Ale, like a lord of the soile,
       In the country shall domineere.

Anon

The Best Ale – Warrington

I've ben crammed with good things like a wallet,
    And I've guzzled more drink than a whale;
But the very best stuff to my palate
    Was a glass of your Warrington ale.

– Derby

Cobblers and tinkers
Are your true ale drinkers.

– Nottingham

I grant that fair Nottingham once bore the bell
For our grandsires that tasted the sweets of good ale –

– Birmingham

Ye mortals who never in all your wild trips
With good humming liquor saluted your lips
Give ear to my story, ye strangers to cheer,
The pleasure I sing of is Birmingham beer;
'Tis here the salutis of Life's to be found;
For merchants who circuit the kingdom around
Declare, on their travels from Thames to the Tweed,
That Birmingham stingo all others exceed.

– Burton upon Trent

The Abbot of Burton brewed good ale,
On Fridays when they fasted.
But the Abbot of Burton never tasted his own
As long as his neighbour's lasted.

– Yorkshire

O Yorkshire Yorkshire: Thy Ale is so strong,
That it will kill us all if we stay long:
So they agreed a journey far to make
Into the South, some Respit for to take.

Yorkshire Squares

Yorkshire beer has long held a fine reputation for its quality, well beyond the boundaries of the country. Historically, this may in no small part be due to the almost unique use by the county's brewers, of the Yorkshire Stone Square method of fermentation; a system which only spread to a very limited extent to the counties of Lancashire and Nottinghamshire, but not, seemingly, elsewhere. The method adopted almost universally throughout the rest of the country, is known as the skimming system. In this system, the head of yeast formed during the beers' fermentation is skimmed off its surface into outlets at the side of the fermentation vessels. The only other truly regional fermentation system, is the Burton Union System, in which the fermentation takes place in long rows of interconnected casks known as Unions. The particular suitability of the Union System to the production of pale and strong ales, led to its almost complete adoption by the brewers of Burton on Trent, though brewers from other areas may have shared in contributing to its ultimate high level of development.

The invention of the 'stone square' system of brewing is attributed to Timothy Bentley of the Lockwood Brewery near Huddersfield, in a brief history of Bentley & Shaw Ltd., the company founded by Timothy Bentley, and in a history of Bentley's Yorkshire Breweries Ltd., founded by one of his sons, Henry Bentley. The Lockwood Brewery history also suggests that Timothy Bentley was acquainted with Doctor Joseph Priestley, or had at least made full use of the scientist's work relating to the brewing industry. Sigsworth, in considering the possibility of a collaboration between the two men concerning the development of the stone square system, states that there is a close resemblance between the experiments conducted by Priestley and the principles upon which the stone square system works, in particular the impregnation of the beer with carbon dioxide. He concludes that the work conducted by Priestley whilst living close to the Meadow Lane Brewery of Jacques and Co., Leeds, is adequately substantiated, but that the Bentley's connection with the scientist is attested only by the reference in the two advertising brochures, published at least a century later.

The yeast used in the Yorkshire system is unusual in that it acts particularly slowly and requires frequent rousing and aerating if it is to work properly. This action is due in part to the yeast's strongly top fermenting qualities, which cause it to rise rapidly to the surface of the fermenting wort and thereby reduce its ability to perform its task of converting sugar into alcohol and carbon dioxide. The beers produced by the system, however, 'drink very full for their gravities, and which, since they retain large quantities of carbon dioxide, are full of life.' The effervescent nature of the beers brewed by the stone square system help to protect them from airborne infection during fermentation; it may also offer an explanation for another, peculiarly Yorkshire tradition, that of dispensing beer by means of hand-pumps fitted with autovac equipment, utilising a very tight sparkler. The agitating action of the handpump displaces much of the dissolved carbon dioxide gas and at the same time introduces air into the beer. It is the air which produces the smooth texture to the beer and supports the long lasting, creamy head, so beloved of all serious beer drinkers in the Yorkshire area.

The stone square is so called because the fermentation vessels themselves, were once constructed from large slabs of hard local stone, such as were the products of the quarries of the Elland flagstones. This type of stone is, even today, much prized as a paving material for the streets of London. The square consists of four large slabs of stone for the sides and a fifth for the base, all being fastened together by means of recesses cut into the stone and secured laterally by iron bolts. A second square, about three or four inches less in height, is constructed so as to surround the first, leaving a narrow gap of about two inches all round the external surface of the first square. Into this space either warm or cold water can be introduced thereby acting as an attemperator; surplus water simply flowing away over the top.

Above the inner square is placed another horizontal slab surmounted by a second chamber; of the same area as the outer square beneath, about thirty inches deep and constructed in a similar manner. In the centre of the base of the upper chamber (which acts as a yeast trough) there is a man hole of eighteen inches diameter, surrounded by a stone collar of about six inches in height, into which fits a stone lid with a handle. Close to one of the corners of the covering slab are located two valves of about three inches diameter to which chains are attached. A long pipe extends beneath one of the valves to within a few inches of the bottom of the lower chamber; it is known as the 'organ-pipe.' The whole massive weight of the structure is carried on large stone pillars, and the chambers themselves rendered watertight by the application of water resistant cement to all the joints. An additional item required for the use of stone squares, is a simple pump of three inches diameter and six inch stroke, which is used to pump wort from the lower to the upper chamber.

W J Sykes, in his book the *Principles and Practice of Brewing*, gives the following description of the operation of the Yorkshire stone square:-

'The wort is pitched with 1 to $1\frac{1}{2}$ lb of yeast per barrel at a temperature of 58 to 59 degrees Fahrenheit. The valve at the upper end of the organ-pipe is closed and a portion of the wort run into the upper chamber; the yeast is then thoroughly roused (vigorously mixed) in with this, the valve opened, and the mixed yeast and wort allowed to flow into the lower chamber. When the whole of the wort has been collected and pitched, it is left undisturbed for 36 hours, at the end of which it should have risen to about 62 degrees Fahrenheit. It is now roused for the first time, the rousing being repeated every two hours during the next twelve hours, at the expiration of which (48 hours after pitching) pumping commences. Before starting the pump the valve of the organ-pipe is shut, and as much wort pumped into the upper chamber as is delivered by fifteen strokes of the pump; it is then well *roused, so as to mix in the yeast which has risen through the man hole, after which the valve is opened and the wort allowed to flow back into the lower chamber. Pumping and rousing are repeated every two hours, the number of strokes of the pump being increased at each repetition of the operations, beginning with fifteen strokes for the first pumping, and increasing by ten at each pumping. This is continued until the wort has reached a gravity of some 1 to 1½ degrees higher than that required to finish. During the whole period of fermentation the temperature of the wort is kept within the necessary limits by means of the attemperating jacket. When the pumping and rousing stage is passed the organ-pipe valve is closed and the yeast which rises through the man hole removed every four hours. After each removal the valve is opened for a short time to allow the beer which has drained from the yeast to run down into the lower compartment. When, by observing the surface of the beer, the yeast appears fully removed, the temperature of the beer is gradually brought down by attemperating to 60 degrees Fahrenheit, or a little lower. The manhole is then covered with the cap, and the contents of the square allowed to remain undisturbed for two days, by which time the beer is ready for racking into trade casks.'*

Stone squares of the type described above, were probably in use from the latter years of the 18th Century and were well established by the 1830's. A lease taken out by Samuel Webster in May 1838 describes the working room of the Fountain Head Brewery as containing – three double cisterns, with a cistern on top of each to hold yeast, three large cocks and pipes for water. By the beginning of the present century, slate began to replace stone as the material for construction of squares, an internal attemperator being used instead of a surrounding water jacket. By the 1920's, although very expensive, aluminium began to be introduced for the construction of fermenting vessels. The new material was much easier to keep clean and maintain than either stone or slate, and it did not suffer from the same restrictions in dimensions. With the new material came changes in the design of the squares, the upper yeast chamber disappearing on the grounds of cost and easier cleaning. Many breweries, however, continued to rouse and aerate their beers as had been done with the stone square system, but the yeast trough was replaced by the more commonplace skimming system. Probably the last remaining user of the Yorkshire squares, though of slate construction, are Samuel Smith of Tadcaster who pride themselves on the traditional nature of their brewing techniques. Near neighbours, John Smith, have retained a single stone square, along with its ancillary equipment, which is on display in a museum type gallery in their new brewhouse, formerly the square room. One or two sets of stone squares have survived on the sites of former breweries in a derelict state, no doubt owing to the expense and difficulty of removing them, and await the attentions of brewery and industrial historians.

Peter Robinson *Brewery History Society Journal*

Keats and Chapman

Keats and Chapman were conversing one day on the street, and what they were conversing about I could not tell you. But anyway there passed a certain character who was renowned far and wide for his piety, and who was reputed to have already made his own coffin, erected it on trestles, and slept in it every night.

'Did you see our friend?' Keats said.

'Yes,' said Chapman, wondering what was coming.

'A terrible man for his bier,' the poet said.

Flann O'Brien *Irish Times*

The Bar of the Hotel Belman, Mazatlan, Mexico

I wandered entirely unprepared into what seemed a vision of the past – a high, cool, scrupulous bar, presided over by angels in white, *real* bartenders with linen coats, affable exterior, everything. Two excellent English cock-fighting prints on the wall and the inevitable stoutish nude lady stepping over a brook, whose name used to be legion in the good old days.

I stood hat in hand in the sanctified twilight of that spacious and cleanly haven, like a good Catholic would in a cathedral after his return from arid and heathen ports; and, after the proper genuflexion, ordered a glass of beer. It was hotter than blazes outside, real tropical, depleting heat. Here, within that exquisitely appointed grot, all was peace and zephyrous coolness. The beer arrived – *draft* beer – in a tall, thin, clean crystal of Grecian proportions, with a creamy head on it.

I tasted it, dear reader, black or white. It was heaven. It was liquid manna. It had the frou-frou of ambrosia, the tender unctuousness of a melted pearl. The planets seemed to pause a moment in their circling to breathe a benediction on that Mexican's brewer's head. One felt some great rubato, sweet yet vibrant, in the celestial orchestra of the revolving spheres. It was like a slight ecstatic sigh from the left lung of the Cosmos. Then the universe went on its wonted way again. Hot Dog! But that *was* a glass of beer!

John Barrymore *Yachting log*

The Beer List

'No wine,' said Acton. 'But I'd like to have a look at the beer-list, please.'

'I beg your pardon, Sir?'

'Surely the biggest hotel in the biggest beer-drinking city in the world has a beer list?'

'I'm afraid not, Sir!'

'Incredible.' Acton shook his head sadly. 'Well, please ask the cellar-master if he has a bottle of '61 Foster's. It was a memorable year for Victorian beer, with that delicate flavour of bushfires in the hops. The '61 Foster's is a really superb lager, brut, mon, charnu, petillante, fino, pizzicato, and faintly amertume. It has that nobly fading straw-like pallor which is less a colour than a vestment, *la robe*: and an aroma that is distinctly Bouverie Street. The bouquet is a discreet cuir russe, or Old Harness. It is urbane but quietly persuasive, and with a notable wet finish, soft on the taste-buds, and on the pocket, too.'

The '61 Foster's was exhausted, but Acton found a tolerable '62 Melbourne Bitter to go with the coffee. He assured the wine-waiter that, though it lacked chiaroscuro and clangtint, it had a compensatory verve, good-humoured spritzig, and almost the panache of a pre-war Export Bass.

Cyril Pearl *Pantaloons and Antics*

Ale for Cricketers

The ale, too – not the modern horror that drives so many men melancholy mad, not the beastliness of these days that makes a fellow's inside like a quaking bog – and as unsteady! Ale that would put the soul of three butchers into one weaver! Ale that would flare like turpentine – genuine boniface. This immortal viand was vended at two-pence a pint!

John Nyren, Landlord of The Bat and Ball, Hambledon, in *The Young Cricketers Tutor 1833*

The Price of Ale

I confess I lost my temper yesterday at Rotterdam, where I had to pay a florin for a bottle of ale (the water not being drinkable, and country or Bavarian beer not being genteel enough for the hotel); I confess, I say, that my fine temper was ruffled, when the bottle of pale ale turned out to be a pint bottle; and I meekly told the waiter that I had bought beer at Jerusalem at a less price. But then Rotterdam is eighteen hours from London, and the steamer with the passengers and beer comes up to the hotel windows; whilst to Jerusalem they have to carry the ale on camels' backs from Beyrout or Jaffa, and through hordes of marauding Arabs, who evidently don't care for pale ale, though I am told it is not forbidden in the Koran. Mine would have been very good, but I choked with rage whilst drinking it. A florin for a bottle, and that bottle having the words 'imperial pint,' in bold relief, on the surface! It

SEIT 1040

BAYERISCHE STAATSBRAUEREI

Weihenstephan

ALTESTE BRAUEREI DER WELT

Bierkarte

**Bierkenner aus aller Welt schätzen Weihenstephaner Bier als
traditionsreiche Bierspezialität.**

	Inhalt l	Preis DM
Weihenstephan Edel-Pils Sorgfältig ausgewählte Rohstoffe und eine jahrhundertlange Brauerfahrung geben dem Weihenstephan Edel-Pils den besonderen feinherben Geschmack. Seine Hopfenblume ist berühmt. Weihenstephan Edel-Pils ist ein großes bayerisches Premium-Bier, das mehrfach die Goldmedaille der DLG verliehen bekam. Fragen Sie bitte, ob Ihr Wirt dieses Bier vom Faß führt!	0,5	2,60
Weihenstephan Export hell Aus erlesenen Rohstoffen ist „Weihenstephan Export hell" zu einem Spitzenbier bayerischer Braukunst ausgereift. Der edelbittere Geschmack hat „Weihenstephan Export" zu einer Bierspezialität für anspruchsvolle Bierkenner werden lassen.	0,5	2,40
Weihenstephan Hell Ein leichtes bayerisches Lagerbier, das aus besten Rohstoffen von erfahrenen Braumeistern gebraut wird. Gut gehopft bleibt es ausgewogen im Geschmack.	0,5	2,20
Stephansquell Für Bierkenner ist dieser helle Doppelbock ein ganz besonderer Genuß. Beste Rohstoffe garantieren ein sorgfältig abgestimmtes Hopfenaroma.	0,5	2,80
Korbinian Der Doppelbock „Korbinian" ist ein dunkles Starkbier von ganz erlesener Güte. Eine Bierspezialität, malzaromatisch und süffig zugleich. Ein besonderer Hochgenuß für Starkbierliebhaber.	0,5	2,80
Alt-Weihenstephan Export dunkel Nach alter überlieferter Tradition gebraut. „Alt-Weihenstephan Export dunkel" hat ein aromareiches, abgerundetes Bouquet. Eine echte Freude für den Liebhaber dunkler Biere.	0,5	2,40
Weihenstephaner Kristall Weizenbier Durch ein selbstentwickeltes geheimes Gärverfahren bleibt dieses edle Bier hefefrei und kristallklar. Es erhält dadurch seinen unverwechselbaren Charakter und seinen perlenden, prickelnden Geschmack. Das erste seiner Art.	0,5	2,40
Weihenstephan altbayerisches Weißbier Für alle Genießer und Freunde altbayerischer Lebensart wird dieses erfrischende und zugleich belebende Weißbier gebraut. Der feine hefeblumige Geschmack erfreut jeden verwöhnten Gaumen.	0,5	2,40
Weihenstephaner Kristall Weizenbock Diese obergärig gebraute Bierspezialität verbindet die prickelnde Bekömmlichkeit des Kristall-Weizenbieres mit der Süffigkeit eines Starkbieres. Weihenstephaner Kristall-Weizenbock ist für den echten Bierkenner eine Gaumenfreude von ganz erlesener Art.	0,5	2,80

Mit Weihenstephan fängt Bier an.

The Beer List: the Bavarians do it right

150

was too much. I intended not to say anything about it; but I *must* speak. A florin a bottle, and that bottle a pint! Oh, for shame! for shame! I can't cork down my indignation; I froth up with fury; I am pale with wrath, and bitter with scorn.

William Makepeace Thackeray Notes of a Week's Holiday

Life isn't all beer and skittles; but beer and skittles, or something better of the same sort, must form a good part of every Englishman's education.

Thomas Hughes Tom Brown's Schooldays

The Arrival of Hops, the Birth of Beer, 1524

Turkey, carps, hops, pickerel, and beer
Came into England all in one year.

Hops, Reformation, Bays and Beer,
Came to England all in one year.

Hops and turkeys, carp and beer
Came into England all in one year.

Hops, Reformation, Bays and Beer
Came to England in one bad year.

Hop-growing in the sixteenth century

The Hop Plant

Hop is the name given to a number of species of plant belonging to the genus *Humulus*. They are twining, perennial plants in the same family as the stinging nettle (family Urticaceae, 'if it stings you, it 'urts you!' – not that hops do sting). The hops used in beer are the mature cones (or flowers) of the common hop, *Humulus lupulus*, and its many varieties. It has been used almost exclusively for brewing for 1,200 years or more, and there is evidence that it has been used in Eastern Europe as a yeast preservative in baking and in brewing for 2,000 years or more. Hopped beer first reached England from the Low Countries in the early part of the fifteenth century, and boiling hops with the wort had become the general practice by the sixteenth century. The value of the hop cones in brewing stems from the essential resins, oils and tannins present in the glands called *lupulin* at the base of the bracts of the cone. The resins are responsible for the bitterness and preservative qualities; the hop oils confer a delicate flavour and aroma; and the tannins assist in the precipitation of protein which could otherwise cause a slight haze in the beer. In fact the chemistry of the flavour and preservative value of the hops is extremely complicated and there is still much scope for further investigation. As has been mentioned before, hop extracts are commonly used nowadays. They are convenient and economical, but are by no means a proper substitute for the natural hop. Present-day extracts may confer a bittering flavour, but they do not give the full aroma and flavour of the natural hop.

The common hop is a climbing perennial plant which may produce for as long as 10–20 years. It has a large rootstock, and this 'hill' or 'stock' has many vegetative buds which give rise to shoots (often called bines). New bines are produced each season, and die after maturity. New hop fields (called hop gardens in south-east England and hop yards in the West Midlands) are created from root cuttings or sections of underground stems, and the young vines or bines are trained to climb strings which are renewed annually and are supported by a permanent framework of wooden poles and wires. They have a phenomenal speed of growth and under favourable conditions can grow six inches or more in twenty-four hours, but the growth-rate is very much dependent on the weather.

The hop is called dioecious, which means that the male and female flowers are on separate plants. The male flower is very small and burr-like and appears in July, and the cone is the fruit which develops on the female plant after flowering. It is 2–4 inches long with overlapping yellowish-green bracts or scales. Cones may be produced without seeds by the exclusion of male plants from the hop gardens, or with seeds by planting male plants at a rate of one to 100 or 200 female plants. Seeded hops are grown in England and seedless hops on the Continent. An advantage of seedless hops is that the brewer does not have to pay for the weight of the seeds, which may be as high as 15 per cent. By tradition they have always been used for the brewing of lager, so most countries prefer them to seeded hops. However, they are not essential for lager-brewing, and although most hops for lager are imported, English brewers do also use seeded hops for some of their lager. It has been claimed that seedless hops give a finer flavour, but no direct comparison has been made and the claim is unsubstantiated. Seeded hops could be a nuisance in continental brewing techniques, but there would seem to be no advantage in changing to seedless hops in Britain as there is already a tremendous difference in flavour between varieties. Actually it would be virtually impossible, because as anyone who has examined a Kentish hedgerow would realise, wild male hops are growing all over the hop-growing countryside.

The hop cones ripen during August and September and nearly all the picking is now done by machines. At this time they contain 65–80 per cent of moisture and they have to be dried down to a moisture content of 10 per cent. If they were not dried they would be certain to heat up, discolour and go off. In England the hops are dried in brick buildings with a tapering roof surmounted by a pivoted wooden cowl which helps to prevent a back draught in windy weather. These buildings are called oast-houses. After drying, the hops are stored for several days for curing, when the moisture content is equalised throughout the cone, which becomes tougher and more pliable for baling or bagging.

Brewers who do not own hop gardens have to buy their annual requirement from a hop merchant who may have a large number of small packets from each farm, and the selection of the exact quality depends upon the skill of the brewer. On the Continent the merchant buys up the entire crop of a larger number of growers who partially dry their harvest, and then the merchant finishes off the drying and packs them himself. In this way the Continental merchant has large quantities of the same quality.

Hops like rich, alluvial and well-drained soils and are grown commercially in Australia, Belgium, Czechoslovakia, England, France, Japan, New Zealand, South Africa, South America, Spain, Poland, the USA, the USSR and Yugoslavia. The USA is the biggest producer and this country together with Germany and England account for about three-quarters of the world total, which is in the region of 150,000 acres. In England about 20,000 acres are grown, most of which are in Kent, then the West Midlands (Herefordshire and Worcestershire), then North Hampshire. Hops are not grown north of the Midlands because they like a warmish climate; neither do they grow in the tropics.

The hop cone has a delightful fresh smell which is very familiar to residents of brewing towns. Not everyone may find it agreeable but it would be hard to dispute that a hop garden in summer with its attendant oast-houses is a part of the rural scene that adds piquancy to the hop-growing countryside.

Frank Baillie *The Beer Drinker's Companion*

Malt in the Brewer's Art

Malt is the basic ingredient for the manufacture of beer, and for hundreds of years the maltster has made the best malt from the best barley. There are several reasons why barley is the most suitable cereal. Firstly it has always been considered that malted barley produces the most desirable flavours. Barley has a husk which maize and wheat do not have, and this husk forms a filter bed when the malt is mashed in the brewery, which is an essential part of the brewing process. Also barley is the most readily available cereal in the UK. With wheat malt the germ breaks easily, allowing undesirable moulds to flourish. But for one reason or another cereals other than barley are in use and certainly have some influence – not always bad – on the palate of the beer. Some wheat beers in Germany are labelled as such and have quite a different palate from barley beers. There may be a case for the declaration of ingredients by brewers.

The malting process itself is a very skilful operation and consists of a controlled germination of the barley which is finally stopped by heat. The hard barley is transformed into tender malt with a pleasant biscuity flavour, but the malted grain has the same outward appearance as the original barley. The insoluble starch in the barley corn is converted during germination into soluble starch which the brewer can easily convert into a fermentable sugar solution. Finally the malt is 'screened' to remove the rootlets which form during germination. Traditional maltings are very conspicuous buildings, and it is in these that the maltster soaked the barley in water for about sixty hours and then spread the grains on the malting floor in a thick and even layer to await germination. The art of the maltster was to control the temperature of the growing malt with the greatest care by turning and spreading the barley with various shovels and forks. The maltster often walked barefoot on the malting floors to avoid damage to the growing grains which could then become mouldy. The process of flooring lasted about ten days after which the temperature was allowed to rise to about 68°F (20°C) to stop further growth. The 'green' malt was then loaded on to a kiln where it was dried. The purpose of this was to stop the growth and to cure the malt which gave it its characteristic biscuity flavour. This was a very critical operation before thermometers came to the aid of the maltster, because the temperature had to be high enough to cure the malt but not too high, otherwise the enzymes in the embryo would be destroyed (they would be necessary in the brewing process to come, for converting the starch into sugar). This is the basic malting process and it is the same today except that modern methods have become very scientific and mechanised. The modern maltster may treat his barley with certain additives which give him more control over the germination, and temperatures as high as 210°F may be needed for roasted malt. Many brewers still use malt made by traditional methods without short cuts, but the old art is gradually disappearing.

Frank Baillie *The Beer Drinker's Companion*

Stout as a Beverage and Medical Adjunct

Guinness's Extra Stout is a pleasant beverage. It has a character quite its own, and it appeals to the palate. The alcohol, the solid constituents, and the extractives present a finely adjusted balance which has gained for it a worldwide reputation. Its stimulating action on the secretions, when taken in moderation, is such that it may be regarded as a food product of much value and it is unquestionably an aid to digestion. Its sustaining effect on manual workers is equally well known, an effect which is believed to be due to the presence of Vitamin B, and to the Acid Phosphates, which are valuable energizers.

The publications of leading dietists and the strongly expressed opinion of many eminent Physicians of the present day have proved how valuable Extra Stout is in cases of debility arising from mal-nutrition, faulty metabolism, and deficient vital secretions.

The experience gained by the medical profession over a series of years has shown the manifold therapeutic uses of Stout as a medicinal agent in many forms of ill health; indeed, the opinion has been frequently expressed that successful treatment might be effected more readily and surely by the prescribing of Extra Stout than by well-known and often expensive drugs.

It would appear from evidence collected and facts ascertained after the most careful enquiry that Extra Stout has been found most useful in the following types of cases:–

1.–DYSPEPSIA.

As a tonic and stomachic in cases of sluggish action of the alimentary canal, Extra Stout has often a wonderful effect. In addition to its nourishing constituents and probable high vitamin content, the Hop Extracts which it contains are believed to act as a stimulant of the bile secretion. Extra Stout stimulates the secretion of the Pancreas, which is instrumental in breaking up the important food principles – proteins, starches, and fats – and the presence of acid phosphates is believed by many medical men to render Extra Stout the ideal tonic.

2.–INSOMNIA.

The wearing and devitalizing results of want of sleep are well known. The soporific effects of Extra Stout are sometimes remarkable, and doctors have declared that it is preferable to Opium, inducing a more natural and healthy sleep, while avoiding the establishment of a drug habit. The modicum of alcohol, in addition to its sedative influence, renders Extra Stout a valuable remedy for overworked and overtired people who are bad sleepers.

3.–GENERAL DEBILITY.

In convalescence after long or acute illness, when vitality is low, sleep disturbed, digestion impaired, and nerves are in a state of irritability, the vitalizing properties of Extra Stout have proved to be of immense help. Its addition to the resources of the physician in the following cases has been fairly established:-

> In Neurasthenia and allied Neuroses; in Pulmonary Tuberculosis; after Influenza and Bronchitis – especially in elderly people; after Pneumonia and the Fevers; in the prevention of Senile Decay, and as a restorative and stabilizing agent in exhausting diseases. Surgeons of repute have also found that Extra Stout is valuable in post-operative debility and following serious injuries associated with 'shock.'
>
> *Guide to St James's Gate Brewery, 1928*

On Ale

> Of this strange drink, so like the Stygian lake,
> Which men call Ale, I know not what to make.
> Folk drink it thick and void it very thin.
> Therefore much dregs must needs remain within.
>
> Anon

Raising the Living

If British beer is unique then so are the methods used for serving it. The best-known English system, the beer engine operated by a handpump on the bar, once travelled widely to help serve cask-conditioned beer throughout the colonies. But as the world lager revolution spread, cask beer and its engines became confined to their country of origin. The beer engine arrived on the pub scene early in the 19th century. It coincided with and was prompted by the decline of the publican brewer and the rise of the commercial companies that began to dominate the supply of beer to public houses. The common brewers expected a healthy return on the sales of their products. They also wanted the beer to be stored and served in exemplary condition in the pubs they supplied. And as the brewers' profits grew and beer prices rose, the publicans found that their margins were being squeezed. In order to sell more beer and maintain their livings, publicans looked for faster and less labour-intensive methods of serving beer.

In *The Brewing Industry in England, 1700–1830*, Peter Mathias records that 'most beer had to be stored in butts in the publicans' cellars for the technical reason that it needed an even and fairly low temperature, even where convenience and restricted space behind the bar did not enforce it. This meant, equally inevitably, continuous journeying to and from the cellars by the pot-boys to fill up jugs from the spigots: a waste of time for the customer and of labour and trade for the publican. Drawing up beer from the cellar at the pull of a handle at the bar at once increased the speed of sale and cut the wage bill'.

The first person to attempt to invent a system for raising beer from cellar to bar was Joseph Bramah who took out a patent for a beer pump in October 1797. Bramah had successfully patented such socially useful devices as the hydraulic press and an improved water closet, but his beer engine created as many problems as it sought to solve. Specifications for Bramah's pump show a man at ground level filling a jug with beer from a pipe that leads to storage vessels below the ground. The pipe ends in a tap and the beer was to be drawn from the cellar by an elaborate system of heavy boxes of sand raised on pistons that fitted into voluminous storage containers. As the boxes pressed down on the beer in the containers it forced it through pipes up to the bar. This sytem of 'sand pressure' had obvious drawbacks: it required cellars with considerable height to accommodate the containers and pistons, while normal butts or casks delivered by the breweries were not suitable as they did not have vertical sides. Publicans would have had to transfer beer from butts to the new containers, activity that would have been as troublesome and labour-intensive as fetching beer from the cellar in jugs. Bramah's invention did not get out of the cellar let alone off the ground. But his idea encouraged others to find a solution to the problem, though Mathias wondered why it had taken so long to be invented: 'One of the few technical devices of importance to come into it [the public house] since the publican stopped brewing his own beer was the beer engine. It was, from the first, a simple manually-operated pump, incorporating no advances in hydraulic knowledge or engineering skill, similar in design to many pumps used at sea, yet perfectly adapted to its function in the public house. It was brought into this environment by the need for speed and efficiency caused by the intensive demand in a busy city tavern. One wonders why such a thing had not been used before, particularly in ports where seamen, all too familiar with pumps, often became publicans; or even more where brewers, who used many pumps about their breweries, themselves controlled public houses.'

By 1801, John Chadwell of Blackfriars Road, London, was registered as a 'beer-engine maker' and soon afterwards Thomas Rowntree in the same area described himself as 'a maker of a double-acting beer-machine.' A. G. Green, again in the Blackfriars region of London, was similarly registered by 1809 and it is likely that the 'patent brewing-machine warehouse' of Needham, Rawlings and Co was engaged in the same manufacture. Yates and Greenaway were also early beer engine manufacturers. In his *Treatise on Mechanics*, published in 1806, Olinthus Gregory referred in passing to 'beer-drawing machines – nothing else than an assemblage of small pumps, either sucking or forcing.' A 'patent beer engine' was among the fittings offered for sale with a public house in 1801 and one with 'four motions' was sold in 1806. In 1812 a valuation of the equipment in the Crown in Fleet Street listed a 'three-motion' beer engine with 'Pewter Sink, Lead Pipe, Screw Cocks and apparatus complete, fixed in a neat, inlaid Mahogany Case.' By this time trade directories in other major English cities such as Bristol and Birmingham were listing beer engine makers. The *Pantalogia* of 1813 reported that such machines were 'very common in London and other large towns.'

One had been installed in a rural pub in Tewin in Hertfordshire as early as 1806. Peter Mathias commented sourly: 'Considering its rapid adoption at the turn of the century, encouraged then, no doubt, by the profit margins of publicans falling as prices rose, we may perhaps think that the device had been held up so long only by an instinctive conservatism and an irrational conviction that pumps were only for water, that engines pumping beer savoured of fountains flowing with wine – fictions fit only for continental extravagance.'

There is no recorded evidence of consumer objection to the beer engine. At a time when public houses were open for long periods and demand for beer was insatiable, customers seemed to value a system that served their drinks quickly and refreshingly cool. By the 1820s, beer engine service had become standard throughout most of urban England and Gaskell and Chambers, the world-renowned makers of drink dispensing equipment, had taken the lead in their manufacture. Such was the demand for engines that during Victorian times Gaskells had more than 700 employed in their Birmingham works alone. By the end of the century some vast London and other big city taverns had banks of 40 to 50 handpumps pulling and heaving to meet the demand for beer. Because of the effort involved a popular form of beer engine was the 'cash register' variety, a bank of three of four pumps mounted with short handles high on the bar, which needed less physical strength to operate them. The George in Southwark, South London, still has a 144 year-old working cash register engine.

The earliest system of engine survived until as late as the 1940s. This comprised lead pipes connected to the casks in the cellar and to a 'leather-bucket' engine below the bar. As early as 1795 Sir George Baker had shown that the illness known as 'Devonshire colic' was in reality lead poisoning, but lead pipes continued to be used in beer engines until well into the 20th century, when their use was banned by law. They were replaced first by porcelain or glass pipe sections about four inches in length, interconnected by rubber tubes. They were followed by stainless steel pipes and today the universal type of piping is micro-bore plastic. Leather bucket engines also disappeared, giving way to all-metal piston engines. In the late 1970s the possibility of EEC legislation prompted brewers and engine manufacturers to replace gunmetal working parts with stainless steel or plastic. The modern beer engine is a perfectly safe method of serving beer if all the working parts and the pipes are cleaned regularly. Some brewery companies – Banks and Hansons of the West Midlands are the best-known examples – prefer, however, to serve their cask beers by electric pumps.

It was a similar and possibly misplaced concern for hygiene that prompted the introduction of the electric pump in the 1930s. It does exactly the same job as a manual engine but without the effort. It comes in two versions – the free-flow pump, which draws the beer until the tap on the bar is switched off, and the metered pump with a diaphragm that moves to and fro inside the mounting on the bar, measuring precise half pints. Electric pumps are rare in the south of England, widespread in the Midlands and often found in Wales and the north. The only possible objections to them are that they lack the aesthetic appeal of a tall handpump and that it is difficult, sometimes impossible when you are in strange territory, to distinguish them from pressurised fonts serving keg or bright beer. It was the introduction of keg beer that almost killed off the beer engine. Fred Bryant, former sales director for Gaskell and Chambers, who worked for the company for 43 years, remembers pressure dispense as far back as 1934, when the Downham Tavern in Grove Park, London, had no fewer than 30 pressure points on its bars. In the post-war years the spread of keg led to cutbacks in traditional beer engine manufacture. Gaskell and Chambers were on the point of phasing them out completely in 1966 but were persuaded not to by Fred Bryant who was convinced that the keg tide would turn. The tide was a slow ebb at first. As publicans discarded their beer engines to make way for such tongue-tingling delights as Watney's Red, Double Diamond, Worthington E, Tartan, Tavern and Trophy, Gaskells bought the engines for 2s 6d each and either sold them for scrap or for £6 a piece to the United States, where they were in demand as lamp standards. Today a new, single-pull engine costs around £120. Although Gaskell and Chambers have ceased to trade, their legendary Dalex engines are made by another firm and are in great demand, built by craftsmen from 70 year-old moulds. Firms such as Homark have introduced simplified styles of engine, including the type that clips on to the bar, which has found favour with landlords keen to experiment with real ale but not so keen to saw away a substantial part of their counter. In its various guises, the beer engine remains the rock on which the real ale revolution has been built. It is the symbol of all that is best in English and Welsh beer and the enduring sign of its quality and tradition.

The difference in serving traditional draught beer in Scotland is even more marked than the tastes and names of the beers themselves. Although beer engines can be found in some bars and Scottish and Newcastle promotes McEwan's cask beer on posters with a picture of a handpump, the tall font primed by air pressure is the traditional and distinctive method of serving Scottish beer. The water engine arrived in the 1870s as the Scottish brewing industry grappled with the same problem as the English one: how to keep and serve beer in the best condition. Ballinghall of Dundee was the first company to use air pressure and its original water engines were designed to produce pressures ranging from 121 lbs per square inch to 40 lbs per square inch. Other firms that moved quickly into water engine production were John McGlashan and Co, Gaskell and Chambers (Scotland) and Laidlaw and Sons. Aitkens of Edinburgh produced an engine and another was manufactured by Allan and Bogle of Glasgow. Two small engines, with the splendid names of Big Wonder and Little Wonder, were built in the United States and exported to Scotland, mainly for the Aberdeen area.

These engines were all similar in concept, a lavatory cistern in reverse, with water pressure being converted into air pressure. As water enters the casing or cistern, it raises a ball-cock and forces air through a float chamber to the air pipe connected to the cask, the process aided by an aptly-named snifter valve. The process is repeated until the required air pressure in the cask drives the beer to the bar. Water engines are now rare and have been replaced by electric air compressors, though many bars keep water engines in reserve in case of a power cut.

The other end of the system, the tall font on the bar, meets the requirements of ancient Scottish legislation that beer should be served in full view of the customer. The most distinctive and handsome font is the McGlashan Albany, still used to serve Maclay's cask beer. The font has a two-way tap. When the tap is operated it draws beer direct from the cask and any beer that overflows the glass goes into a return tray and is served through a second beer line when the tap is moved in the opposite direction. Many bars use a Cornelius font, originally designed for use with gas pressure systems of dispense but now widely used for cask beer too. As with the electric pump in England and Wales, it is not always possible to detect whether a Cornelius font is serving the real or the dead McCoy. If you don't like to ask then you have to pay your money and let your tastebuds do the rest. If they are immediately atrophied by Arctic bubbles then you know you have struck unlucky.

Scottish bars range from the bare and the brash to the splendidly ornate but when they serve cask beer they are united by their system of dispense that is as singular and proud as the English one. If you still harbour any doubts about air pressure then visit the justly famous Athletic Arms in Edinburgh, known as the Diggers because it is opposite a graveyard. You do not order verbally but merely raise the necessary number of digits for pints required as you enter the hallowed portals. The air pressure dials on the wall rotate and the phalanx of 13 fonts ensure that your glasses of McEwan's 80 shilling are ready and waiting as you reach the bar. Don't grab for your drink. Wait for the swirling rush of beer to settle and separate into bright liquid and tight white head. Then drink and savour Scottish beer, traditionally served, and wonder how the same company can dare lay claim to Tartan Bitter and Kestrel Lager.

Roger Protz *The Great British Beer Book*

Not turning taps, but pulling pumps,
Gives barmaids splendid busts and rumps.

Entry in a New Statesman competition

How to Taste and Judge Beer

To stare too intently at a glass of beer, or sniff it too obviously, in a bar or pub can be a questionable enterprise, but those are the first steps in appreciation. All food and drink is enjoyed with the eyes and nose as well as the mouth, and beer is no exception.

A glass of beer should look good. Some drinkers look for a deep, dense, uneven head on their beer. The Germans, who know something about beer, call it a 'beautiful flower.' If the flower is sufficiently beautiful, it will not quickly fade. As the beer is enjoyed, each swallow will leave behind what brewers call 'Brussels lace.' The bubbles in the beer will be small and sustained, and there will be no 'carbonic bite.' In most styles of beer, these are easily recognizable signs of a fresh, natural brew, though some of the finest English Bitter ales do not have a big head.

Therein lies the difficulty: every style of beer has its own balance of characteristics. They can be very different from one style to the next. Every beer is intended by the brewer to be in one style or another. It can be judged only according to the style it affects.

Every style has its own typical range of *colour*, but within that some interpretations are more subtle, complex, even beautiful, than others. A bright, clear, golden Pilsener can look especially appetizing, but so can an opaque, ebony Stout. In their blend of malts, brewers aim for certain levels of colour in their beer. They express these according to a scale agreed by the European Brewery Convention. A single brewery may make a Pilsener with six E.B.C. units of colour and a Porter with 80 or far more. These figures are a useful guide, but they cannot tell us what the eye sees: whether a beer has an earthy, autumnal russet colour or the richness of mahogany.

Nor does *clarity* count for much in a style of beer that is meant to be sedimented, or even hazy. The question is: which presentation is appropriate to the style?

All beers should have a *bouquet*, but this is more important in some styles than in others. It is most central to the Pilsener type. In all beers, the bouquet should be pleasant and appetizing. In a Pilsener, it should be fragrant, flowery, herbal, hoppy. In the Bavarian styles, there should also be some maltiness in the bouquet. In a Wheat Beer or ale, there should be some fruit.

In all styles, there should be a complex of these elements. Every time the glass is raised, new notes should be noticed in the bouquet, and the same goes for the *palate*. The accent of hop, malt and fruit in the palate should vary according to the style. So should the character of the hoppiness (fragrant, herbal, bitter?), maltiness (sweet, drier, spicy, coffeeish, roasty?), and fruitiness (subtle or assertive, citric, apple-like, a hint of banana?). Many lager brewers would worry about the apple notes, even more about the banana, but these are part of the character of some styles. In whatever style, the elements should find their own balance. A hoppy beer should not simply be harshly bitter. A malty one should not merely be sweet and sticky. A fruity one should not be all acidity and nothing else.

More than 120 descriptions for flavour elements in beer have been jointly agreed by the European Brewery Convention, the Master Brewers' Association of the Americas and the American Society of Brewing Chemists. Hundreds more have been identified by flavour specialists. The recognition of these elements gives some measure of beer's complexity of character. To the drinker, the same can be evident in one mouthful of a truly wonderful beer: the senses are aroused; the appetite quickens; and the subtleties of flavour, like all pleasures, defy captivity. They are the beer's soul.

In body, a Berliner Weisse should be light, but not thin. An ale might be light-bodied or full. A Märzen or a Bock should certainly have some malty 'mouth-feel'. Again, it is a question of style. Carbonation may vary, too. Continental European brewers measure this in grams per litre. English-speakers talk of volumes. One volume equals just under two grams per litre. The range can extend from 0.75 volumes to more than 3.0.

After it has been swallowed, no beer should altogether vanish. As the glass is put down for a moment, the pleasure of the beer should linger. There should be some *finish*. All the elements contribute to the finish, but the dryness of the hop is most important in several styles, especially English Bitter and Pilsener. The hop offers aroma and flavour as well as bitterness, but that is what the brewer can most readily measure, again according to a scale agreed by the European Brewery Convention. A beer with 10–15 European Units of Bitterness will be bland; one with 40 or more will be packed with flavour.

Inexperienced lovers can be intimidated. Untrained eaters can dislike oysters. Unaccustomed drinkers can pronounce: 'That beer tasted funny. Sort of bitter.' They have probably just encountered a classic.

ORGANIZING A TASTING

In almost every brewery of any size, a group of workers from different departments gathers at 11 o'clock each morning to check the latest batch of beer, often alongside its immediate competitors. They sample at this time because the immediate flavour of breakfast has gone, and hunger is beginning to arouse the palate. Mid-morning is the best time to sample, but not the most convenient if the tasting is to be among friends at home, or in a restaurant or club. For a sociable tasting, the time before the evening meal is ideal.

The daily tasters are not all brewers. They are picked not for their knowledge but because they have shown that they have sensitive palates. Special knowledge is not necessary: anyone can taste, and perhaps discover some surprising sensitivities to flavours. The tasters at the brewery often use opaque mugs, so that they will not be prejudiced by the colour, or perhaps recognize the beer by its hue. For the sociable taster, the opposite is required: the colour is part of the pleasure. Glasses that are not coloured, engraved or otherwise decorated should be used. Wine glasses are best, because their curve helps to retain the aroma.

A sample of two or three ounces of each beer is enough, and will look more than adequate in a small, narrow wine glass. This will also be sufficient for the taster to judge head formation and lacework. Five or six beers is plenty, ten or a dozen the maximum. If different styles are being compared, the lightest in overall character should be sampled first.

In breweries, the tasters often sample the beer at room temperature, because its flavour will be most fully expressed that way, defects and all. In a sociable tasting, the beer should be served at its appropriate temperature: it is being judged as it is normally consumed.

Professional tasters may be required to score a beer on 25 or even 50 points. Sociable tasters should have a simple score-sheet, awarding points on bouquet, palate, finish and fidelity to style. If that is thought too basic, appearance and body (or 'mouth feel') can be added. Some tasters like to clean their palate with bread or crackers between beers, but this can leave the floury taste of stale beer. Plain water, and lots of it, is better. It also guards against hangovers if the tasting becomes rigorous.

STORING BEER

Most beer is brewed to be consumed immediately, not to be stored. It may not deteriorate, but it is vulnerable from the moment it leaves the brewery. Some brewers recover their beers from the trade after three months, whatever the 'sell-by' date says.

Only a handful of beers, always strong and usually sedimented with living yeast, are made to be laid down, and they are usually vintaged-dated. Many Belgian specialities, some Imperial Stouts and Old Ales, and one or two Barley Wines are examples. Most reach a peak within 18 months to five years, though some will evolve for 25 years.

All beer should be stored in the dark. Conventional beers should be kept upright, so that the beer is not in contact with the crown bottle-top. Beer in wine bottles should always be stored on its side, so that the cork is kept moist.

Sedimented beers should never be kept in a refrigerator; the yeast will not work, and the beer will 'die.' They should be kept at a consistent temperature, preferably in a cool cellar. A sedimented ale should not be brought home from a shop and served immediately. It will need several hours, possibly a day to settle. German Wheat Beers *mit Hefe* are normally served with the yeast in suspension. Lager beers should be kept in a refrigerator, but ideally not at too cold a temperature setting. In very cold temperatures, a high-quality, all-malt, lager may become hazy. Once it is removed from the refrigerator, this 'chill haze' will gradually vanish, but no beer likes extremes of temperature.

DEFECTS

The most common defect in bottled or canned beers is staleness caused by oxygen. This imparts a floury, papery, damp-cardboard aroma and taste. If the beer has been newly-purchased, it should be returned to the retailer. He is probably not rotating his stock on the proper basis of 'first in, first out.' New bottles should not be stacked in front of old ones.

A very common defect in bottled beer is known by Americans as 'skunkiness.' This aroma, less graphically compared with over-cooked cabbage, is caused by sunlight or supermarket lighting. Bottles should not be kept in shop windows or other places where they are exposed to direct light.

CANS VERSUS BOTTLES
The strongest argument against cans is that they are aesthetically unpleasant. Deep in their hearts, most brewers also still harbour misgivings about the lengthy contact of beer and metal. When a batch of beer is not quite up to par, as inevitably happens in even the best-run establishments, some brewers will send it to the canning line. The theory is that consumers are less likely to return cans than bottles.

BOTTLES VERSUS DRAUGHT
Some styles of beer are by nature draught products. The classic example is British cask-conditioned ale. Most beer-lovers prefer draught because it is less often pasteurized (though practice varies from one country to another) and more likely to be fresh. Brewers do not install draught systems in outlets with a slow turnover. A publican who does not clean his lines will ruin his beer. In that respect, bottled beer is less vulnerable – but it, too, has to be well kept.

ADDITIVES
Like the food and wine industries, the beer business has occasional scandals over additives. In all three areas, additives are perhaps less fashionable among producers than they were.

Many brewers say they use no additives whatever, and some indicate this on their labels. One difficulty is to define an additive. Tannic acid, for example, occurs naturally in brewing, but may also be added to clarify beer. Most additives are used to clarify or preserve beer, or improve head retention. At best, they are 'beauty aids' where none should be needed. At worst, they may be used clumsily, though there is no such thing as 'chemical beer.'

No additive currently used has been proven to be harmful, though some could trigger allergies or other health problems. This is the strongest argument for ingredient labelling, which would also discourage the use of additives and allay public fears.

Michael Jackson *New World Guide to Beer*

We don't really need a beer vocabulary for some opinions!

Cooking with Beer

The French turn quite naturally to their wine when they start to cook, so why don't we in Britain automatically reach for the beer? I tell you that the British pint is probably more versatile than French plonk when it comes to the cooking pot, for beer used in recipes not only enhances the flavour and texture of the dish but by its very nature as a living product containing natural carbon dioxide, can be a lightening agent as well. Just sloshing a drop of ale into a casserole will no doubt improve its flavour, but isn't that a bit too easy? It is far more interesting – and delicious – to have a look at the different types of real ale on offer in your area and match them to the dish you want to make. Dark milds go beautifully with strong flavoured meats such as stewing beef and venison – and it is fortuitous that in winter when we want to make warming casseroles we get strong, full-flavoured ales to add to them. I quite envy all the cooks in the Maidstone area with Goacher's Old and Dark Maidstone Ales to bring a marvellous malted barley flavour to thick, rich stews. It may seem obligatory to put chicken into white wine or cider, but it isn't – a light smooth bitter will produce a more savoury taste that you will find makes an intriguing change.

Cakes and ale really go together, as any maker of rich fruit cakes will tell you – but I am impressed by the Cumbrian publican who uses beer to make his own bread, served with home-made soup in his pub. Neil Walmsley at the Old Dungeon Ghyll Hotel in Great Langdale says you can quite easily replace water with beer, or half and half, when making your dough. At his own pub he can turn to Theakston, Yates, Younger and Marston – it's definitely brown bread and obviously does not suffer for want of yeast.

Talking of home-made soup, Hazel Milligan at the Falkland Arms at Great Tew in Oxon sent me this simple yet extremely tasty (and filling) recipe for **Cheese and Ale Soup** (a large quantity – you could halve it):

Ingredients: butter; two large onions; two slightly heaped tbsps of plain flour; 1 pint ale; 1 pint stock; 1 pint milk; 1 lb cheese; 1 teasp English mustard; salt and pepper; pinch of mixed herbs.

Method: Slice onions and cook in butter until soft; stir in flour, then stir in beer, stock and milk and add the mustard, seasoning and herbs. Bring to the boil then simmer, stirring, until thickened; add cheese chopped in small pieces and continue stirring gently over a low heat until it is smooth.

Cheese and beer really are made for each other, so here is another recipe from an enthusiastic real ale cook, Doreen Scott at the Bell at Odell, Beds.

Welsh Rarebit with Abbot Ale:
Ingredients: $2\frac{1}{2}$ oz butter; $2\frac{1}{2}$ oz plain flour; $\frac{3}{4}$ pint of milk; 4 oz grated Cheddar cheese; $\frac{1}{2}$ teasp cayenne pepper; $\frac{1}{2}$ teasp mustard powder; $\frac{1}{2}$ tbsp Worcester sauce; 1 egg yolk; $\frac{1}{4}$ pint Abbot Ale.

Method: Melt the butter in a saucepan, gradually add the flour, mix and cook for a few minutes. Gradually add the milk and mix to a thick, smooth sauce. Simmer, stirring, for a few minutes. Add the grated cheese and allow to melt over a low heat. Add the cayenne pepper, mustard powder and Worcester sauce; stir well. In a separate small saucepan boil the Abbot Ale until it has reduced to about a tablespoonful, then add it to the cheese sauce and stir it in. Allow it to cool and thicken before using. Spread thickly on buttered toast and brown under a hot grill. Comments Doreen: 'Of course you can use any beer for the rarebit but it goes without saying Abbot Ale's the best!'

Before we leave cheese, don't give the Swiss all their own way with the fondue. Create a thoroughly English version using a pint of bitter and cheddar – here is my recipe to serve four people:

Ingredients: One pint of a strong flavoured bitter; 1 lb Cheddar, chopped small; one small onion, finely chopped; one crushed clove of garlic; one teasp finely chopped fresh coriander; one teasp dry mustard; black pepper.

Method: Sweat onion and garlic in butter then add beer and heat; add cheese and cook slowly until it has melted (if it doesn't seem thick enough add a little cornflower mixed with milk). Add the dry mustard and fresh coriander and stir well; season with plenty of freshly ground black pepper. As a dip use fresh-baked, crusty mixed grain bread.

Beer comes into its own when making batter. In the interests of this guide I experimented by pouring a drop of bitter into my Yorkshire pudding batter instead of the cold water I usually add last, after the milk has been whisked in. The results were very good – I do believe the puds rose slightly higher than usual and had a more savoury flavour.

Here is another way of using beer in batter from the Crown at Melton Mowbray for coating wings of skate before frying (to coat 12 pieces):

Ingredients: 4 oz flour; salt and pepper; 1 tbsp olive oil; 7 fl oz/$\frac{3}{8}$ pint beer; 2 egg whites; a little fresh dill.

Method: Sift the flour into a bowl and season with salt and pepper; make a well in the centre of the flour. Add the oil and gradually whisk in the beer, working from the centre outwards. Whisk only for as long as it takes to produce a smooth batter, do not overwork the mixture. Leave the batter to rest for about an hour at room temperature, otherwise it will shrink away from the fish pieces and provide an uneven coating. Add the fresh dill and beat the egg whites until the form soft peaks and fold them gently into the batter mixture just before using.

Last and probably least, my own contribution to cooking with beer. I chose oxtail, a cheap and under-rated cut of meat which produces the most delicious, slightly glutinous gravy, particularly when cooked entirely in mild. The landlord from the McMullen pub opposite my house brought me a pint of AK and as I write the cooking aroma is guaranteed to set the mouth watering, but I suspect it would be an even better dish using a dark mild such as Morrells in Oxford. Anyway, here it is: **Oxtail with Mild** for six people:

Ingredients: 2 lb chopped up oxtail (you can buy it in supermarkets in packs containing pieces of rather uniform size, but I prefer my butcher's way of chopping up the whole tail so you get huge lumps reducing to little bits); one large onion, sliced; approx 1½ large carrots, sliced in rounds; one small swede, diced; 2–3 oz small button mushrooms; 1–2 leeks; one pint dark mild; seasoned flour; one bay leaf.

Method: Fry the sliced onion in dripping in a large ovenproof casserole until softened, then remove with a slatted spoon. Add a little more dripping if necessary, coat the oxtail pieces in seasoned flour and fry a few at a time until browned on all sides. Add onion, mild, carrots, swede and bayleaf and cook in a low oven, 300F, gas mark 4, for at least three hours, until the meat is tender; during the last half hour add the washed button mushrooms and sliced leek so that the leek remains slightly crisp in contrast to the long-cooked root vegetables. Serve with creamed potato.

Susan Nowak *Good Pub Food*

GUINNESS'S CHRISTMAS PUDDING

This delicious

Christmas pudding

is ideal for the festive

season.

Serves 10-12 people.

Here's what you need

10 oz fresh breadcrumbs
8oz soft brown sugar
8oz currants
10oz seeded raisins (chopped)
8oz sultanas
2oz mixed peel (chopped)
10 oz shredded suet
½ level teaspoon salt
1 level teaspoon mixed spice
Grated rind of lemon
1 dessertsp. lemon juice
2 large eggs (beaten)
¼ pint milk
½ pint Guinness

1 Mix together all dry ingredients in a large basin.

2 Stir in lemon juice, eggs, milk and Guinness

3 Mix thoroughly and turn into two 2½ pint well greased pudding basins. Tie pudding cloths over the basins, or cover tightly with greaseproof paper and foil. Leave overnight.

4 Steam for 7½ hours. Puddings are then ready for the table.

5 If not serving immediately, cool puddings, recover and store in a cool place. When required resteam for 2-3 hours before serving.

The History of Beer Labels

The use of a paper label to advertise products in bottles appears to stem from the 17th century. Early drug phials contained a label which covered the glass entirely but early in the following century, patent medicine vendors were using paper labels widely. The progression to alcohol seems to have come in the middle of the 18th century. Alec Davies, in *Package & Print*, suggests that a black and white label was being used for port wine in 1756. Yet it was not until 1860 that single bottles of wine were allowed to be sold and the law required each bottle to bear a paper label.

Beer labels were unknown to the 1840's. Until 1834, when the duty on glass was repealed in England, beer was not bottled to any large extent. The customer had his own bottles which were impressed with his own seal – usually showing a coat of arms or name, together with date – just below the neck of the bottle.

After 1834, bottles were still manually sealed and, in lieu of any label, bore the name of the brewer and a description of the contents stamped into the neck of the wax seal. Expanding trade called for a quicker method and a metal foil capsule, similar to those still in use today for the bottling of wines and spirits, was soon introduced. This depicted the brewer's name and nature of contents. The disadvantage was that, with rough handling the cap soon became illegible; printed paper labels were therefore the answer. Brewers recognised the importance of identifying their products properly. British settlement in India gave rise to the export of a light ale specially brewed for the climate, appropriately named 'East India Pale Ale.' Extensive use was made of bottled beer, and earliest labels usually advertise this brew. The growth of cities caused by the Industrial Revolution enabled brewers to 'mass produce' their beer, while in rural districts the decline of home brewing increased the sales of country brewers.

By 1843, Bass of Burton-on-Trent were using a small circular printed label similar to the wax seal and affixed to the bottle in the same position. From then on, labels grew in size and became more colourful, particularly when used for export. However, small circular labels similar to the Bass labels – which were printed black on white – were in use for Guinness Stout into the 1930's. The cork was usually sealed with wax or foil cap and wire where natural gas was liable to build up; in particular, export ales were so sealed. In 1885, the screw stopper was invented by Barrett and this began to replace the cork although corks were still in general use in the third decade of the 20th century; indeed Gales of Horndean still use corked bottles for their Prize Old Ale, and Hardy Ale, when it was introduced by Eldridge Pope in 1968, appeared in similar bottles.

In 1892, Crown corks were invented by the American, Painter, and they further reduced the use of ordinary corks. With the general use of the screw stopper, there followed the top strap label over the stopper and in the early 1900's, with the passing of the Children's Act, it became necessary for all bottles which were capable of being easily opened to bear such a strap label; indeed, some strap labels even mentioned the Act. In the United Kingdom during the Second World War, many brewers, due to the paper shortage, ceased to issue labels and designated the type of beer, in small bottles, by the colour of the crown cork. Others, such as Trumans and Ind Coope & Allsopp, reduced the size of their labels and spelt out the reason for it:– 'Miniature label necessitated by War Conditions.'

In the early days of bottled beer, the majority of brewers did not bottle their beer, but left it to individual shops, public houses and wholesalers. It was not until the early 20th century that brewers established their own bottling stores, with one notable exception – Whitbread, who had founded their own stores in 1868. The early labels of Barclay Perkins and Combe & Company of London bear the names of the bottlers.

Labelled bottles were probably in general use by 1855 due to the extensions of the railways and canals which allowed the brewers to extend their markets. Labelled bottles were being exported in quantity during the Crimean War. A bottle of that period 'well corked and wired and bearing a faded trade label of the house on its dusky sides' is retained at William Younger's Brewery in Edinburgh. The quality of the best ales was highly prized, but unfortunately, imitations were sold, particularly Scotch Ale on the American market. Cut throat competition increased with trade expansion. The use of a distinguishing mark was an open invitation for it to be copied and used on an inferior products. Guinness, William Younger, and above all, Bass, suffered from imitations, and a book of forged labels is still retained at Bass's Brewery at Burton.

Yet perhaps that was the price to be paid for a company who had ensured that its trade mark was to become the most famous in the World. The Bass red triangle Pale Ale Label is perhaps the World's best known label; the designer of the trade mark sat on the steps of the Registrar's Office all night to ensure that the red triangle was the first trade mark to be registered under the Trade Marks Act 1875; Bass's Diamond trade mark was the second entry. Both trade marks had, however, been used for many years previously.

But the Bass label has another claim to fame: it is depicted on a bottle in Edward Monet's famous painting of 1881, entitled *Bar at the Folies-Bergère*. This illustrates only too clearly the popularity of British beers on the Continent at that time.

With the introduction of machinery for the purpose, bottled beer production expanded greatly between 1880 and 1890. About one third of all the breweries date their first labels from that period. At that time, designs for labels were prepared at the brewery and printing contracted out to a local jobbing printer. Owing to the amalgamation of many breweries after the First World War, and loss of overseas markets, there was a considerable decrease in the number and variety of labels used. Prior to the Second World War, label design had become the responsibility of commercial agencies and specialist printers.

Just prior to the 1939–1945 War, bottles with 'fired-on' labels were introduced. Whilst they were of some use during the wartime paper shortage, they did not prove popular, owing to the time spent in sorting at the bottling store. Brewers which made use of the fired-on label included Bullards, Steward & Patteson and Youngs Crawshay & Youngs, all of Norwich.

Today the beer label is still basically a selling instrument. The essentials of a good label are simplicity and boldness – it must be prominent on the bar shelf or counter to attract the required custom. There is a tendency for special brews to give rise to a special label – in many countries, foil has been used but British labels still tend to be rather conservative, though this may be an advantage as far as the collector is concerned. Whereas most of the World's labels tend to be pictorial. British labels generally depict the brewer's name, and trade mark or motif, together with brand name, although the introduction of regulations affecting contents and country of origin has led to further wording on labels and has, in the opinion of some, devalued the design to a certain extent. Perhaps one of the most famous designs which changed little on the label between 1907 and 1965 was the head of a Cape Buffalo, depicted on the Rustic Ale originally brewed by Brandon's Putney Brewery and later continued by Mann Crossman & Paulin and subsequently Watney Mann. Yet perhaps the most unusual design was that of a French beer label; when artist Jean Cocteau was commissioned to design a label for the De Luxe beer brewed by the Pecheur Brewery, he produced merely a drawing with no wording or advertising except for his signature.

Keith Osborne *The Beer Drinker's Guide to Labology*

The History of the Beermat

Beermats in the form we know today started in Britain in about 1920 with Watneys of London producing two mats, one advertising Watney's Pale Ale and the other Reids Stout. Beermats were however in use on the Continent many years earlier. The first woodpulp beermat was produced in 1892 by Robert Sputh of Dresden. Before the invention of the relatively cheap wood pulp mats, pottery or porcelain tankard stands were in use, and known as 'bottle coasters.' The term coaster is still in use in America and Australia. The bulk of present day mats are made from woodpulp but they have been made from other absorbent materials, such as, foam plastic, foam rubber, cork, leather, felt, wood, paper, linen, cardboard and cellulose wadding, and also a few non absorbent materials such as rubber, plastic and metal.

The early beermats were all on fairly thick woodpulp sometimes up to a quarter of an inch thick and mostly were printed in one colour. The earlier mats also had the printer's name on them in small writing at the bottom. If the printer's name was 'A. Brown' this indicated that the mat was most likely to have been issued prior to 1936. Mats bearing the name of Regicor (Reginald Corfield) were most likely printed during the period 1935–1950. The other name on beermats of this period was 'Tresises' although this name persisted on mats up to at least 1955. There are several beermat printers in existence now, but by far the largest is 'Quarmbys' whose name incidentally is found on most early Guinness mats.

Since 1939 most beermats have been printed on woodpulp approximately an eighth of an inch thick but the type of surface has changed. Mats with a pitted or stippled surface were probably issued before 1955 whilst those with a bleached (very white) surface have been issued only in the last few years. In the immediate years most mats were printed on a dull white woodpulp.

Another major change over the years has been the development from single-colour, worded mats to multi-coloured, pictured mats. As printing processes have improved so also have the beermats.

Unfortunately with the cost of woodpulp rising steadily and with most of the pulp coming from Scandinavia, beermats are now becoming relatively expensive to produce and with there being far fewer breweries to issue mats the hayday of beermat production has probably passed.

Michael Powell The Beer Drinker's Guide to Tegestology

Tegestology is the name given to the study of beermats. The name derives from the Latin word 'Teges' which literally means small rug but which collectors have freely translated as simply 'mat.' Collectors are also often called Dripsomaniacs.

The Versatile Beermat

The beermat is a wondrous invention. It can be far more than a collector's treasure or just a preventer of drips from falling in your trousers; this humble piece of fibrous card is at once comforter, weapon, piece of sporting apparatus, notepad, furniture-wedge and indicator of a pub's standards. A virtuous wad indeed.

It is probable that the kind of nervous tension which can be relieved by nail-biting is responsible for the mutilated remains seen on pub tables at chucking-out time. My spell in the trade taught me that different people vent their tensions on the poor old mat in distinct ways. There are the rough, heavy-handed types who tear the thing bodily into scraps, the delicate ones who pick at the edges with fingernails (if they have any left,) the sadists who spear the mat with a cocktail stick and the subtle artists who carefully peel the printed layers off the faces of the mat, leaving an untorn but plain mat and two wrinkled labels as mementoes of their triumphs. One could probably judge the anxiety level of a district by counting the mutilated mats in pub dustbins. I wonder if the number would rise when redundancy threatens, or the beer's rough, or United lose again?

The beermat's aerodynamic properties when spinning across the room render it an accurate, though hardly potent, weapon. Competitions akin to discus-throwing are clearly a possibility here. Tests of dexterity are sometimes seen in which beermats, poised on the edge of the table, are flipped upwards by the fingernails and grabbed as they spin in the air; skills can be measured by adding more and more mats to the flipped pile. Square mats can be built up like card-houses. A veritable mini-Olympics could be held using beermats.

I have observed scribblings on beermats ranging from simple sums of how much the next round will cost through shopping-lists and betting-slips to the strangest, most obscure messages (one I saw recently said 'J 42 Pete not in.') We should encourage this as an alternative to paint-spraying on walls.

A folded beermat is the ideal wedge for a rickety table, though finding the right number of thicknesses can be tiresome. Regulars in pubs with uneven floors can become quite annoyed when the cleaners keep removing their improvised wedges, and have been known to hide the tatty old things behind curtains and elsewhere, a form of hide-and-seek which gives cleaners endless fun. Landlords could help here by marking the legs of their tables with the required number of beermat-thicknesses to achieve a stable table.

But finally, one can learn a little about the care taken in a pub by observing whether the landlord frequently issues clean mats or allows the same old dirty things to do duty for weeks before finally being thrown out – or meeting one of the fates described above. It's only a small, unimportant matter, but beermats don't cost much.

Cheap it may be, but the undervalued beermat is a versatile instrument. If you can think of any further uses for it (not too abstruse or rude) don't keep them to yourself. Share your idea with others; write it on a beermat, and leave it about.

Tony Scholes

The Brewer's Dray

The most familiar symbol of the brewing industry in the past was, perhaps, the giant dray-horse pulling its load of beer barrels and making an impressive sight in the brewing towns of bygone years. Today they can still be seen at agricultural shows and even delivering beer in several towns up and down the country. And what a colourful sight they are! Some brewers have reasoned that, apart from any prestige value, they have other advantages for local deliveries within a few miles of the brewery. When a horse is held up at traffic lights he is resting, but a lorry is burning up expensive fuel; and if a dray-horse could speak he would surely support such a logical argument, because they seem to enjoy their work which they perform with pride and a touch of dignity.

The brewer's dray-horse belongs to one of the five main types of modern horses – the Draught (or 'Heavy' or 'Work' or 'Cart') horse. (The other types are Saddle, Light Harness, Heavy Harness and Ponies, and each of these types includes various breeds.) Draught horses are large, bulky and tall. They are strong and were bred for industry, and for pulling ploughs and waggons.

Perhaps the most famous of the heavy breeds is the Shire, which hails from central and north-east England and is a descendant of the war-horses of the Middle Ages. The Shire is usually bay or brown – less often black or grey – with great tufts of hair or 'feather' on the pastern (the section of the foot between fetlock and hoof). It was commonly used both as a farm and dray-horse and can still be seen today delivering Thwaites' beers in the Lancashire town of Blackburn, and in London taking casks of Young & Co's beers to thirsty customers around Wandsworth and Whitbread's beers to parched denizens of the East End. In the south-west a shire type delivers out of Plymouth Breweries, which now belongs to Courage Ltd; and in Leeds, Tetley uses them on town deliveries.

Another breed used for pulling brewer's waggons is the Percheron, which hailed from La Perche in Normandy and is a composite of the medieval Great Horse and French Coach Horse with some oriental ancestry. It has shortish legs without hair and its colour is grey or black. Percherons deliver the beer of Vaux & Associated Breweries in Sunderland and Edinburgh (Thos. Usher) and also Adnams' Ales in and around Southwold in Suffolk.

The Suffolk or Suffolk Punch is another typical heavy English breed originating in Suffolk and existing as far back as the sixteenth century. Its colour is a uniform light or dark chestnut with a flaxen mane and tail and it is the only clean-legged British draught horse. Although Suffolks were more often used on the farm than for delivering the stuff required to quench the thirst of our ancestors, it was not so long ago that they could be seen delivering Truman's beers in London's East End. Now they have been relegated to the comparative peace of the Essex countryside around Colchester.

The Clydesdale is a native of Lanarkshire, but is said to have been founded by a Dutch stallion brought from England in the eighteenth century. It is usually brown or black with prominent white markings and long fetlocks with feather. It is the breed which the Hull Brewery has used for many years – and still uses – for local deliveries in the town.

These are not the only breeds, and countries such as Belgium, France, Holland and Russia developed their own styles of work-horses with individual characteristics which, unfortunately, are becoming less and less common. They may be an enigma to some motorists in a hurry, but when he hears those impatient hoots on the horn the old dray-horse will not take much notice – he can't go any faster. Perhaps the pressure of modern traffic will, in the end, relegate the few remaining teams to the showground. That will be a pity and the loss of a colourful symbol of the past.

Frank Baillie *The Beer Drinker's Companion*

A Young's dray leaving the brewery

Hands off The Tetley Horses

Tuesday, 7 December, 1971, was a fairly quiet day for local news in Yorkshire, but an event that was to rouse The Great British Public to a rare fury was showing the first flickering flame of the conflagration to come.

Almost always when the public are stirred enough to rise in protest, it is the result of someone in authority completely misreading what that mysterious and powerful force called public reaction is likely to be in a particular situation.

The spark which started the outcry and resulted in the Yorkshire Evening Post receiving the most protest letters from readers in its history – three mail bags full – was a statement from the then chairman of the Leeds Corporation Planning and Traffic Management Committee saying that the Corporation were to seek 'the cooperation of Tetley's Brewery in limiting the number of horse-drawn vehicles because they had received complaints from motorists about the horse drays holding up traffic.'

The chairman said: 'There is no law under which we could ban them, but we might have to consider introducing one if there is no improvement. No-one should expect to be held up in this modern day by a horse-drawn vehicle.'

And that lit up the city as if it had fired a tanker full of high octane fuel.

The next day letters poured into the Yorkshire Evening Post, into local radio and television offices and through the letterbox of the corporation chairman.

And of these thousands of letters not one agreed with the suggestion that the Tetley horses should even be restricted let alone banned.

'Hands Off the Tetley Horses' said a Page One leader in the Yorkshire Evening Post.

Reporting teams from the Evening Post, television and Radio Leeds climbed aboard drays pulled by Tetley horses and toured the city streets to see what drivers of other vehicles had to say about the 'hold-ups' alleged to have been caused by the horses.

And of all the people interviewed not one complained.

A truly amazing tribute to the Tetley horses.

The B.B.C. TV commentator said: 'The Council really should have known better, for they were hitting the Englishman, not to say the Yorkshireman, on one of his touchiest points – his love of horses.'

Derek Naylor, feature writer on the Yorkshire Evening Post, wrote:

> I have just taken part in a leisurely, majestic and sentimental procession through Leeds – riding shotgun on a Tetley's brewer's dray. In an hour's progress around Briggate, Boar Lane, City Square, The Headrow, Vicar Lane, and back over Crown Point Bridge, I saw what a pair of beautiful grey shire horses can do for a city.
>
> Everywhere we went we were wrapped in a great big smile. Pensioners yelled: 'You tell that councillor chap to . . .'

Traffic wardens beamed huge grins I never thought they could flash, motorists happily gave way as we changed lanes and, best of all, were the wonder-filled eyes of small children as they caught sight of the horses – Randy and Majesty – plodding along at a hypnotic three m.p.h.

I had taken the ride after the rumpus caused by a council committee's suggestion that the horses held up traffic and should be limited in their numbers and use.

At once the Evening Post was swamped by the indignant cries of the Leeds public which loves its horses and is prepared to put up with any minor inconvenience the horse-drawn drays might cause.

In a bulging and continuing Postbag we received not one letter which did not support the horses.

My ride through the city centre in mid-afternoon confirmed that high feeling. Time and again pedestrians shouted up to us 'Good luck!'

See 'em in hell

The Tetley horses and their drivers became the heroes of the day. People in the streets stood and cheered as they passed . . .

'Keep going,' 'You're all right,' 'See 'em in hell, first,' and even more bellicose words of encouragement were shouted at the draymen.

Every delivery of mail to the Evening Post brought hundreds more letters of protest and in one edition two columns of letters appeared under this introduction:

Rarely has a subject provoked such a voluminous response from our readers. Tetley's horses are certainly not without friends – it is rather like the charge of the write brigade . . .

Here are some of the comments made in the letters:

'These horses also have an aesthetic quality in our highly mechanical society. Magnificent creatures, they are far more beautiful and durable than their man-produced, potential scrap-iron competitors. Many people thrill at the sight of them. Hands off the horses. I myself am a motorist' – Colin Anderson, Leeds 16.

'How many of my fellow motorists have the effrontery to complain of the famous brewery horses? I suspect they are bittermen from the south, probably in the pay of a foreign brewery. Our children's faces light up at the sight of these magnificent animals . . . 'Ands off the 'osses, and to 'ell with cars.' – J. H. Jose, Bramley, Leeds.

'Shire horses in harness are a majestic sight. And if they are pulling drays they are doing a good job as well.' – Andrew Loudon, Headingley, Leeds.

'These beautiful animals with their gentle strength are a precious part of our heritage and surely should be pemitted to give some pleasure and colour to our ever more drab, dreary and even poisoned environment.' – Mrs M. E. Teal, Shadwell, Leeds.

'As a motorist who covers some 33,000 miles a year I find it refreshing to see the horses working their way through Leeds.' – Jack Ellis, Rothwell.

'These magnificent horses were plodding the streets of Leeds long before cars were thought of. Why not ban cars?' – M. S. Wynn, Leeds 15.

Within three days the battle to save the Tetley horses had spread to the national newspapers, and within four days the letters to the Evening Post had become petitions.

And by the fourth day the Leeds Planning and Traffic Management Committee had decided that in the face of this onslaught by the public of the city the time had come to retreat with honour. They made a declaration of peace and said it was never their intention to ban the horses ... 'they only wanted to emphasise that the roads should be kept clear during peak periods.'

Christmas was now only days away and the Tetley horses paraded the streets and made a special visit to their champions, the Yorkshire Evening Post, with a sign on the back of their dray saying: 'We, the Tetley horses, say Thank You to all who have come to our support ... and wish everybody a Good, Old-Fashioned Happy Christmas.'

Clifford Lackey *Gentle Giants*

Epitaph

Here sleeps in peace a Hampshire grenadier,
Who caught his death by drinking cold small beer,
Soldiers, take heed from his untimely fall,
And when you're hot, drink strong, or not at all.

Winchester churchyard

CHAPTER 6

DRINKING, DRUNKENNESS AND TEMPERANCE

It was my Uncle George who discovered that alcohol was a food well in advance of modern medical thought.

P G Wodehouse *The Inimitable Jeeves*

Keats and Chapman

Keats and Chapman once climbed Vesuvius and stood looking down into the volcano, watching the bubbling lava and considering the sterile ebullience of the stony entrails of the earth. Chapman shuddered as if with cold or fear.

'Will you have a drop of the crater?' Keats said.

Flann O'Brien

Winterreise

I was back in beer-territory. Half-way up the vaulted stairs a groaning Brownshirt, propped against the wall on a swastika'd arm, was unloosing, in a staunchless gush down the steps, the intake of hours. Love's labour lost. Each new storey radiated great halls given over to ingestion. In one chamber a table of S.A. men were grinding out *Lore, Lore, Lore*, scanning the slow beat with the butts of their mugs, then running the syllables in double time, like the carriages of an express: '*UND – KOMMT – DER – FRÜHLingindastal! GRÜSS – MIR – DIE – LORenocheinmal.*' But it was certain civilian figures seated at meat that drew the glance and held it.

One must travel east for a hundred and eighty miles from the Upper Rhine and seventy north from the Alpine watershed to form an idea of the transformation that beer, in collusion with almost nonstop eating – meals within meals dovetailing so closely during the hours of waking that there is hardly an interprandial moment – can wreak on the human frame. Intestine strife and the truceless clash of intake and digestion wrecks many German tempers, twists brows into scowls and breaks out in harsh words and deeds.

The trunks of these feasting burghers were as wide as casks. The spread of their buttocks over the oak benches was not far short of a yard. They branched at the loins into thighs as thick as the torsos of ten-year-olds and arms on the same scale strained like bolsters at the confining serge. Chin and chest formed a single column, and each close-packed nape was creased with its three deceptive smiles. Every bristle had been cropped and shaven from their knobbly scalps. Except when five o'clock veiled them with shadow, surfaces as polished as ostriches' eggs reflected the lamplight. The frizzy hair of their wives was wrenched up from scarlet necks and pinned under slides and then hatted with green Bavarian trilbys and round one pair of elephantine shoulders a little fox stole was clasped. The youngest of this group, resembling a matinée idol under some cruel spell, was the bulkiest. Under tumbling blond curls his china blue eyes protruded from cheeks that might have been blown up with a bicycle pump, and cherry lips laid bare the sort of teeth that make children squeal. There was nothing bleary or stunned about their eyes. The setting may have reduced their size, but it keyed their glances to a sharper focus. Hands like bundles of sausages flew nimbly, packing in forkload on forkload of ham, salami, frankfurter, krenwurst and blutwurst and stone tankards were lifted for long swallows of liquid which sprang out again instantaneously on cheek and brow. They might have been competing with stop-watches, and their voices, only partly gagged by the cheekfuls of good things they were grinding down, grew louder while their unmodulated laughter jarred the air in frequent claps. Pumpernickel and aniseed rolls and bretzels bridged all the slack moments but supplies always came through before a true lull threatened. Huge oval dishes, laden with schweinebraten, potatoes, sauerkraut, red cabbage and dumplings were laid in front of each diner. They were followed by colossal joints of meat – unclassifiable helpings which, when they were picked clean, shone on the scoured chargers like calves' pelvises or the bones of elephants. Waitresses with the build of weight-lifters and all-in wrestlers whirled this provender along and features dripped and glittered like faces at an ogre's banquet. But all too soon the table was an empty bone-yard once more, sound faltered, a look of bereavement clouded those small eyes and there was a brief hint of sorrow in the air. But succour was always at hand; beldames barged to the rescue at full gallop with new clutches of mugs and fresh plate-loads of consumer goods; and the damp Laestrygonian brows unpuckered again in a happy renewal of clamour and intake.

I strayed by mistake into a room full of S.S. officers, Gruppen- and Sturmbannführers, black from their lightning-flash-collars to the forest of tall boots underneath the table. The window embrasure was piled high with their skull-and-crossbones caps. I still hadn't found the part of this Bastille I was seeking, but at last a noise like the rush of a river guided me downstairs again to my journey's end.

The vaults of the great chamber faded into infinity through blue strata of smoke. Hobnails grated, mugs clashed and the combined smell of beer and bodies and old clothes and farmyards sprang at the newcomer. I squeezed in at a table full of peasants, and was soon lifting one of those masskrugs to my lips. It was heavier than a brace of iron dumb-bells, but the blond beer inside was cool and marvellous, a brooding, cylindrical litre of Teutonic myth. This was the fuel that had turned the berserk feeders upstairs into Zeppelins and floated them so far from heart's desire. The gunmetal-coloured cylinders were stamped with blue HB conjoined under the Bavarian crown, like the foundry-mark on cannon. The tables, in my mind's eye, were becoming batteries where each gunner served a silent and recoil-less piece of ordnance which, trained on himself, pounded away in steady siege. *Mass*-gunfire! Here and there on the tables, with their heads in puddles of beer, isolated bombardiers had been mown down in their emplacements. The vaults reverberated with the thunder of a creeping barrage. There must have been over a thousand pieces engaged! – Big Berthas, Krupp's pale brood, battery on battery crashing at random or in salvoes as hands adjusted the elevation and traverse and then tightened on the stone trigger-guard. Supported by comrades, the walking wounded reeled through the battle smoke and a fresh gunner leaped into each place as it fell empty.

My own gun had fired its last shot, and I wanted to change to a darker-hued explosive. A new *Mass* was soon banged down on the board. In harmony with its colour, it struck a darker note at once, a long Wagnerian chord of black-letter semibreves: *Nacht und Nebel!* Rolling Bavarian acres formed in the inscape of the mind, fanning out in vistas of poles planted pyramidally with the hops gadding over them heavy with poppy-sombre flowers.

The peasants and farmers and the Munich artisans that filled the tables were much nicer than the civic swallowers overhead. Compared to the trim, drilled figures of the few soldiers there, the Storm Troopers looked like brown-paper parcels badly tied with string. There was even a sailor with two black silk streamers falling over his collar from the back of his cap, round the front of which, in gold letters, was written *Unterseeboot*. What was this Hanseatic submariner doing here, so far inland from Kiel and the Baltic? My tablemates were from the country, big, horny-handed men, with a wife or two among them. Some of the older men wore green and grey loden jackets with bone buttons and badgers' brushes or blackcocks' feathers in the back of their hatbands. The bone mouthpieces of long cherrywood pipes were lost in their whiskers and on their glazed china bowls, painted castles and pine-glades and chamois glowed cheerfully while shag-smoke poured through the perfor-ations of their metal lids. Some of them, gnarled and mummified, puffed at cheroots through which straws were threaded to make them draw better. They gave me one and I added a choking tribute to the enveloping cloud. The accent had changed again, and I could only grasp the meaning of the simplest sentences. Many words were docked of their final consonants; '*Bursch*' – 'a chap' – for instance, became 'bua'; 'A' was rolled over into 'O', 'Ö' became 'E', and every O and U seemed to have a final A appended, turning it into a disyllable. All this set up a universal moo-ing note, wildly distorted by resonance and echo; for these millions of vowels, prolonged and bent into boomerangs, sailed ricochetting up through the fog to swell the tidal thunder. This echoing and fluid feeling, the bouncing of sounds and syllables and the hogsheads of pungent liquid that sloshed about the tables and blotted the sawdust underfoot, must have been responsible for the name of this enormous hall. It was called the *Schwemme*, or horse-pond. The hollowness of those tall mugs augmented the volume of noise like the amphorae which the Greeks embedded in masonry to add resonance to their chants. My own note, as the mug emptied, was sliding down to middle C.

Mammoth columns were rooted in the flagstones and the sawdust. Arches flew in broad hops from capital to capital; crossing in diagonals, they groined the barrel-vaults that hung dimly above the smoke. The place should have been lit by pine-torches in stanchions. It was beginning to change, turning now, under my clouding glance, into the scenery for some terrible Germanic saga, where snow vanished under the breath of dragons whose red-hot blood thawed sword-blades like icicles. It was a place for battleaxes and bloodshed and the last pages of the *Nibelungenlied* when the capital of Hunland is in flames and everybody in the castle is hacked to bits. Things grew quickly darker and more fluid; the echo, the splash, the boom and the roar of fast currents sunk this beer-hall under the Rhine-bed; it became a cavern full of more dragons, misshapen guardians of gross treasure; or the fearful abode, perhaps, where Beowulf, after tearing the Grendel's arm out of its socket, tracked him over the snow by the bloodstains and, reaching the mere's edge, dived in to swim many fathoms down and slay his loathsome water-hag of a mother in darkening spirals of gore.

Or so it seemed, when the third mug arrived.

Patrick Leigh Fermor *A Time of Gifts*

Longevity

> The Horse and Mule live thirty years,
> And nothing know of wines and beers.
> The Goat and Sheep at twenty die
> And never taste of Scotch or Rye.
> The Cow drinks water by the ton
> And at 18 is mostly done.
> The Dog at 16 cashes in
> Without the aid of rum or gin.
> The Cat in milk and water soaks
> And then in twelve short years it croaks.
> The modest, sober, bone-dry Hen
> Lays eggs for nogs, then dies at 10.
> All animals are stricly dry
> And sinless live and swiftly die.
> But sinful, gin-full, rum soaked men,
> Survive for three score years and ten,
> And some of us, the mighty few,
> Stay pickled till we're 92.

Anon

The Plagues of London

It followeth in Fitzstephen that the plagues of London in that time were immoderate quaffing among fools, and often casualties by fire. For the first, to wit of quaffing, it continueth as afore, or rather is mightily increased, though greatly qualified among the poorer sort, not of any holy abstinence, but of mere necessity, ale and beer being small, and wine in price above their reach.

John Stow

If all be true that I do think,
There are five reasons we should drink;
Good wine, a friend, or being dry,
Or lest we should be by and by;
Or any other reason why.

Henry Aldrich, Dean of Christchurch 1648–1710

When ale is in, wit is out.

Anon

I pray thee let me and my fellow have
A Haire of the dog that bit us last night.

John Heywood, 1546

How can I, who drink good wine and bitter beer every day of my life, cooly stand up and advise hard-working fellow-creatures to take the pledge?

W E Gladstone, Prime Minister

Epigram on an Academic Visit to the Continent

I went to Frankfort, and got drunk
With that most learn'd professor – Brunck:
I went to Worts, and got more drunken
With that more learn'd professor – Ruhncken.

Richard Porson

Hogarth

Beer Street

Beer, happy produce of our Isle,
Can sinewy strength impart
And wearied with fatigue and toil,
Can chear each manly heart.

Hogarth

Gin Lane

Gin Cursed Fiend with a Fury fraught,
Makes human Race a Prey;
It enters by a deadly Draught,
And steals our Life away.

The Drunkard's Prospective

Drink beastiates the heart, and spoils the brains,
Exiles all reason, all good graces stains,
Infatuates judgement, understanding blinds,
Perverts the wits, and doth corrupt the minds.
It doth surprize the thoughts, and it doth all
The powers and faculties of soul enthrall.

Drunkards for nothing that is good are fit,
In all the world of earth, the barens't bit,
Like to a dumb Jack in a virginall,
They have no voice in commonwealth at all.
They've no more use of them throughout the land,
Than Jeroboam had of his withered hand.

Health out o' the body, wit out of the head,
Strength out o' th' joints, and every one to bed.
All money's out a purse; drink out o' th' barrels,
Wife, children, out of doors, all into quarrels.

To you churchwardens, constables, and others
That love the Lord, the Church, the State, your brothers,
Your selves, your sons, the people of the land,
Put forth against this sin your helping hand.
Help, help the Lord, the lawes, some ground to win,
Against I say, against this mighty sinne.

> Joseph Rigbie, Clerk of the Peace of the County Palatine of Lancaster, 1656

Pubs to get Drunk in

There hath been great sale and utterance of wine,
Besides beere, and ale, and ipocras fine,
In every country, region, and nation,
But chiefly in Billingsgate, at the Salutation;
And the Bore's Head, near London Stone,
The Swan at Dowgate, a taverne well known;
The Mitre in Cheape; and then the Bull's Head,
And many like places that make noses red;
Th' Bore's Head in Old Fish Street, Three Cranes in the Vintry,
And now, of late, St. Martin's in the Sentree;
The Windmill in Lothbury; the Ship at th' Exchange,
King's Head in New Street, where roysters do range;
The Mermaid in Cornhill, Red Lion in the Strand,
Three Tuns, Newgate Market; Old Fish Street, at the Swan.   Anon

The Irish Pig

'Twas an evening in November,
As I very well remember,
I was strolling down the street in drunken pride,
But my knees were all aflutter,
So I landed in the gutter,
And a pig came up and lay down by my side.

Yes, I lay there in the gutter
Thinking thoughts I could not utter,
When a colleen passing by did softly say,
'Ye can tell a man that boozes
By the company he chooses.'–
At that the pig got up and walked away!

Anon

Being drunk – some synonmyms

*(There are more than 3,000 in various lists and the following 50 are simply a
selection of the ones that attracted and amused me. I claim one as my original.)*
BP

Arseholed

Back teeth afloat

Been at the top shelf

Bit by the barn-weasle

Brahms and Liszt

Breath strong enough to carry coal with

Burning with a low blue flame

Can't hit the ground with his hat

Can't see through a ladder

Decks awash

Discomboozelated

Drunk as a brewer's fart

Drunk as a fiddler's bitch

Drunk as a lord

Due for drydock

Elephants

Enjoying a rest from sobriety

Feeling no pain

Five sheets to the wind

Flown with the wild turkey

Full as a boot

Full as a catholic school

Gambrinous

Half-seas over

Has his head on backwards

He hath seen the French king

He hath swallowed a tavern token

He's eaten a load and a half for breakfast

He's had a date with John Barleycorn

He's had a thump over the head with Samson's jawbone

He's had his nose painted

He's so drunk he opens his collar to piss

In uncharted waters

Isle of Wight

Knows not the way home

Lit up like a Christmas tree

Loaded to the Plimsoll line

Obfuscated

One over the eight

Pissed as a handcart

Pot-valiant

Put to bed with a shovel

Reached a hundred proof

Sniffed the barmaid's apron

Somebody stole his rudder

Taken by the head

Tired and emotional

Under the affluence of incohol

Walking with his head back (so as not to spill any)

Zonked

Hangover Cures

Take the juice of two quarts of whisky . . .

Eddie Condon

A martini made of 1 part vermouth, 4 parts gin and one olive, to be taken around the clock

W C Fields

Stick thirteen pins into the cork of the bottle you were drinking from.

Haitian Voodoo cure

Moderation is true temperance.

Motto of Yates's Wine Lodges Ltd

Report of the Committee of the Brick Lane Branch of the United Grand Junction Ebenezer Temperance Association

'Your committee have pursued their grateful labours during the past month, and have the unspeakable pleasure of reporting the following additional cases of converts to Temperance.

'H. Walker, tailor, wife and two children. When in better circumstances, owns to having been in the constant habit of drinking ale and beer; says he is not certain whether he did not twice a week, for twenty years, taste "dog's nose," which your committe find upon inquiry, to be compounded of warm porter, moist sugar, gin, and nutmeg (a groan, and "So it is!" from an elderly female). Is now out of work and penniless; thinks it must be the porter (cheers) or the loss of the use of his right hand; is not certain which, but thinks it very likely that, if he had drunk nothing but water all his life, his fellow workman would never have stuck a rusty needle in him, and thereby occasioned his accident (tremendous cheering). Has nothing but cold water to drink, and never feels thirsty (great applause).

'Betsy Martin, widow, one child, and one eye. Goes out charing and washing, by the day; never had more than one eye, but knows her mother drank bottled stout, and shouldn't wonder if that caused it (immense cheering). Thinks it not impossible that if she had always abstained from spirits, she might have had two eyes by this time (tremendous applause). Used, at every place she went to, to have eighteen pence a day, a pint of porter, and a glass of spirits; but since she became a member of the Brick Lane Branch, has always demanded three and sixpence instead (the announcement of this most interesting fact was received with deafening enthusiasm).

'Henry Beller was for many years toast-master at various corporation dinners, during which time he drank a great deal of foreign wine; may sometimes have carried a bottle or two home with him; is not quite certain of that, but is sure if he did, that he drank the contents. Feels very low and melancholy, is very feverish, and has a constant thirst upon him; thinks it must be the wine he used to drink (cheers). Is out of employ now; and never touches a drop of foreign wine by any chance (tremendous plaudits).

'Thomas Burton is purveyor of cat's meat to the Lord Mayor and Sheriffs, and several members of the Common Council (the announcement of this gentleman's name was received with breathless interest). Has a wooden leg; finds a wooden leg expensive, going over the stones; used to wear second-hand wooden legs, and drink a glass of hot gin and water regularly every night – sometimes two (deep sighs). Found the second-hand wooden legs split and rot very quickly; is firmly persuaded that their constitution was undermined by the gin and water (prolonged cheering). Buys new wooden legs now, and drinks nothing but water and weak tea. The new legs last twice as long as the others used to do, and he attributes this solely to his temperate habits (triumphant cheers).'

Charles Dickens The Pickwick Papers

He left his pint in there!

Don't go out tonight dear father

Don't go out tonight dear father,
Don't refuse this once I pray,
Tell your comrades mother's dying,
Soon her soul will pass away.
Tell them too of darling Willy,
Him we all so much do love,
How his little form is drooping,
Soon to bloom again above.

Don't go out tonight dear father,
Think Oh think how sad we'll be,
When the angels come to take her,
Poppa won't be there to see.

Tell me that you love dear mother,
Lying in that cold, cold room,
You don't love your comrades better,
Cursing there in that saloon.
Oh dear father do not leave us,
Think Oh think how sad we'll be,
When the angels come to take her,
Poppa won't be there to see.

Don't go out tonight dear father,
Think Oh think how sad we'll be,
When the angels come to take her,
Poppa won't be there to see.

Morning found the little pleader,
Cold and helpless on the floor,
Lying where he badly struck her,
On that chilly night before.
Lying there with hands uplifted,
Feebly uttering words of prayer,
Heavn'ly father please forgive him,
Reunite us all up there.

Don't go out tonight dear father,
Think Oh think how sad we'll be.
When the angels come to take her,
Poppa won't be there to see.

Anon

Teetotal Taverns

The White Swan in Well Lane (Chapel Allerton) had a chequered history. It lost its licence in 1867 possibly because of rowdiness and turned full circle to become a teetotal social club, one of the first of the British Workmans Public Houses, with a sign that bore the inscription:

'A Public House without the drink
Where men may read, and smoke, and think
Then sober home return;

A stepping stone this house you'll find,
Come leave your rum and beer behind
And truer pleasures learn.'

It sold drinks that imitated the more famous alcoholic ones – Winterine was the temperance wine, Anti-Burton was the beer and aerated milk the champagne!

Barrie Pepper *Old Inns and Pubs of Leeds*

What will the drunkard do for ale?

What will the drunkard do for ale?
Shall I unfold my dreadful tale?
Yes! I'll unfold it if I can,
To benefit a drunken man.
What will a drunkard do for ale?
It'll make a sober man turn pale.
Sell his hat and pawn his coat
To satisfy his greedy throat,
Sell his stockings and his shirt,
Strut about in rags and dirt.
Sell his shoes from off his feet,
And barefoot go about the streets.
What will he do to gain his end?
He will deceive his dearest friend.
His crafty plans he will devise,
And tell the most atrocious lies.
What will a drunkard do for ale?
Dark and dismal grows my tale.
Sell his bedstead and his bed,
Nor leave a place to lay his head,
Sell his blankets and his sheets,
Lie in barns or walk the streets.

His thirsty soul will cry for more,
He's starved and miserably poor.
He'll beg for ha'pence when he can,
And say he is a dying man,
But if three ha'pence he has got,
He'll go and find another sot
As mean and shabby as himself
A dirty, ragged, drunken elf,
In some alehouse corner seated,
Waiting, longing to be treated.
They freely enter into chat
If they can but catch a flat.
With everyone they will be friends
If they can but gain their ends.
Then with his bosom full of strife,
Each man goes home to beat his wife,
The children beat and sent to bed,
Because the wretches have no bread
No meat, no butter have they got,
Such is the dwelling of a sot.
The wife in tears and ragged too.
Say drunkard, is my story true?

I prefer temperance hotels – although they sell worse liquor than any other kind of hotels.

Artemus Ward

I'm only a beer teetotaller, not a champagne teetotaller.

George Bernard Shaw *Candida*

People who don't drink are temperance to the shilling.

Alan Thompson

WEST MIDLANDS CAMPAIGN FOR FULL ALE

THE LAW

SAYS A PINT OF BEER CAN INCLUDE THE HEAD. THE WEST MIDLANDS CONSUMER SERVICES DEPARTMENT WANTS BEER DRINKERS TO GET WHAT THEY PAY FOR— WITHOUT ASKING FOR MORE!

West Midlands County Council
CONSUMER SERVICES DEPT.
D.I.Y. BEER GAUGE
PLACE AGAINST BEER MUG RIM

BLISS! ——

DO YOU NEED A TOP UP? ——

DO YOU NEED A TRADING STANDARDS OFFICER ? ——

DO YOU NEED ANOTHER LOCAL? ——

West Midlands drinkers fight back

CHAPTER 7

CAMPAIGNING

Publicans versus Public

During the last few months there has been a series of incidents in London and elsewhere, which has focussed public opinion on the licensing trade and the laws which presumably govern it. The trade has enjoyed a sheltered existence, and while the revenue materially helped to balance each year's Budget, successive governments were not apparently concerned with the rights of the public-house user or the responsibilities of the licensee.

During the war the average licensee has had the time of his life, with demand exceeding supply, and with little or no control over the prices charged to customers. In hundreds of pubs, full or fair measure has been the exception, and any customer who had the temerity to demur at short measure was disregarded or insulted. Drippings from other customers' glasses have been served up after being 'topped-up' from the tap, and spirits and bottled beers served at prices determined by the licensee alone. The sale of spirits has been nothing less than a ramp, some public-houses charging 2s. 6d. for a nip, which gives the licensee a profit of £2 17s. 6d. on the bottle.

At the recent Brewster Sessions at Epping, a customer complained he had been charged 4d. per pint extra for mild ale in the saloon bar, although, as there were no glasses, he could not be served in the public bar. He further complained of short measure, and although he pointed this out to the licensee, the latter made no effort to give him full measure. Having been overcharged and given short measure, he had to suffer the indignity of being refused further service by the licensee. The Bench over-ruled the objection and told the objector:-

1. The question of charges was a matter for the licensee and the brewer.
2. Short measure should have been reported to a police officer or inspector of weights and measures.
3. Refusal to serve was a matter for a civil court.

In regard to (1), the brewers state that they do not propose to make any statement; (2) the public-house in question is situated in a country district, where it would puzzle anyone to find either a police officer or a weights inspector! The dictum of the Bench in this case is made more interesting by the fact that they have just stated 'that the Bench have decided to make periodical visits to the licensed premises in their division.' Comment would be superfluous.

But an even more flagrant case comes to us from Luton, where a weights and measures inspector summoned licensees for short measure, averaging from 5 per cent. to $7\frac{1}{2}$ per cent. The facts were not disputed, but counsel put up the extraordinary defence that, whilst they must not give short measure, they were under a penalty if they gave over measure. Apparently no one thought of asking how it was possible to give over measure in legally marked pint or half-pint glasses! These cases were dismissed on payment of costs, but if a grocer had given one ounce short in a pound of margarine, or if a milkman had served milk deficient in fat, there would surely have been convictions with heavy penalties.

The Shaftesbury Avenue case is well in the public eye, where our hon. secretary, who has used the pub regularly for thirty years, was refused service.

Although there have been several prosecutions lately, Customs and Excise would be well advised to make a thorough investigation regarding the dilution of spirits, and the Income Tax authorities might make further inquiry regarding the profits of licensees. If assessed on the normal profits of their sales prior to the war, the question naturally arises: 'What has become of the additional profits made during the war as the direct result of short measure and gross overcharging?'

The campaign to deal with bad publicans has met with a wide and active response. Hundreds of letters have been received from all over the country, and quite a number have come from tenants or managers of licensed premises. Whilst we have neither the desire nor the intention of harming any licensee carrying on his business in a fair and just manner, we are determined to stop the extortionate methods adopted by others. There is no logical or other reason why the publican should not be compelled to give full measure, charge fair prices, and be as courteous as other traders.

We have already appointed 128 investigators and their efforts must be implemented by real assistance from the weights and measures inspectors everywhere. Whilst it may be true that inspectors have made hundreds of domiciliary visits and have tested thousands of glass measures, the fact still remains that they take no notice of the liquid content of the glasses served to customers. If this statement is challenged by the authorities, and they will provide us with the services of a few inspectors, we guarantee to provide them with hundreds of instances where short measure is given.

The vast majority of public-house customers are workers, manual or otherwise, and the present Government could introduce legislation which would end the majority of the evils of the pub. Beer comes under the Sale of Food (Weights and Measures) Act, 1926. It certainly is one of the staple foods for workers and surely some control should be placed on the cost. I wonder if anyone would agree with any publican who, having no glasses in the public bar, charges 5d. per pint extra in the saloon bar! And the right of the publican to serve a respectable citizen, with or without cause, should be reviewed. Under the existing law, the publican has the legal right to serve prostitutes or other undesirables, but can refuse a well-conducted person. In one case the publican refused to serve a gentleman who had complained of overcharging and short measure. If this is not a travesty of justice, then any proved or suspected delinquent can openly insult any minion of the law who calls upon him.

With a strong and resolute President in the person of Mr Fred Potter, and Messrs. Wm Vickery, Ewart Wheeler, and Townley Searle as our principal

Executive officers, we are determined to *end this corrupt system and secure justice for the Man-in-the-Pub.*

Manifesto of the short-lived Pub Users' Protection Society, May 1946

Pint in Hand

Keg, or not to keg; that is the question.
Whether 'tis nobler for the gut to suffer
The effect of CO_2 in dustbin beer
Or take arms against the sea of bubbles
And, by boycott, to end them . . .

Society for the Preservation of Beers from the Wood (founded 1963)

London Beer

The state of London beer is a telling microcosm of London itself. The old small breweries have largely been swallowed up and their individual tastes have been replaced by mass-produced flavours, which in London tend to be unpleasantly tinny, without any bouquet. The stuff is undeniably strong, but whoever drank beer just to get drunk? Of the big breweries the best is Whitbread's – very good when on form, but be careful, because not all Whitbread pubs sell Whitbread bitter. From the smaller breweries, the best beer by far, to my taste, is Fuller's London Pride, brewed next to Chiswick Church and sold over a wide area of West London. But when in doubt, go for the two Burton standbys, Draught Bass and Worthington E. One will give you more kick at the time and one will give you less kick the morning after and I suggest you find out which is which.

All this refers to proper draught beer. If you are forced into drinking keg, which is a kind of bottled beer in big cans – some London pubs sell only keg, especially if they want to put on airs – then my advice is the same: Canister Bass or Canister Worthington E, and also Flower's Keg, which comes from Stratford-on-Avon. Draught Guinness, from Park Royal, is of course in a class by itself. Good drinking!

Ian Nairn *Nairn's London, 1966*

Politicians at Work

EARLY DAY MOTION 27th February 1973

Mr Roy Mason
Mr Douglas Jay
Mr George Darling

Mr Goronwy Roberts
Mr Frederick Willey
Mr George Thomas

That this House views with concern the growth of the Tied-house system in regard to beer supply; notes that HMG has not adopted the recommendations of the Monopolies Commission which concluded that the Brewers' Tied-house system operates against the public interest, restricts competition, is detrimental to efficiency in brewing, wholesaling and retailing and is especially detrimental to the interests of the independent supplier and consumers; is further concerned that the brewery monopolies are riding roughshod over consumer interests by closing regionally based breweries, thereby depriving consumers of their local brews; invites local authorities to use their powers to deprive such monopolists of sites for expansion; and calls upon HMG to carry out the Monopolies Commission recommendations without delay.

(Total signatories: 166)

K.B. v GROTNYS...

The Death of the English Pub

There is a pub in north-west London, which I sometimes visited during the early stages of research for this book. The public bar was a favourite gathering place for pensioners in the area, who used to enjoy a couple of drinks and a natter or a game of cribbage or dominoes. In the middle of 1972 the elderly tenant and his wife retired, and the pub was immediately closed for 'extensive alterations' according to the contractors notice outside. When it re-opened three months later, the public bar had been knocked through into the saloon, and the whole area covered with wall-to-wall carpeting. The tenant had been replaced by a manager who no longer kept the dominoes or the cribbage board behind the bar – nor even the darts, for this board too had been removed. the beer pumps had vanished to make way for a set of keg dispensers and all the prices were several pence up on those charged before the closure.

During the first lunchtime session after the pub reopened, the pensioners arrived one by one to renew their old habits. They were told immediately that their custom was no longer wanted, that the pub was aiming for a different trade. In spite of a petition on their behalf signed by several hundred people, and sympathetic coverage in the local press, they have been thrown out for good. Those who can travel to other pubs in the area do so in smaller groups: those who can't, stay at home.

This is not an isolated case. There are thousands of similar instances, many not quite so devastating to the local community, some even worse. The nature of most of the pubs that we know and have used has been changed out of all recognition in the last ten years and the bulldozer still seems to be gathering power and pace. People sit in bar corners bemoaning the declining strength and flavour of their pint. Articles about the destruction of character in old pubs appear in the press from time to time. When a tenant is given notice to quit by his brewery so that a manager can be installed, his regulars usually get up a petition. With a few exceptions, however, people have not effectively resisted the changes that have been forced upon their pubs. On the face of it, the reason could be that they do not care about these changes, even that they welcome them. Anyone who knows a pub that has been tarted up and given the gimmick treatment, or where a longstanding and popular tenant has been sacked, or where the local beer has been discontinued after a takeover, will know that this is not true. People do care greatly about what happens to their local. The problem is that where English men and women are quick to organise effectively when their home is threatened by a road scheme, or their work by a redundancy plan, they quite naturally prefer to take a more casual approach towards their leisure facilities, in the relaxed but misplaced belief that these will not be spoilt.

The growing band of environmentalists, while they are beginning to achieve so much in so many areas, have a blind spot where the pub is concerned. Its preservation should be among their highest priorities. After home and work-place most people probably spend more time in their local pub than anywhere else, more so even than the supermarket, the cinema or the local beauty spot. Some people may disapprove of this, but it is nevertheless a fact. What happens to a happy spirited pub, however smoke-filled the atmosphere, and even if too much alcohol is occasionally consumed, is just as much an environmental issue as the future of Covent Garden, or what we do about pollution in the River Trent.

This is not to say that all change should be blindly resisted on the assumption that what is old is always best. Of course the pub is bound to change in some ways, and indeed needs to do so if it is to keep its vitality in the future. A great deal of money has been well spent in providing kitchen facilities so that people can have a snack as well as a pint. The standards of modern sanitation are obviously preferable to those of the nineteenth century on grounds of both hygiene and comfort. Not all old pubs are cheerful and welcoming, and those which are not can certainly benefit from a careful facelift. But items such as these account for only a small proportion of the brewer's massive spending on their tied estate. Much of this budget is used to force unwelcome change on unwilling consumers, and this is what the argument is about.

This situation has arisen because of the way the brewing industry has changed as a result of the unprecedented spate of mergers and takeovers in recent years. Fifteen years ago the industry consisted of hundreds of individual companies competing with one another locally and regionally, each producing local beers to suit local tastes. Today seven companies account for more than 80 per cent of beer sales in this country. They are: Allied Breweries, Bass Charrington, Courage, Guinness, Scottish and New-castle, Watneys and Whitbread. Guinness is excluded from the broad scope of this book's argument, firstly because it owns no pubs, and secondly because its major product has not been reduced significantly in strength or flavour. The behaviour of the remaining companies, the 'bix six' as it is convenient to call them, is the root cause of the death of the English pub. They each own several thousand pubs, and partly because of their very size, have lost touch with the real needs and wants of their customers. None of them is any longer run by a brewer. They are commanded partly by marketing men, whose objectives are to banish quality and variety and to replace them with consistent mediocrity. Even the *Financial Times* has described the 'big six' as

> 'the major brewers whose goal is to own no more than half a dozen national brands each, all being pumped out non-stop by the most up-to-date methods available.'

The approach of the marketing men is matched by that of the accountants, who view their companies' pubs as good objects for the application of their property development mentality, and refer to houses that don't fill up until nine o'clock as 'redundant units.'

The 'big six,' of course, employ hordes of public relations men whose function is ultimately to persuade people to settle for what they don't really want. These P.R. men are given to bland generalisations about the changes that their companies are making. This approach completely misses the point because you can't generalise about pubs, the people who use them and their differing tastes in beer. That is why this book aims as far as possible to deal with individuals and small groups of people as the basis for its arguments.

When you order a pint of beer and hand over your money, you are paying for a complicated package deal. As well as the beer in your glass, the deal includes the barmaid's smile or the landlord's bonhomie, the opportunity to buy a sandwich or have a game of darts, the chance either to find a corner to chat with friends or stand at the bar and meet a stranger to the pub. In other words to enjoy the intangible but crucial feeling which is called atmosphere.

The pre-requisite of 'atmosphere' in any pub is that it should serve a good pint of beer. Writing about drink is to risk the pitfalls of pretension and pomposity, as many wine correspondents of the posh Sundays have found to their cost, and as 'Pseuds Corner' in *Private Eye* has discovered to its delight. These pitfalls are best represented by the ridiculous figure in the Thurber cartoon, who, while opening a bottle of plonk as his guests sit down for dinner at his table, announces: 'It is only a naive domestic Burgundy without any breeding but I think you'll be amused by its presumption.'

In writing about the different approaches of individual breweries and the beer they produce, I have not found it necessary to construct a league table of taste or quality. Taste varies and so, therefore, do judgements of quality. But there is one trend in the making and serving of beer that deserves to be wholeheartedly condemned. This is the application of carbon dioxide pressure to the barrel to force the beer to the point of dispense. This gas gets into the beer, putting an unpleasant tang where flavour should be, and causing acidity in the stomach. Pressurisation is alien to a well-brewed and well-kept pint of draught beer, and yet it is now the rule rather than the exception in most parts of the country. It is an innovation that is designed to cover up the weaknesses of an inferior product, served by a landlord who cannot be bothered to keep his pipes clean. It is part of the trend to standardisation (rather than variety, quality, and even eccentricity of flavour) which is killing the English pub.

This trend to standardisation affects all aspects of the pub, its facilities and activities, as well as the beer itself. More and more tenants are being replaced by brewery-employed managers. The manager can be told what items to stock, while the tenant is freer to order the products his customers demand, and serve them in the way they like. The tenant furnishes his own pub, while the managed house is kitted out in fabrics and designs bought in bulk and repeated in pubs in dozens of towns. More and more small breweries are taken over each year. Local beers are discontinued and replaced with tasteless national brands. There are so many ways in which the trend to standardisation in our pubs expresses itself, and most of them are covered in subsequent chapters. Standardisation, of course, means elimination of choice and is the enemy of the distinctive but infinitely variable atmosphere that is the hallmark of the really good pub. As the major brewers have increased in size, they have become less and less accountable to the public it is their job to serve. They are already guilty, in my view, of what would elsewhere be termed robbery and violence. They have robbed the public of so many vital aspects of their leisure, and their violence has already caused the death of thousands of pubs. There are still many corners of excellence and variety in the brewing industry and the licensed trade. But if the major brewers are allowed to move with as much freedom and as little accountability in the next ten years as they have for the last ten, then the death of the English pub, which has already happened in many parts of the country, could well be accomplished everywhere.

Christopher Hutt, 1973

The Quest for a Decent Pint

Every drinker has heard it said that there is no bad beer, but some is just better than the rest. It's an old tale, which has never borne any truth. But today it is even further off the mark than ever.

Two major developments are threatening to kill off good ale once and for all:

the large-scale promotion of characterless keg and tank beers at an advertising cost of millions of pounds a year; and

the transfer from traditional methods of serving draught beer to pumps using carbon dioxide pressure, which makes ale gassy and sickly.

On top of which, the closure of dozens of breweries in England and Wales in the past few years has robbed the beer drinker of much of the choice he used to have. Six companies now own more than 60 per cent of our pubs and because they have started to standardise our beer, it is becoming more and more difficult to find a pint with any character. Large brewing factories near the motorways are supplying beer for whole regions of the country, where once there were dozens of little breweries each producing ales of different strengths and flavours.

The big brewers say there is plenty of choice – more than 1,500 brands of beer currently available in Britain. But this is no consolation for the man in a little Norfolk town who can find nothing but the fizzy products of one big group within a ten-mile radius of his home. Nor does it cheer up the poor fellow visiting London for the weekend who can find plenty of apparent choice, but nothing that he can call enjoyable.

This guide is designed to help people who are searching for a decent drop of ale anywhere in England, Wales or the Isle of Man. It is not just another pub guide recommending the unsuspecting traveller to places cluttered up with horse brasses or landlords who won a runners-up medal in the 1949 FA Cup Final. It is for the millions of people who spend millions of pounds a year between them on beer – and deserve a product of quality.

The Good Beer Guide is completely independent of any interest in the brewing industry or licensing trade. Pubs have been selected entirely on the merit of their beer – and, unlike one guide published in recent times, no one has been given the chance to buy his way into it. Some pubs have even been included despite the landlords' insistence on their exclusion. This guide is for the benefit of beer drinkers – to guide them towards good beer – not to please brewers or licensees, though in many cases this will undoubtedly be a welcome by-product.

The guide has been drawn up from reports compiled voluntarily by members of the Campaign for Real Ale. It is not suggested that the 1,500 or so pubs listed are the best in the country – nor that every town or village has been covered. Some towns have, in fact, been covered inadequately. The guide does, *however*, contain the names of the best pubs that have been found. If you find others which are more worthy of mention, please write to CAMRA and they'll be considered for possible inclusion in future editions.

A final word of warning about the pubs you are likely to find if you follow the Good Beer Guide. Some of them are, quite honestly, rough; others may be too posh. But in between these two extremes, there are pubs to suit all tastes. And beers to suit most palates.

John Hanscomb, Editor, Good Beer Guide, 1974

Good Things

When I was almost fifteen my elder brother took me to a pub. This made me feel very bold, and I could hardly refuse the even more grown-up offer of half a pint. I'd had bottled beer at home, but never draught bitter. The first sip was horrific. I vividly remember the shiver that went down my spine at the appalling bitterness of the stuff, and the dismay with which I registered the sheer quantity that was half a pint. We were somewhere near Westerham at the time, so it was probably a Fremlin's pub, or else Westerham Ales (which no longer exists). In any case it was probably strongly hopped, as was usual in the hop-growing county of Kent. Somehow I got through that half, but I'm sure I didn't have any more that day. Over the next year or two the experience was repeated and I came to tolerate and then actually enjoy the taste.

This must be a fairly common experience. In *A Sort of Life* Graham Greene describes his first taste of beer:

> I was offered beer first by Lubbock, my riding master, whom I visited one evening in summer. I hated the taste and drank it down with an effort to prove my manliness, and yet some days later, on a long country walk with Raymond, the memory of the taste came back to taunt my thirst. We stopped at an inn for bread and cheese, and I drank bitter for the second time and enjoyed the taste with a pleasure that has never failed me since.

I have no idea who brewed any of the beer I drank in the years immediately before, during and after my time at university, with the single exception of an especially delicious pint of draught Bass in a pub somewhere underground near Charing Cross station. In those days one chose a pub more or less at random and simply asked for bitter. I did, however, have a friend I considered unduly fussy who used to make a point of avoiding Watney's pubs.

Cambridge and a couple of years knocking about in London was followed by a spell abroad in Sweden and France. In Paris the drink was naturally wine. It's the best in the world and at that time was cheap, whereas the beer was expensive and in the case of the *pression* (draught) tasted of metal polish. By the time I returned to England in the mid-1960s I was looking forward to getting back to English beer – only to find that I didn't like it. I attributed my disappointment to a change in taste caused by a year in Paris, and accordingly drank wine and spirits and sometimes, without much pleasure, beer. Looking back I can remember two experiences which should have shown that it was not me that had changed but the beer. Some time around 1965 I went for a holiday which took me by train through Germany, Czechoslovakia and Austria. This was before Dubcek's time, and Novotny's Prague must have been a tough place to live in. To me it seemed delightful. The setting of the city was magnificent, the architecture grand without being intimidating; the eye was not constantly assaulted by advertisements, nor the lungs, ears and human life itself endangered by roaring, polluting automobiles. The food was stodgy, low in taste and protein, but my God the beer was good. I had only intended to stay in Prague for two days: I knew no one there, I hadn't much money and there was little to do. I stayed nearly a week, going from place to place drinking this wonderful beer and feeling more and more like the good soldier Svejk.

At least I liked Czech beer. I liked some English beer too, for it must have been around the same time that my brother, who had emigrated to Australia, returned home for the first time in five years. One evening we took my mother out from Whitstable, where she was living, to a place we had spotted in the *Good Food Guide*. It was a pub called the Red Lion at Wingham, and before the meal we had some beer. Ten years is a long time, memory blurs and taste changes, but I would still say that it was the best beer I've ever drunk. At a time when I thought I didn't like English beer, I liked it. My brother, who had come back making unfavourable comparisons between English beer and Australian, liked it. My mother, who probably drinks as much beer in ten years as a Sheffield steel-worker in a weekend, liked it. We had intended to have wine with the meal, but all agreed to go on as we had started. It was the very poetry of beer.

Later I learnt that it was brewed by Gardner's of Ash, which supplied only two or three pubs. Shortly afterwards Gardner's was taken over by Tomson and Wotton, which was in turn swallowed by Whitbread's. The Red Lion now serves Whitbread Trophy.

If the Czech experience had shown me I still liked beer, the Gardner's one should have shown me that I still liked English beer, though not what was in most of the pubs in London. I now realize that the reason I went off beer in

ANNOUNCES
THE INAUGURAL MEETING
of the
BANGOR BRANCH
to be held in
THE BULKELEY ARMS
Caernarfon Road Bangor
at 8·15 on Wed 2lst Jan
Croeso I Bawb I Gyfarfod Cyntaf
Yn Y Cylch O Ganeng Cwrw Gwir

YMGYRCh
CWRW GWIR

The Movement grows...

general in the mid-1960s was that without my knowing it I was drinking something different. By merely asking for bitter, or mouthing a name I had seen in television advertisements, I was getting something sweet and gassy which I didn't like – in short, keg beer. A friend once tried to explain it all to me, but it seemed rather technical: besides, I was growing to like bottled Guinness.

In 1972, while suffering from a severe cash-flow crisis, I undertook some hack-work for an American firm on a guide to London pubs. The book never appeared, but going round a number of pubs was an educational experience. First I was appalled by what the brewers had done to pubs I hadn't visited for years: then I gradually began to realize what they had done to the beer. The familiar hand pumps were rapidly vanishing, being replaced by top-pressure CO_2 systems that made the beer fizzy. Even worse, the traditional draught beer (in whatever way it was served) was becoming hard to find and the much-advertised, gaudily-presented keg beers were being vigorously promoted.

There was still good beer to be found, even in London, but you had to look for it. In central London most of it was in Bass Charrington pubs, where real beer was often still delivered by hand pumps. Further out were the Young's pubs, mostly in the Wandsworth area, and Fuller, Smith and Turner's over at Chiswick. These independent breweries showed that not all beer tastes the same.

I awoke to what was happening to English beer at about the same time as many other people. The idea of writing a beer column started in a fairly jokey kind of way. A reader had written to the *Guardian* pointing out that there were plenty of wine correspondents about but no one to lead the beer drinker through the thickets. I talked about it with Michael McNay and Harold Jackson of the *Guardian* and we agreed it was a good idea. One could have a go at the big brewers; one could point to the surviving local brewers of traditional beer; there was pub architecture; pub games, pubs in literature – oh yes, there was material for several weeks at least. Accordingly in the summer of 1973 I started writing a weekly column, appearing on Saturdays, on beer, pubs and allied topics.

It quickly became apparent that the idea interested far more people than we had expected. Letters poured in, full of suggestions, information, appreciation and encouragement. I take no particular credit for the fact that 'Boston on Beer,' as the column came to be called, acted as something of a catalyst. The same would have happened if the column had been much better or much worse. By a chance that for me was a happy one, there was nothing else like it anywhere around. Thanks to the *Guardian* and its readers I was able to collect and pass on information about breweries that were still producing traditional beer (mostly the surviving independent regional breweries), to attack what the big companies were doing to beer and pubs, and generally to write about the subject in a way appropriate to what is after all a major part of the nation's leisure activities.

Teasing and baiting the big breweries was great fun, but what was also needed if they were to be made to feel the weight of the consumers' demands was some kind of organized body, and this was provided with skill and some panache by Camra (the Campaign for Real Ale).

I think that three years ago the most anyone hoped for was that our protests and derision might, even if only ever so slightly, slow down what the big bad brewers were doing to beer and pubs. Within two years it was apparent not only that this was happening but also that the brewers were actually changing tack and reversing previous policies. The consumer revolt against the big brewers that has taken place in the past three or four years is unique. I know of no other industry of this size that has been checked in the direction it had taken by the massive resistance of the customers. This is gratifying to beer drinkers, but the achievement is one that is important to others as well. It has demonstrated that we need not be endlessly manipulated by the forces of the state or big business.

We should be able to take the simple things for granted. It is ridiculous that we have to seek out a good loaf of bread as though hunting for a gastronomic luxury, but it's no exaggeration to say that in some parts of the country good bread is as rare as truffles. Unless you can find a health food shop or one of the diminishing number of one-man bakeries you're almost certain to find yourself with presliced bread wrapped in waxed paper: it is never really fresh but it takes a long time to go stale (it usually goes mouldy first); it's expensive, has no taste, and on being eaten forms a wedge like a clenched fist high up in the chest where it can cause acute discomfort for hours.

The sausage is increasingly a standardized product, low in flavour and dubious in contents. As Jane Grigson says (in her book from which I have borrowed the title of this chapter), 'It is easier to put no seasoning to speak of into a sausage – it offends nobody, everybody buys it. This is the theory. We're back to the primitive idea of eating to keep alive.'

Eggs are pale in shell and yolk, and are laid by hens in concentration camps. Kippers are dyed and packed in plastic: the real thing is almost unobtainable. Instead of those wrinkled, scarred, funny-shaped green-and-red delicious tomatoes you get in Italy, we are sold tomatoes that are perfectly red, perfectly round and almost perfectly tasteless.

What all these things have in common is blandness, an absence of character. They're not sweet and they're not sour, they're not stale and they're not fresh. They are offensive for their inoffensiveness, like the Laodiceans denounced by St John the Divine in *Revelation*: 'I know thy works, that thou are neither cold nor hot: I would thou wert cold or hot. So then because thou art lukewarm, and neither cold nor hot, I will spue thee out of my mouth.'

Today you have to go out of your way to find real bread, or Cheddar cheese with a rind on, or fresh chickens, or eggs from free-range hens. The battle for these things was lost without a shot being fired. This resulted partly from a shameful indifference on the part of the consumer, partly from defeatism. Standardized, mass-produced and extremely expensive convenience foods have replaced varied, and variable, local produce. The reasons why the major brewers were keen to replace traditional beer with what is called keg beer will be explained later. Here it is sufficient to say that keg beer is a Laodicean product in every respect except that it is not lukewarm: usually it is served rather cold, in order to disguise its lack of taste. Its character, however, is utterly lukewarm. Whereas real beer can be very good or very bad, keg is consistently mediocre. It is an exaggeration to say that much-promoted drinks like Watney's Red, Allied's Double Diamond, Courage's Tavern, Younger's Tartan, Whitbread's Tankard and keg Worthington E are revolting. The exaggeration is pardonable but it is still an exaggeration. They don't actually make your gorge rise, which the very worst of real beer could conceivably do. But they are sweet and gassy, like Coca-Cola and all sorts of mineral waters which I don't personally like but which I can drink without vomiting. What I want when I ask for a pint of bitter is something quite different, a beer that is fairly flat in appearance, that is served at about room temperature, that smacks of hops and tastes bitter.

Unlike the consumers of bread and cheese, beer drinkers woke up in time to protest successfully against standardization. By the beginning of 1975 I began to feel that so far as my *Guardian* column was concerned, I could let up a little. The information had been put across, in so far as it was ever going to be, and the polemical points had been made. Accordingly the column ceased to be exclusively about beer and pubs, and turned to other matters while continuing to make frequent trips to Publand. That inexhaustibly fascinating country is the subject of this book. In spite of the worst the big brewers have been able to do, there is still fine English beer, and there are still fine English pubs. Though there is much to criticize, there is still more to celebrate.

Richard Boston *Beer and Skittles*

Official Recognition

Restrictions:
1. To sell bottled beer of all descriptions and draught beer that is brewed from the traditional materials and allowed to mature in the barrel after leaving the brewery, and served to the consumer without the introduction of extraneous gas.

From the licence of the Brahms and Liszt public house in Leeds, granted in March, 1976

The Biter Bit

DD is 4 U

1976 advertising gimmick for Double Diamond

DD is K9P

CAMRA response

CAMRA spreads its wings

STATEMENT BY THE CHAIRMAN

INTRODUCTION

In 1974, the National Executive of CAMRA decided to promote the launch of a Company whose main purpose would be to acquire and operate public houses specialising in the sale of traditional draught beer, in simple and unfussy surroundings. The Company was to be financially and legally separate from CAMRA, so that both organisations could concentrate on their own functions, and so that members' and shareholders' money could be accounted for separately, and their different rights defined. The close link between the two organisations was recognised in the assurance given by the Directors of the Company that they saw their operations as being 'a development of CAMRA's own activities', and that they would act, 'according to the spirit of CAMRA itself.'

CAMRA (Real Ale) Investments Limited was incorporated on 17th October 1974. A Prospectus was published on 24th October 1974 in connection with the issue of up to 250,000 shares of £1 each at par. This issue was largely successful in that 190,680 shares were subscribed for during a period when the investment markets were in their most depressed state since the last war. The vast majority of the Company's inaugural shareholders were also members of CAMRA. The Company began with many small shareholders rather than a few large ones, and this we consider to be a source of strength. The largest shareholder accounts for fewer than 2 per cent of the Company's issued shares.

Introduction to the Report and Accounts of CAMRA (Real Ale) Investments Limited, 1976

What's Brewing – the Programme

Barrie. We present Tap Room Tales by Gerry Garside – an endless saga of the fight to preserve the traditional aspects of beer and pubs

Episode one – The price of a pint.

The scene is the tap room of the Plastered Parrot, a real ale pub in a working class suburb of a West Riding town. The time is half an hour before closing time on a weekday evening.

Let me introduce you to the cast.

Nora Nockers is an occasional barmaid; Yorkie Bale is a retired shoddy merchant, Shufflem Round is the pub domino captain and Barum Hall is the landlord. Charlie Chock, Gordon Spile, Andrew Mallet and Peter Barrel are members of the Campaign for Real Ale. Girlington Gertie is an aging ex-chorus girl and we present Lars Torders a Swedish Steel worker.

door open and close/footsteps

Quietly . . . Charlie, Gordon and Andrew have just entered and are leaning on the bar talking to Nora. The landlord lingers in the background reading the Morning Advertiser. Shufflem and three others are playing dominoes and Girlington Gertie is perched on the edge of a corner stool with a part consumed glass of Guinness.

Charlie. Three pints of bitter please Nora.

Nora. (handpump sound) Eighty-seven pence please.

Charlie. My God has it gone up again?

Barum. Aye, Brewery's put another penny on.

Gordon. What excuse this time?

Barum. Increased cost of CO_2 cylinders.

Andrew. Its always us what suffers – I don't want any CO_2 pressurised ale. It's ridiculous. And when's that lager going to be taken out?

Barum. It's not. Can't afford to. Lose too many best room customers.

Gordon. Has lager gone up as well?

Barum. No, brewery say public won't stand for a penny on lager, it has to go on beer.

Charlie. Anyway, bitter here's still fourpence cheaper than that Twitbreads in the Bloated Baboon up t'road.

Andrew. That's by the way, we never drink t'stuff. (drinks) Three more pints of your overpriced bitter please, Nora.

Nora. Don't take it out on me, I only pullem.

Gordon. There's no answer to that.

Barum. Come on lads you know Nora's a good worker and never let's us down in a crisis.

Charlie. There's no answer to that either.

Barrie. Yorkie Bale comes in in a raincoat and an old trilby, puffing on a curved pipe which emits an evil smell

(coughs from several players)

Yorkie.   Pint of mild.

Nora.   Twenty seven please.

Yorkie.   That's nearly six bob – has it gone up again?.

Barum.   Aye, brewery increase.

Yorkie.   (Slowly) I remember when you could get four pints, ten fags, a box o' matches and *still* have change out of half a crown.

All.   Oh, not again.

Shufflem.   Better drink that up quick Yorkie in case it goes up in t'next five minutes.

Yorkie.   I wouldn't be capped at that, neither. (Footsteps away) Inflation – strikes – falling pound – foreign cars everywhere – incompetent government. I tell you, its only ale that keeps me from committing suicide.

Shufflem.   What are you talking about. You've made your pile & retired.

Yorkie.   Never. Anyway, what do you think its worth now. NOWT.

(Door opens and closes, footsteps)

Gordon.   Why it's Peter Barrel, a founder member of the old West Yorkshire branch of CAMRA. Haven't seen you for ages, Pete, where've you been?

Peter.   Working down south.

Andrew.   Oh, don't pull that old gag on us.

Peter.   No honestly. Anyway there is some good ale down there, so that John Brights advert is a load of rubbish.

Gordon.   Three pints please; better make if four, Nora, one for Pete.

Nora.   Hundred and sixteen please.

Peter.   Has it gone up again?

Charlie.   Aye, CO_2 cylinder price increase.

Peter.   Ridiculous.

Yorkie.   I remember the time when . . . (Interruptions of 'Oh No/Not again)

Charlie.   And its different everywhere, 29 here, 33 in't Bloated Baboon, 30 in the Easy Swallow.

Peter.   What about doing a survey to see how it varies and which places do the cheapest pints?

Gordon.   Great idea.

Peter.   Four pints of bitter please.

Barum.   (Quite loudly) Last orders please.

General milling around, with glass clinking, sounds off of 'Four pints Barum,' and lady says 'Guinness, Nora luv' . . .

Charlie.   Right, we'll start tomorrow, now how many pubs are there in the area?

Gordon.   Well the Medley's pubs are the Easy Swallow, the Clinging Top and this one.

Andrew.   Sam Smooths have the Mellow Pint and the Pull and Swiggitt.

Charlie.   And Timtays have the Electric Hop and the Riverside Experience.

Gordon.   Then there's the Hillock Sparrow, that's a Grabsters house and Chas Barrington have the Sadbrick.

Charlie.   Thats the real ale houses, but we ought to do the rest as well
Peter.   Include me out.
Charlie.   No fairs fair, we'll each do some. Gordon & me can do the John Bright's pubs – there's the Malt Extract . . .
Gordon.   . . . the Severed Head and the Hangmans Arms.
Andrew.   OK – Pete and I'll do the Twitbreads – that's the Bloated Baboon and the Klowdy Keg.
Peter.   And don't forget the Griping Gut on Bottom Dribble Road.
Charlie.   The only other one is Grabsters, The Pushbutton. We'll do that.
Andrew.   No there's the Ugly Rumour at Whispertown. I'll do it with Pete.
Gordon.   That's it then. Meet here at half past nine tomorrow and we'll compare prices.
Barum   Time Gentlemen (hesitantly) and er Lady, please.
Barrie.   At this moment Lars Torders the Swedish Steelworker comes in.
Barum.   Sorry Lars, towels are up.
Lars.   Bloddy hell, late again.
Barrie.   What will the survey show? Is there a cheaper pint than the Plastered Parrot. Listen to next month's thrilling installment when all is revealed.
Nora.   Watch it!

> Gerry Garside: Script of *Tap Room Talks*, episode 1 – *The Price of a Pint*, What's
> Brewing? programme, BBC Radio Leeds, August 1977

BEER LOVER

The Real Thing
(Definitely not Coke)

Some go to 't pub just to swill and carouse,
Some to escape from their nattering spouse,
Some to throw money in greedy machines,
Some to chew beermats to small smithereens,
Some just sit silent and ogle the birds,
But we've come to show them we're not lost for words.

We're all here for the real thing,
That's why we're singing this song
Just to show all those
Fancy TV promotions
That the customer's not always wrong,
So you'd better not
Give us pale imitations
Or gas us with chemical beer.
So just give us a pint of the real thing landlord,
'Cos that's why we're ruddy well here.

What pubs get up to to entice us along,
We're here to show them they've got it all wrong.
Those big busted barmaids are wasting their skills
Just pumping out all that push-button bilge.
We'll sing and we'll show them whenever we call
If we can't sup the real stuff we'll not sup at all.

We're all here for etc.,

Eddie Lawler

Peter Austin

Peter Austin, the father of the new brewery revolution, thought he had finished with malt and hops when he retired as head brewer of Hull Brewery in 1975, after 30 years, following the takeover of the company by Northern Foods.

'It was sold down the river,' he recalls. Disillusioned, he upped anchor from the mash tun and, his fishing rods across his shoulder, started a Hampshire sea-angling business. 'But it was too embarrassing. You see, there are no fish off this coast.

'Then the *Boston on Beer* column in *The Guardian* mentioned that they were looking for a brewer. And that's how, in 1977, I came to design a small plant for Monty Python comedian, Terry Jones, at Penrhos in Herefordshire.

'I remember the first brew very well. It was five o'clock one morning with bats flying about as we got up. It was the last possible day for brewing because the grand opening had to be before Terry Jones went to America.

'We got the mash in at six. The plumbers were ahead of us connecting up the next vessel. By 8am we were in the copper – it took hours to get it to boil – we were using oxibottles and every source of heat we had. It was a 20-hour marathon in all, but we did it.'

He added: 'Penrhos proved you can brew excellent beer on that sort of scale. It's a bit like making an omelette: it can be very difficult with only one egg; you could do it with a million eggs but it wouldn't be very good; but six to eight eggs is ideal.'

From there he not only set up his own brewery, with its famous Ringwood Best Bitter and Old Thumper, but spawned many more as he sold his equipment and consultancy skills far and wide. The list is endless: Archers, Ballards, Bourne Valley, right through the alphabet to Woods. He has helped set up over 40 breweries in 10 years, one every three months.

And he did not stop in England. It was one hop to Hilden in Belfast, and then another across the Atlantic to Newman's brewery in New York state, sparking the revolution in North America. When I arranged an interview with him in 1986, it was a case of fitting in a visit between his return from Nigeria, where he has established the 500-barrel a week Mopa Brewery, and his flying out to China, where he is working to set up small communal breweries.

The Chinese build his equipment under licence, for production in rural areas. 'Previously all their beer was lager from big breweries built by the Germans in the Thirties. Now they are brewing ale from a 40 per cent rice mash. It's simple. Customers come along with one-gallon containers on their bikes. Fill up and ride off.'

The big African brewery stretched his resources to the limit. It is so 'up country' that it was 230 km down a dirt road to the nearest telephone. And then you had to queue for eight hours. 'It was a week's work to get two nuts and bolts.'

Other contracts for 'Austin Rover,' the global brewer, include an experimental plant for a big German brewery; a home-brew pub in Leuven (the Belgian home-town of Stella Artois); and a real-ale brewery in France, La Brasserie des Deux Rivieres in Morlaix.

While spreading the gospel of good beer abroad, Peter Austin is concerned that the market for new beer at home is being strangled. 'Unless the tied-house system is broken, we will all start cutting each other's throats. We have enough new breweries in most parts of the country, and many are under-capitalised.'

Yet as the first chairman of the Small Independent Brewers Association, he is a great believer in new breweries. 'The re-introduction of small-scale brewing does not imply that some of the developments in technology used in large-scale brewing cannot be applied. Examples are the use of stainless-steel plant, in-place cleaning techniques and better understanding of the management of yeast.'

Among innovations of his own, he has produced a small cask washing machine, the Roundabout, and designed a new heating system to avoid charring hops. He is convinced small is beautiful.

'We have retained the basic principle of traditional brewing: we brew our beer using only malted barley, hops and yeast as did our forefathers. With our localised trade we do not need the wholly unnatural extension of shelf-life so vital to the operation of the giant brewing complexes. We do not find it necessary to filter, carbonate or pasteurise our beer, and it is all the better for it.

'Everything stems from the big brewers demand for beer that will last for weeks as it is transported round the country. It's the same all over whether it's milk or bread. You can do it by filtering and pasteurising. But the result is so boring you have to fizz it up. It's expensive to do and the dispensing systems are costly as well, but the beer is so bad they have to do it. It all stems from trying to operate from a few big breweries.

'Beer should be a local, natural, fresh product, not a mass-marketed liquid.'

Brian Glover *New Beer Guide*

When is a Pub Guide not a Pub Guide?

In William Younger's Book of the Bar ('a useful guide for everyone involved in running a bar' distributed by the Scottish & Newcastle owned brewery), there is an interesting little aside. Explaining what kinds of beer bar staff might encounter, traditional draught ales are described thus: 'often called real ales, though why is a mystery, because all beer is 'real' otherwise it wouldn't be beer.'

Questions of philosophy aside, there is no mystery surrounding the use of the word to describe the beer to which this guide is dedicated. We now live in a consumer climate in which terms like Real Food have common currency. Real in this case has little to do with Descartes and everything to do with quality, simplicity, integrity, the non-processed and the delicious. Real ale is to keg beer – whose only virtue is that it makes life easier for the people who aren't expected to drink it – what a fine mature farm-produced cheddar is to a sad lump of cling-clung yellow wax in a supermarket chill cabinet. Precious little mystery there.

The Good Beer Guide 1990 has something for everybody. As ever, 5000 Great British pubs with stunning real (and we mean real) ale, – that almost goes without saying. What is new is the attempt to provide you with more of the benefit of our knowledge and expertise, by setting out to describe and evaluate the real ales of Britain. A good chunk of the beers listed in the breweries section have for the first time been tasted – rather than just quaffed – by Good Beer Guide panels all over the country. Their fruity, toffee, honey, flowery and no doubt controversial findings are exclusively unveiled here, and their 50 favourites designated the Good Beer Guide 1990 Beers of the Year.

Also in this Guide, well known wine fancier Oz Clarke explains why we need to develop a beer snobbery; the beer drinkers vocabulary offers useful terms like Cooked Veg, Tom Cat and Skunk, and Beer for Beginners is just what it says it is. We've got writers on real (and we mean real) bottled beers, Real Mug Awards to outstandingly bad advertising, the riches to rags (to riches) story of Scottish brewing, an absorbing account of a brewery's day, an appetising guide to European lager ... what other pub guide offers this much?

Cheers!

Andrea Gilles, Editor, *Good Beer Guide, 1990*

The man who ordered lager at his first CAMRA meeting.
(with apologies to H. M. Bateman)

CHAPTER 8

NEW WORK

Jazz and Pubs – a Relationship of Convenience?

Ronald Atkins

First, a quiz. Below are the titles of eight tunes you may hear jazz musicians play. Which is the odd one out?

Lullaby of Birdland;
Mahogany Hall Stomp;
Six Bells Stampede;
Going To Minton's;
Swinging At The Copper Rail;
Bohemia After Dark;
Royal Garden Blues;
Roseland Shuffle.

The answer should cohere thematically with the subject of this dissertation. So if I had any polyester poodles or plaster-cast Napoleons to hand out, winners would be those among you who picked No. 3. Each title contains the name of a building with jazz connections, but of these the Six Bells is the only pub.

Music in pubs goes back a long way. There is the participative sort, where pianist or singer guides the drinkers through the melody. Then you have the pure performance. In the days when there were no radios, television sets, cars nor railways, a musician had to travel to where the people lived and find a building locally where they could gather.

Jazz, like Music Hall, straddles both camps. The average pub-goer should have no trouble visualising six or seven men (rarely women, apart from singers), wearing open-necked shirts and corduroy or demin trousers. A trumpeter sports a bushy red beard and at some point bursts into song. If the pub has a piano, it's an upright model with a glass of beer resting on the top. The tunes will be at least vaguely familiar, and the bandleader will in any case tell you what most of them are called and even ask you to join in an occasional chorus.

Such a band complements the drinking and the camaraderie. Things may be done differently elsewhere. Perhaps in a room over the bar where a guitarist, head down, spends the evening twiddling intently with the knobs on his amplifier. The drummer squats on the floor surrounded by trinkets – like a toddler in a play-pen, happily banging bits of plastic together – as often as he sits at the drums with a stick in each hand. Violins, cellos, bass-clarinets and bassoons may be among the instruments. No announcements, nor any tunes that are remotely recognisable. While musicians play, hardly a word is spoken.

These more abstract pieces, and the fact that people enjoy listening intently to them, don't rate many inches outside the arts columns and the specialist magazines. But when we snap our fingers in time to *Didn't He Ramble* or *The Onions* at our local, we are witnessing what the mass media identify as the symbiotic relationship that exists between pubs and jazz. Stereotypes on the lines of our red-bearded trumpeter are the lifeblood of journalism, and jazz is classified by the media as fun music provided for the pleasure of a certain type of eccentric. When Jazz FM radio came on the air in London, for instance, the hacks scrambled over each other in the race to resurrect the hirsute fan, complete with duffle-coat, sandals and CND badge.

To understand how this relationship took root, you have to go back to the most tear-jerkingly cockle-warming episode in the story of British jazz. The Red Barn is an ordinary pub, capacious as the name implies, in the extremely ordinary suburb of Barnehurst on the fringe of South-East London. Bexley-heath & District Rhythm Club used to hold jam sessions there and, towards the end of Hitler's war, a group called George Webb's Dixielanders played during the intervals. Their music sounded dreadfully old-fashioned to the others and, being amateurs, they were often mocked.

A relic of this derision survives in the pen-name of the band's clarinet player Wally Fawkes, famous as the cartoonist Trog: short for 'troglodytes', which his music was denounced as being performed by and suitable for. Any ill-feeling between traditionalists and the rest vanished long ago so that Webb, a pianist who worked during the day in a local factory, now receives full credit for launching the crusade that led to the great New Orleans revival. The Red Barn itself has been bereft for many years of trumpets, clarinets and the like. However, a plaque on the wall round the back of the pub commemorates 'in tribute and with thanks' Webb and his men who 'came together to play the almost forgotten music known as Jazz.'

The Dixielanders and their disciples were serious about music but played for the love of it. At the time, they attracted those who were rebelling against what they saw as the commercialisation of the music industry. Attitudes and lifestyles surrounding revivalist jazz even anticipated, in a modest way, the yearning for a so-called alternative society that later drove people to quit the rat race and form communes deep in the countryside.

The same love in making music, without the socio-political connotations, is found today among the hundreds who come home from office or factory, grab an instrument case from the cupboard and go down the pub for a blow. One of the beauties of jazz as improvised music is there are no absolute levels of skill. Take someone like Art Tatum, whose remarkable technique is drooled over by classical pianists. Compare him with Jimmy Yancey, who could play only a few tunes in a few keys and who worked as groundsman for the Chicago White Sox baseball team. Just as nobody dazzled the senses like Tatum in full flight, so could nobody wring more poetry out of a slow blues than Yancey.

Issues of money and professionalism have to be faced, though, and this is where ambivalence creeps into our relationship. A landlord is not going to splash out heavily on a band the customers hear for free. He may even pay nothing at all, so the band rely on someone passing round the hat on their behalf. A semi-pro. musician finds this quite acceptable, but it limits the range and, to some extent, the quality of music available to pubs.

The state of the piano can act as another deterrent. A reason why those electric keyboards you lug around became so popular with pianists is they never slip unwittingly out of tune. Then, how much amplification will the patrons put up with? For their part, musicians may not wish to play over the noise and through the smoke of a typical pub crowd, a feeling such crowds are likely to reciprocate.

A separate room offers one solution, where the audience underlines its dedication by paying at the door. Many publicans have rooms they rent out at a fee reasonable enough for the promoter, often one of the musicians, to be able to pay the band from the gate money and have enough over to cover costs. The pub sells more drinks and everyone is happy.

Indeed, by a delicious irony, the culture that gave birth to British Trad also nurtured the development of free improvisation. What these superficially opposed idioms have in common is that, of all the outcomes planned for by those taking part, an instant financial bonanza gets low priority. All they need is a room detached from protesting neighbours and enough space in which to spread the instruments around and to fit in those who wish to listen.

Derek Bailey, who deconstructed the systems used by other guitar players and evolved a style utterly his own, has set the pace in this field since the early 1960s. Bailey is quite obsessive on the subject of improvisation. He even persuaded Radio 3 to let him present a series on its role in different musics throughout the world, and later turned the result into a book. *Improvisation*, published in 1980 by Moorland, will also form the basis of a TV series to be shown on Channel 4.

Included in the book is an account of how his ideas crystallised during the time he worked with a trio in his native Sheffield, and the passage describing what happened when they got together is one that all *habitués* of such sessions will recognise. The pub in question is the Grapes Inn.

'Some of the playing we did . . . was carried out in the upstairs room of a pub in which we organised a weekly performance throughout the two and a half year period. During that time we collected a small audience which attended these performances with astonishing regularity and faithfulness, the bulk of them coming to the 'club' throughout its existence.'

Pubs now have many rivals among licensed premises when it comes to catering for jazz, but are far from being eclipsed. In London, the Lord Napier in Thornton Heath, which boasts a mural over the stage declaiming 'Britain's Leading Jazz Pub' draws the traditional fans. The Bull's Head in Barnes has a room at the back where the finest of those musicians loosely classified under modern jazz perform nightly. Both are Young's pubs, selling beer from South

London's popular independent brewers. The Prince Of Orange in Rother-hithe often hires big bands. Many others, like the Duke of Wellington in Islington, put on the freer stuff once or twice a week.

This is repeated throughout Britain. The Old Duke in Bristol was re-named in honour of Duke Ellington. The Trumpet is a one-bar pub with a jazz motif in Bilston, just outside Wolverhampton, that features live music each night. It has the distinction of being owned by Holden's, a small Black Country brewery that turns out some of the tastiest beer around.

Jazz and good beer often go together, a truism that sounds dangerously like the cue for another stereotype: extend the paunch on our bearded trumpeter's stomach and you incarnate the media's favourite CAMRA member. Blowing into wind and brass instruments is thirsty work, as anyone who frequents pubs near concert halls or opera houses will know. To slake that thirst, jazz musicians tend to drink in bulk and, by and large, they prefer real ale: it's unpredictable, like improvised music, but the best is better than anything else. The National Youth Jazz Orchestra has even dedicated an album to the quality products of British breweries.

That takes us back to our quiz for starters because *Six Bells Stampede*, composed by Spike Hughes in the 1930s, honoured those musicians who dashed between the Chenil Galleries recording studio in King's Road, Chelsea and the nearest pub to get the ale (or whatever) in. No doubt they left it until the last possible second to dash back again. Like the Copper Rail in New York, the Six Bells was in those days a musician's hangout rather than a musical venue. Mahogany Hall, incidentally, was a brothel in Basin Street, New Orleans, where Jelly Roll Morton and other pianists would be hired to entertain or divert the customers; others on my list were all clubs or dance halls.

In the 1960s, the Six Bells did allow groups to perform in a room upstairs. By then, the King's Road was becoming even more of a shop window for posers to preen themselves in, and neither jazz nor pubs were what they were after. From the street, the Six Bells retains today the original black-and-white facade with oddly protruding leaded windows, run up in the 1890s when architectural throwbacks were the ultimate fashion. Behind this, the much-gutted interior has succumbed to yet another blast of Watneyfication. A mid-Atlantic hybrid wherein the canned music blares, Henry J Bean's (yes, it's now one of those) wins rave notices from the Good Pub Guide and, to be fair, packs them in on Saturday afternoons.

Other pubs will doubtless go the same way. Jazz is not all that suffers when long-serving tenants leave or when the fingers of a brewing conglomerate's design supremo get that itchy feeling. How encouraging, then, to learn about a viable alternative. Brain's, the Cardiff brewers, were having a problem with one of their large hostelries in the city centre. This they solved by turning it into a major jazz venue, symbolised by the change of name to Four Bars Inn, and by putting the Welsh Jazz Society in charge of the nightly sessions.

All the best local musicians play at the Four Bars Inn, which also slots into the national touring network. So successfully has the formula worked for everyone involved, the Society hopes to be doing the same in Swansea by the time you read this. As jazz continues to grow both more visible and more audible than at any time in my experience, pubs in other towns and cities – jazz audiences do drink, after all, and are well-behaved with it – may be tempted to join in.

Somebody, some day, may even write a song about them.

Ronald Atkins has written on jazz for the *Guardian* for more than 20 years as well as for the *Financial Times*, the *Economist* and various jazz magazines. He has contributed to several books on the subject notably to *Modern Jazz – the Essential Records*. He has also written on beer for the Guardian and for three years was co-editor of CAMRA's *London Drinker* magazine.

Pub Jazz: The Adelphi Hotel, Leeds

Flat Caps, Whippets and Woodbines

Mark Dorber

One variation on the theme 'how should we characterise the mild drinkers of yesteryear?' resulted in the cliché above and provided the title for a festival of mild beers held at The White Horse on Parson's Green, Fulham in March 1990. Sadly, the festival produced only two flat caps one of which was proffered in jest and not worn. Absent the whine of whippets and the whiff of Woodbines (or should it have been Wills?). So who are the mild drinkers?

Many people had certainly travelled 'milds,' a dialect variation of mile, and generally satisfied the Oxford English Dictionary definition of mild mannered viz: 'Gentle and conciliatory in disposition or behaviour, not easily provoked and giving no offence to others; not rough or fierce in manners'. Although the 'mild boys' from Mitcham and members of CAMRA's national executive were obvious exceptions. Nevertheless, not a pint was returned nor a cross word heard. But how can we explain such behaviour? The poets might answer that meekness and mildness are eternal companions and the clerics that mild and merciful is the example of our Lord Jesus Christ.

However, what seems unusual about the way in which we contemplate mild as a drink is a readiness to confuse it with the quality of 'mildness' which inevitably increases the complexity of our response, drawing on literary and religious imagery to form a picture of mildness as virtue. For example in the proverbial simile 'as mild as a dove,' and in Thomas Hardy's 'a temper as mild as milk' in which mildness achieves a certain purity by dint of its likening to the whiteness of milk. In similar vein the expression 'to draw it mild' means to be moderate in statement or behaviour; to refrain from exaggeration. But what of the beer itself?

In its early use, as a description of beer, mild was said to be 'free from acidity; not sour or stale'. Today mild differs from other beer styles in its relative absence of bitterness and its low alcoholic strength, notwithstanding the exceptions of Merrie Monk (og1043) and Sarah Hughes Dark Ruby Mild (og1058). Mild may be light or dark although perversely the light milds are invariably and ungrammatically called 'best.' Mild achieves greater complexity in its dark form where the nuttiness of roasted malt is set off by a creaminess of texture and the slight sweetness on the palate is underpinned by a barely discernible bitterness. Liquorice, caramel and toffee are the flavours most commonly found in dark milds.

In spite of its distinctiveness as a beer style, mild in London was in decline for many years before Courage in 1979, Fuller's in 1980 and finally Young's in 1982 ceased production of their cask conditioned milds. The tainting of 'Mild's' reputation and one of the chief reasons for falling sales was due to the widespread malpractice of using the darker mild as the dustbin for beer wasted in the normal course of dispense i.e. retrieved from drip trays or from the bellies of inexpertly tilted casks. In extreme cases the recovery of slops from half-finished pints at the end of sessions was also added to the mild. Given the low hopping rates and low alcoholic strengths of the milds they were least able to withstand this persistent abuse and consequently volumes fell leading to the familiar spiral of lower quality. Meanwhile the keg revolution of the 1960's and 1970's promised the drinker the alternative of a consistently acceptable pint in that it was bright and not acetic. Moreover, it gave the modern consumer a modern hygienic drink. Tradition was not the word tripping from people's lips at this time nor was the passive imagery associated with mild likely to stimulate demand in the way that the hearty local boozer imagery used to advertise keg bitters could and did. The colloquial expression 'to do bitters' means to drink beer but also captures a mood of activity, albeit in a rather macho way, as evidenced in the 'Tetley Bitter Men' advertising campaign of the 1970's.

The strongholds of cask mild have historically been the Midlands and the North West and despite the triple assaults of the keg revolution, Tory economic policies in the 1980's and merger activity, they have held up well. However, using the *Good Beer Guide* as a source, the national picture has seen the number of milds regularly available in the last ten years (excluding home brew pubs) fall from approximately 90 in 1980 to approximately 70 in 1990.

The relatively rare sightings of mild in the Capital (six different brews regularly available in 17 outlets according to Roger Warhurst) in early 1990 provided reason enough therefore, to reacquaint ourselves with some old friends and to make some new ones. Thus a festival in March 1990 was seen to serve a number of purposes. It brought together people and beers from different parts of the country thereby extending the tasting experiences of the participants. It enabled a comparative tasting of beers to take place which in turn helped to stimulate debate about regional interpretations of beer styles and the taste boundaries of beer styles themselves. And, oh yes, for those too earnest students of beer who might have forgotten then it reaffirmed the ancient decree that drinking beer is to be enjoyed. Indeed there were some participants actively campaigning to re-establish the definition of festival as 'a time of revelry' in modern usage.

Of the 19 beers advertised two were imposters; one known: Timothy Taylor's Golden Best, a beautifully aromatic light bitter; and one suspected: Premier Ale's Old Merlin, a 'small' porter. The remaining 17 showed an interesting range of colours, aromas and tastes. From the cellarman's perspective one noteworthy feature of the behaviour of 13 of the 17 milds was their high level of natural carbonation, requiring the use of soft spiles to purge them of their excess CO_2. Given that some sweetness is a feature of both dark and light milds then it is perhaps not surprising that the beers should have shown so much liveliness. In fact most of them produced a thick collar of fob when dispensed without any need to use tightly screwed sparklers. A far cry from Dylan Thomas's complaint in a letter of September 1946: 'It is time for the Black Lion but there is only Buckley's unfriskly mild'.

In my experience, the time it takes for beers to drop bright may vary from four hours to a week after the soft pegging process is complete; yet all the festival milds had dropped bright within two days and the only concession demanded by some of them was that of lifting the cellar temperature to 58°F for twelve hours in order to bring a little extra polish to their appearance. The combination of star bright beers ranging in colour from dark amber to deep ruby red and on to brown/black topped with a layer of cream had the effect of stimulating thirst with the same suddenness and intensity as the aroma of garlic frying in olive oil has on the appetite.

If our sample of milds was a fair reflection of cask conditioned mild brewed in Britain today then poor quality can be dismissed as a reason for its continued decline. Rather, the vogue for lighter coloured beers, our recent social history of mild abuse and the imagery associated with this beer style have all contributed significantly to its fall from fashion. The inescapable conclusion is that if mild is to make a comeback it will need to assume a new name. Any suggestions?

Mark Dorber is a business analyst with a firm of solicitors in the city and in his spare time the cellarmaster at The White Horse at Parsons Green in south-west London. Beer analysts say that this pub serves the best pint of Draught Bass outside Burton on Trent. He is presently studying to become a Master of Wine.

Origins

Graham Lees

Revolutions often have improbable starting points. So it was that a hastily arranged, cut price holiday in Ireland one wet and windy week in Spring 1971 became the trigger which sparked a popular uprising against British brewers.

For it was somewhere out there, sheltering in a pub among the most westerly peat bogs of Europe, that four earnest and naive young Englishmen vowed to 'revitalise' beer.

As they guzzled their Guinness (for sipping was not the local custom), the four bachelors ruminated on what was wrong with much of Britain's national drink. Between them, they hadn't got much idea how beer was made or how it reached their pint pots. But they knew enough (from a sampling or three) to sense that all was not well.

They agreed that many of the national brands appearing almost everywhere they went – Double Diamond, Red Barrel, Tartan and the like – lacked something. Only much later would they learn how genuine taste was being replaced with an overdose of carbon dioxide.

Something should be done about it, they told one another in rising voices which momentarily distracted Irishmen from their St. Patrick's Day celebrations. So they formed a club: the Campaign for the Revitalisation of Ale: membership four.

Thus Michael Hardman, James Makin, Bill Mellor and myself returned home from a pleasant but unspectacular Irish holiday, all but forgetting the resolution to get revitalising.

Almost nine months later, membership of the CAMRA club remained steady at four. Then, as Christmas approached, I was persuaded by a colleague in Chester to help boost his fledgling printing business by letting him produce personal Christmas cards for me. What verse would I like, he asked? In a mischievous and irreverent moment I came up with the following daft doggerel to sit between the holly sprigs:

'Whether In City Bar You Sup,
Or In Village Vault You Get Tanked Up,
Be On Your Guard Against Bad Ale,
Or You'll Never Live To Tell The Tale
Of CAMRA.'

Inspired by the success of this mighty message (we tripled our membership to 12 within three weeks), and egged on by my printer friend, we next introduced membership cards – arbitrarily priced at five pence a time. That weeded out the men from the boys and membership growth stalled: most people were still thinking in old money and five pence was a whole shilling with which you could buy half a pint of bitter.

Many of the first 100 members of the Campaign for the Revitalisation of Ale were journalists working on provincial newspapers up and down the country – friends of Hardman, Mellor and myself who were in the same trade. Journalists gather in pubs, talk about CAMRA spread, the subject of beer and disgruntled drinkers found its way on to numerous news editors' lists. Suddenly, startlingly, spontaneously, CAMRA was launched. Predictable but persuasive headlines began appearing, like the Daily Mirror's 'Drinkers Bitter About Their Beer.'

The target of all this rather uncoordinated bitterness was inevitably the big national brewing combines who became increasingly rattled by negative publicity which, slowly at first, was to undermine and finally kill some of the most expensively-promoted national brands of the 1970s.

One highly-paid brewery public relations man, whose future went the way of Watney's Red Barrel, put his foot firmly in his mouth with the immortal statement: 'CAMRA is just a bunch of journalists looking for a story.'

How wrong he was, as the postman of CAMRA's early headquarters – my mother's home in Salford, Greater Manchester – would have willingly testified. The shoebox membership file was filling up fast but the 'bunch of journalists' included bus drivers, businessmen, pensioners and a parson.

By the summer of 1972, a special general meeting had been held, a national executive committee elected, and the first area organisers appointed. The big brewers continued to laugh derisively.

In those days, the organisation of the fledgling CAMRA tended to follow the first chairman, Michael Hardman, and myself and our journeyman journalism as we left our northern homeland for the 'riches' of the south.

I landed, briefly, in St. Albans, where a meeting with another young beer enthusiast who had just completed a 'crawl' of all Young Brewery's London pubs (then 146) to collect a brewery tie, led to this cathedral city becoming the headquarters of CAMRA. John Green eventually became the first fulltime employee of the Campaign.

224

When I moved on – handing over the now wholely inadequate shoebox membership file – Green opened CAMRA's first office, a room over a bicycle shop, for a few shillings rent a week. Membership was soaring away: would it perhaps one day reach the magic figure of 1,000 we wondered? (it actually peaked at about 33,000, and today stands at 22,300 and rising again).

CAMRA is now run by a team of professionals but in the early days it was often all hands to the pumps – like the occasion when several hundred angry members descended on the sleepy town of Stone in Staffordshire for a coffin-carrying funeral to protest against the closure of the local brewery by one of the national brewing giants.

The resident journalistic skills of CAMRA, notably Hardman who also became a full-time Campaign employee, were to play a vital role in promoting the organisation. A monthly newspaper 'What's Brewing' was founded and became required reading in brewery boardrooms; an annual *Good Beer Guide* was launched and has been a best seller for years.

The cause was helped in many ways by members. Like lecturer Peter Linley who reasoned that getting your tongue round 'the Campaign for the Revitalisation of Ale' after a few pints was beyond the call of duty. Thus, we acquired the shortened, crisper title of today.

People lined up for 'active duty' as though they had been training all their lives for this moment. One unforgettable character, now departed to the great pub in the sky whose never-closing door awaits us all, had the energy of 100 campaigners, marching alone into pubs and breweries alike to recruit new members or remonstrate with 'bad' brewers. The pocket-sized V.D.S. Fowler, who tucked away a gallon of ale a day, also engaged in forthright correspondence.

A certain brewer kept insisting that as carbon dioxide was a natural by-product of brewing it was perfectly reasonable for him to inject more of the gas into his brews.

Forthright Fowler's reply was both unequivocal and memorable: 'Sir, shit is a natural product of the pig, but one wouldn't expect to have it served up with the roast pork on Sundays.'

In no time at all, CAMRA had become the marshalling yard of a simmering great British grievance. It wasn't just four northern lads on an Irish holiday who thought summat was up with the pint in their local.

Graham Lees is one of the four founder members of CAMRA – the Campaign for Real Ale. He has been a journalist all his working life, first on regional papers in England followed by spells in Australia, Germany and London. He is now living in Munich where he runs his own news agency. Among other organisations he has founded are the MCC – the Munich Cricket Club, and CIA – Cricket International Auslander.

The Lost Breweries of Edinburgh

Allan McLean

The teacher was alarmed at the discovery that two short-trousered pupils had been on a tour of breweries. But they had an explanation which satisfied him.

He looked at their scrap book full of beer labels and asked them to justify what they had done. They had been told to carry out a project on Edinburgh industry. Why beer labels?

'Well, sir,' came the response of one of the 12-year-olds, 'in your local geography lesson, you said the main industries of Edinburgh were brewing, paper-making, printing and glass manufacture. The beer bottle labels represent the lot.'

If any intrepid youngster today was to set off to call on all Edinburgh's breweries, the exercise would not last long. What the two boys who asked various breweries for labels did not know was that they were just in time. The year was 1959. And the 'Locust Years' were about to begin, when the city which ranked as one of the world's great brewing capitals was to lose brewery after brewery.

Some had closed in earlier times because two world wars had changed international markets and there had been a between-wars slump in the home trade. But the series of takeovers which hit the industry in the decade from 1959 led to closures which many drinkers still mourn, either because they are old enough to remember great ales or because they have heard tell, from drinkers long in tooth and memory, of fine pints of yore.

From their classroom window those pupils could look down on plumes of steam rising from the valley which contains the lower reaches of the Royal Mile, an historic street running from the Palace of Holyroodhouse to Edinburgh Castle. The steam came from breweries, all of which were to fall silent, never again to house that magic which is represented by the mashing of malt, boiling of hops and pitching of yeast. On occasion, the boys could go down into that brewing area with its wonderful aromas of beer in the making, and climb Arthur's Seat, the former volcano which dominates much of Edinburgh like a sleeping lion. From the summit it was possible to look back to the Holyrood area and its brewing heart, and over to the Duddingston and Craigmillar area on the other side of the hill where yet more breweries thrived. All are now closed.

Considerable volumes of ale and lager are still produced in Edinburgh, but the fingers of one hand are too many to count the breweries on. Of the 90 breweries in Scotland in 1880, no less than 37 were in Edinburgh. Now Edinburgh has three breweries, plus a brew-pub, but even this small number represents a greater concentration of brewing activity than elsewhere in Scotland. The biggest Edinburgh brewery today is the Scottish & Newcastle plant at Fountainbridge, capable of brewing two million barrels a year – at 288 pints a barrel. That's equal to the total output of all the breweries in Scotland in 1900!

Fountainbridge is where William McEwan set up business in 1856. The William Younger company, established 1749, was then a rival, but the two united in Scottish Brewers in 1931 and then in 1960 formed the northern end of Scottish & Newcastle. William Younger brands are now brewed at the same Fountainbridge site as those known by the McEwan name; William Younger's Holyrood Brewery having become a casualty of 1980s rationalisation. (William Younger's earlier Abbey Brewery at Holyrood had already ceased brewing, but remains as the site of the S & N head office.)

Edinburgh's other active breweries are also on the west side of town, not far from Fountainbridge. The second biggest in Edinburgh is the Heriot Brewery of Tennent Caledonian, the Scottish arm of Bass. Tennent's main brewery, famous for its lager for more than 100 years, is Wellpark in Glasgow. Heriot – former home to the Edinburgh brewing company, Jeffrey's – also produces Tennent's Lager, as well as ales. Lager was first brewed there in 1902, but the takeovers and amalgamations which brought the Wellpark and Heriot breweries into the same ownership meant that Jeffrey's lager was dropped in favour of the Tennent's brand.

Curiously Jeffrey's Edinburgh Lager – still commemorated in an Edwardian stained glass advertisement in a door at Bennet's Bar, Tollcross, Edinburgh – was sold in bottles sealed with wired tops similar to those still used today for Grolsch, a Dutch lager distributed in Scotland by Tennent's. 'You can't top a Grolsch!' say the advertisements for it. But they 'topped' Jeffrey's!

Both Fountainbridge and Heriot breweries produce cask-conditioned ales, although the bulk of their output is fizzy brewery-conditioned ale and lager. (Although S & N's Fountain Brewery is responsible for a truly great ale, Gordon's Highland Scotch, it is only available overseas, notably in Belgium, its main export market.) For decent beer in Edinburgh, lovers of real ale prefer to seek out the wonderfully-flavoured nectar emanating from the city's third operational brewery, in terms of size, and first in terms of quality. This is the Caledonian Brewery, once home to the Vaux subsidiary Lorimer & Clark. Vaux decided in recent years to pull out of Scotland and make Lorimer's Best 'Scotch' Ale in Sunderland instead of Edinburgh. A management buy-out saved the Caledonian from closure, and a good thing too, because this is more than a production centre for outstandingly fine ale. It is an architectural gem, a piece of living industrial archaeology virtually unaltered since Mr Lorimer and Mr Clark got together in 1869.

Whiffs of brewing do emerge from the heavily modernised mega outfits of Fountain and Heriot, but the scents which waft from the Caledonian carry with them the mouth-watering promise that more great ale is on the way, reminding a certain one-time schoolboy label-collector of the way things once were across on the east side of town at Holyrood, where commercial brewing has now ceased more than 800 years after the monks at the abbey there discovered that Edinburgh water is just wonderful when it comes to making ale.

The 'Caley' brews pure beer, using only water, malt, whole hops and yeast. The results are ales which are satisfyingly rich and malty, and include the three finest examples of those three stalwart Scottish beer qualities – 60/-, 70/- and 80/-. The 'shillings' refer to the prices of barrels in Victorian times and are now a guide to strength, 60/- being in the range of many English milds, 70/- being of the strength of many English bitters and 80/- having the alcohol content of a best bitter of the most distinguished kind. The 'Caley' also has interesting export brews, keeping up the old Edinburgh Ale tradition of sending beer around the world.

Of the three direct-fired coppers at the 'Caley' one is more than 120 years old and the others are exact replicas of 1869 originals. These and other attractive aspects of the building add to its charm – that being an appropriate description, because one of the reasons for its location at Slateford Road was the presence of good underground water within what was known to generations of Edinburgh brewers as 'The Charmed Circle.' That circle once embraced such gone, but not forgotten, breweries as those of Aitchison, Bernard, Drybrough, Maclachlan, Morison, Murray, Steel Coulson, Robert Younger and Thomas Usher.

All these and more, closed since 1960, are sadly mourned. But the most grievous loss was that of Campbell, Hope & King, whose Argyle Brewery in the Cowgate was taken over by Whitbread in 1967 and closed in 1971.

After a short period with British Rail in Yorkshire, Allan McLean returned to his roots and a staff job on the *Scotsman* in Edinburgh. He writes a regular beer column and was the first winner of the British Guild of Beer Writers Gold Tankard award.

Revolting Reds and other Animals

Roger Protz

It's time for all this bad mouthing of Watneys to stop. Is there no gratitude left in the land? Every beer lover should be grateful, down on his bendy bits and praising Bacchus for Grand Metropolitan's brewing division. I mean, where would we all be if Watneys hadn't brewed such awful beer? CAMRA would never have got off the ground, for start.

Just think of the juxtaposition of these two dates. 1971, Watneys launch Red keg bitter. 1972 CAMRA formed.

Within a few years the Campaign had close on 30,000 members and was a power in the land. Watney's Red was laughed into oblivion and the group actually admitted in public that it had got its brewing policy round its neck and would start producing real ale again.

Bill Tidy did his bit. His Kegbuster cartoon strip in CAMRA's newspaper *What's Brewing* fired endless barbed darts at a dreadful conglomerate run by pin-striped smoothies. It was named 'Grotny'. The name stuck. It hurt. Tens of thousands of pubgoers who wouldn't give real ale to their goldfish picked up the wicked soubriquet. Even seaside comedians latched on to Grotnys.

GrandMet brought in Allen Sheppard from Unipart, British Leyland's spare bits division, to give Watneys a much-needed de-coke and oil change.

An expensive public relations firm advised Sheppard to stop painting his pubs red with hideous white lettering and to stop calling them 'Watneys.' Out from under the paint came old brewing names such as Ushers, Wilsons, Websters and Tamplins. They even dreamt up a fictional name for the Norfolk area, the Norwich Brewing Company. It must be the only recorded example of a giant national company hiding its name, as if it had been called Martin Bormann Brewers.

Watney's Red was one of the greatest brewing and marketing disasters of recorded time. Some bright spark, who twenty years later would have slicked back hair, a double-breasted suit and a cellphone, thought the long-running and archetypal keg beer, Red Barrel, needed a facelift and a new image. He had a great wheeze. Let's aim for the youth market, all those kids rampaging over London and other major cities against the Vietnam war and the invasion of Czechoslovakia, Watney's Red, Real cool, man.

The only trouble was, it was 1971, not 1968. I had spent so much time in the late Sixties outside the American Embassy in Grosvenor Square that I had given serious consideration to leaving a camp bed under the bushes. (On one occasion, due to the press of people and police horses, I found myself lying atop a young lady who was so far to the left in those days that she almost defied gravity when she walked. She went on to become editor of both the News of the World and the Sunday People, but I don't blame Watneys for that.)

The Sixties came to an end. The generation it had spawned had grown demo-weary. The Beatles paid mocking benediction to the end of the decade with 'Things Are Getting Better All The Time.' And that was when Watneys decided to launch a new keg beer with the slogan 'The Red Revolution' and backed by lookalikes of Chairman Mao, Nikita Khrushchev and Fidel Castro on giant posters.

It was more a case of reactionary cheek than radical chic. For a start, the youngish generation, even if they were still on the streets, didn't identify with the people on the poster. Apart from a handful who dressed in unisex cotton suits and peaked caps and chanted strange slogans in unison, there weren't many lovers of the Chinese system. We thought more of Che Guevara in the Bolivian jungle than Fidel boring the pants off the Cubans with his nine-hour speeches. And Nikita Khrushchev was about as popular as Lyndon Baines Johnson in a Hanoi casualty hospital.

So the marketing of Watney's Red was risible. Even so, bamboozled and bombarded by the ads, I did set foot in a Watney's pub to sample the new concoction. For a start it was expensive, around thirty pee (I'm convinced that the abbreviation for the new fangled 'pence' had been done with Watneys in mind). And above all, it tasted dreadful. Thin, gassy, sweet, the nearest thing to liquid Mars Bars with a dash of alcohol. After one taste I went straight back to handpumped Charrington's IPA, which in those days was a good ale actually brewed in London.

GrandMet tried to make amends. They started to brew a real ale called Fined Bitter. It tasted like nail polish, but at least they were back on the right

'more reactionary cheek than radical chic'

track. Truman produced a clutch of excellent cask beers for a while. Wilsons was good and I remember a time when a pint of Webster's Bitter was much sought after.

But old habits die hard. 'National branding' became the marketing buzz word of the Eighties. One by one, the real ales disappeared, along with the breweries. 'Yorkshire' was stuck between Webster's and Bitter and popped up in bars from the Lizard to Cape Wrath. GrandMet paid a ludicrous £14 million to buy the pipsqueak Ruddle's brewery in order to have a renowned premium cask beer in their pubs.

We've come full circle. Webster's is a bowdlerised version of its old self, bland and treacly. And you need to extend your overdraft at the bank if you plan to drink Ruddle's County in a Watney's pub.

Now GrandMet have done the decent thing. The timing for once was perfect. Just as the Berlin Wall was falling and the crowds cheered Dubcek and Havel in Wenceslas Square, the combine announced it was getting out of brewing altogether and selling its remaining plants to Courage, now owned by the Foster's lager people.

So the Red Revolution fizzes to an end. But no laughter round the grave, if you please. Be thankful for what Watneys have bequeathed us – a generation of beer lovers who care about their ale and about quality and tradition.

Who will replace 'Grotny?' Who will become the new figure of hate in the brewing world? No problem. Bill Tidy has even come up with the name. Been to a Twitbread pub lately?

Roger Protz is one of the most prolific writers in the burgeoning world of beer writing. He has some dozen books and six editions of the Good Beer Guide to his credit. As well as several periods as Editor of What's Brewing he contributes to many periodicals including the Guardian and the Publican and broadcasts on Radio 4's Food Programme.

Index of Authors and Titles

Acknowledgements

Thanks are due to the following for their kind permission to reproduce their work in this book:

Alisdair Aird and the Consumers' Association for an extract from the *Good Pub Guide, 1990*.
Ronald Atkins for *Jazz and Pubs – a Relationship of Convenience?*
Frank Baillie for extracts from *The Beer Drinker's Companion*.
The Literary executor of James K. Baxter and Oxford University Press (New Zealand) for 'Bar Room Conversation'.
The late Brendan Behan for an extract from Brendan Behan's *Island* published by Random Century Group.
Richard Boston for 'Good Things' from *Beer and Skittles* published by Collins.
Terry Cryer for his photograph of Jazz in the Adelphi, Leeds.
Mark Dorber of *Flat Caps, Whippets and Woodbines*.
Martin Drury for his article 'The Country Pub' from *Time Gentlemen Please*.
Dave Dutton for *Birth of a Plastic Pub*.
Phil Evans for his cartoon.
Donal Farmer for 'Joe McHugh's' originally broadcast on BBC Radio Leeds.
Patrick Leigh Fermor and John Murray (Publishers) Ltd. for an extract from *A Time of Gifts*.
Julie France for three original cartoons.
John Fraser for 'Downtown Boozers – Pre-war' from his *Poems for the People*.
Gerry Garside for the script of an episode of *Tap Room Tales* originally broadcast on BBC Radio Leeds.
Andrea Gillies for an extract from the *Good Beer Guide, 1990*.
Brian Glover for his piece on Peter Austin in the *New Beer Guide* published by David and Charles.
John Hanscomb for an extract from the *Good Beer Guide, 1974*.

Neil Hanson and CAMRA for two extracts from *Classic Country Pubs*.
Michael Hardman for an extract from his book *Beer Naturally*.
Christopher Hutt for the introduction to his book *The Death of the English Pub*.
Michael Jackson for 'How to taste and Judge Beer' from the *New World Guide to Beer*.
Dermot Kelly for the words of his song 'Joseph McHugh'.
Clifford Lackey for an extract from *Gentle Giants*.
Eddie Lawler for the words of his song 'The Real Thing'.
Graham Lees for *Origins*.
Allan McLean for *The Lost Breweries of Edinburgh*.
Peter Moynihan for his article on the Davy Jones Brewery in the journal of the Brewery History Society.
'London Beer' from *Nairn's London* by Ian Nairn, published by Penguin Books.
Susan Nowak for an extract from *Good Pub Food*.
Mrs Elevyn O'Nolan for extracts from works by her late husband Brian O'Nolan (Flann O'Brien).
The late George Orwell and the Evening Standard Company Ltd, for 'The Moon Under Water'.
Keith Osborne for an extract from *The Beer Drinker's Guide to Labology*.
Cecil Parrott for an extract of his translation of Jaroslav Hasek's *The Good Soldier Švejk*, reprinted by permission of William Heinemann Ltd.
Ken Powell for 'The Northern Urban Pub' from *Time Gentlemen Please*.
Michael Powell for an extract from *The Beer Drinker's Guide to Tegestology*.

David Pownall for part of 'The Waggon and Horses' from *Between Ribble and Lune*.

Roger Protz for *Revolting Reds and other Animals* and extracts from his books *Best Pubs in London* and *The Great British Beer Book*.

Peter Robinson for his article on the Yorkshire Stone Square System of Fermentation from the journal of the Brewery History Society.

Tony Scholes for 'The Versatile Beermat' from Parish Pump, the newsletter of Sheffield and District Branch of CAMRA

John Simpson for 'Charlie' cartoons originally published in What's Brewing

The Society of Authors as the literary representative of the estate of James Stephens for 'A Glass of Beer'.

The late Dylan Thomas for an extract from *Under Milk Wood* published by Dent.

Alan Thompson for his quote on temperance.

Bill Tidy for 'Keg Buster' and 'Cloggies' cartoons.

Young's Brewery for a photograph.

Sid Waddell for an extract from *Bedside Darts*

John Watney for an extract from *Beer is Best* published by Peter Owen Ltd.

Join CAMRA

If you like good beer and good pubs you could be helping in the fight to preserve, protect and promote them. CAMRA was set up in the early seventies to fight against the mass description of a part of Britain's heritage.

The giant brewers are still pushing through takeovers, mergers and closures of their smaller regional rivals. They are still reducing the availability and diluting the quality of a magnificent and uniquely British product – real ale. They are still trying to impose brands of beer and larger on their customers whether they like it or not, and they are still closing down town and village local pubs or converting them into grotesque 'theme' pubs.

CAMRA wants to see genuine free competition in the brewing industry, fair prices, civilised licensing laws, and, above all, a top quality product brewed by local breweries in accordance with local tastes, and served in pubs that maintain the best features of a tradition that goes back centuries.

If you are in sympathy with these aims you could be expressing that sympathy in a positive way, by joining CAMRA. We have well over 25,000 members and that's not including our three fully paid-up dogs and two cats! Yet we're pitting ourselves against the power and financial muscle of a multi-million pound, multi-national industry. We desperately need active campaigning members, but we are also grateful for the support of people whose only involvement may be to pay their membership subscription once a year. It's only £10, but each additional subscription helps us to campaign that bit more effectively across the whole spectrum of pub issues on behalf of *all* pub-users.

If you leave it to others, you may wake up one day to find *your* local pub shut, *your* local brewery closed down, *your* favourite beer no longer being brewed. So join CAMRA and help us to prove that the most important person in the brewing industry isn't the megalomaniac chairman of some brewing giant, but that most vital, and under-valued person – the pub customer.

Full membership £10. Life membership £100 I wish to become members of CAMRA Ltd. I agree to abide by the memorandum and articles of association of the company. I enclose a cheque-p.o. for £10/£100.

Name(s) _____

_____

Address _____

_____

_____

_____

Signature(s) _____

_____